Voyage through the Twentieth Century

Voyage through the Twentieth Century

A Historian's Recollections and Reflections

Klemens von Klemperer

Published in 2009 by
Berghahn Books
www.berghahnbooks.com

© 2009, 2014 Klemens von Klemperer
First paperback edition published in 2014

All rights reserved.
Except for the quotation of short passages
for the purposes of criticism and review, no part of this book
may be reproduced in any form or by any means, electronic or
mechanical, including photocopying, recording, or any information
storage and retrieval system now known or to be invented,
without written permission of the publisher.

Library of Congress Cataloging-in-Publication Data

Von Klemperer, Klemens, 1916–
 Voyage through the twentieth century : a historian's recollections and reflections / Klemens von Klemperer.
  p. cm.
 Includes bibliographical references and index.
  ISBN 978-1-84545-584-2 (hardback) — ISBN 978-1-78238-383-3 (paperback) — ISBN 978-1-84545-944-4 (ebook)
 1. Von Klemperer, Klemens, 1916–. 2. Historians—Germany—Biography. 3. Germany—History—20th century. 4. Germany—Intellectual life—20th century. I. Title.
 DD86.7.V66A3 2009
 943.087092—dc22
 [B]   2009014621

British Library Cataloguing in Publication Data

A catalogue record for this book is available from
the British Library.

Printed on acid-free paper.

ISBN 978-1-84545-584-2 hardback
ISBN 978-1-78238-383-3 paperback
ISBN 978-1-84545-944-4 ebook

To Jani, my dear Viennese aunt, who returns often in my memory

Jani always took great interest in my friends' adventures and in mine. In October 1939, when she lived in exile in southern France and I had just begun my studies at Harvard, she wrote to me: "All your ideals will be tested, and I do not doubt that you will manage. Because only what we hold on to when the chips are down (*wenn's hart auf hart geht*) will tell us what it really in the deepest sense of the word was worth to us."

Jani

Contents

Acknowledgments	viii
Introduction	1
1. Beginnings	5
2. School Years	12
3. "O du mein Österreich …"	20
4. America—Coming Down to Earth	36
5. Going To and Fro upon the Earth—On Being a Soldier	45
6. "Du bist ein Wanderer …"	63
7. "Mit dem Gesicht nach Deutschland"	92
8. Living in a "World Come of Age"	112
Afterthoughts	135
Notes	140
Selected Bibliography	158
Index	164

Acknowledgments

Every work I have written has been a communal venture, even this rather personal one. Since I have lived on both shores of the Atlantic, I owe thanks to those in Europe and in America who have accompanied me on my path and have encouraged me to pull together at long last the threads of my rather complicated past. Thanks to them, the story of my life, which might at first have appeared rather disjointed, has become whole.

The brothers Georg Michael and Ekkehard Klausa, with whom I am connected in a third-generation friendship, helped me to give my recollections a sense of continuity. Here in America I have benefited from the encouragement of my friends. Marion Macdonald has reminded me that, as in nature, weeding out is a crucial proposition for every writer. The team of editors at Berghahn Books—Ann Przyzycki, Shawn Kendrick, Melissa Spinelli—has supported me with both rigor and kindness. A novice in the digital world, I have been assisted by Smith College's Information Technology Services whenever help was needed.

As always, I owe thanks to my good wife Elizabeth for never allowing a stylistic blooper to mar what I have put to paper.

K. v. K.

Introduction

The twentieth century was the century into which I was born—*my* century. Now that it has drawn to a close, I am tempted, especially as a historian, to balance the books on it. To do so, I will have to write about a century shattered by two world wars that gave rise to all-encompassing political systems—fascism, communism, National Socialism—sustained by tyrannical ideologies.

But this is not a history of the twentieth century, nor an overview by someone now old enough to be above the fray. It is the story of my experience of that twentieth century, which is that of a generation that was fully adult before World War II and, furthermore, of a particular fraction of this generation—one that was in many ways privileged. For the most part, I am thinking of people who, like myself, enjoyed a better than average education, who had access to the same books and musical performances, the same rivers for rowing or slopes for skiing. It is partly because many of them did not survive to tell their stories that I feel obliged to tell mine: it is also theirs. Like Tennyson's Ulysses, I am a part of all that I have met.

I am keenly aware of the pitfalls of writing a memoir. Inevitably, it borders on autobiography. Here I take comfort in Plutarch's observation that "if the 'know thyself' of the [Delphic] oracle were an easy thing for every man, it would not be held to be a divine injunction." So be it, then. In any case, the burden of this memoir is to be on my experiences of living in troubled times and on my accounting of how they affected me and how I responded to them. I hope to be able to give evidence of having lived the examined life that Socrates thought was alone worth living.

Leafing through the histories of my century, I notice the names of many men and women who, although born after me, had to die long ago. I think of

Hans and Sophie Scholl (born in 1918 and 1921), the two students from Ulm in southern Germany, who, together with their friends in the so-called White Rose group, stood up to Nazi tyranny. In February 1943, they dropped illegally printed leaflets into the inner courtyard of the University of Munich, calling on the public to resist. They were detected by a vigilant custodian and executed within four days.

If I shift the focus to my immediate friends, I cannot help but be moved by the fact that virtually all of their lives were marked by upsets, if not tragedy. Was it their own ill fortune, or was it the troubled times that overwhelmed them? Here I single out a few of them.

Helmut Jörg from Klosterneuburg near Vienna, a singularly clearheaded and dynamic fellow, was the moving spirit among us students trying to stem the Nazi tide in Austria. He was thrown into jail immediately after the German takeover of Austria in March 1938, the so-called *Anschluss*, and then spent three years in the Dachau concentration camp.

Otto Molden was politically no less engaged and exposed than Helmut. He was fortunate inasmuch as his confinement by the Gestapo turned out to be a short one. A letter from his mother, which reached me after I had left for America, gave me a sense of the dispersal of my Viennese friends immediately after the *Anschluss*: "Otto sends many greetings. You will not know that at the end of August he had to go once again for six days where he also had been in March [Gestapo custody]; but he has returned safe and in good spirits. However, he is forbidden to write letters … otherwise you would have had news from him himself.… Fritz [Otto's younger brother] goes to school in the Gymnasiumstraße.… About Helmut one hears that soon he should return to Klosterneuburg; but so far this has not happened." Helmut was released from the concentration camp years later only to fight on the Russian front, where he fell in 1943.

A very different story is that of my two Junker friends, Friedrich and Georg von Schweinitz. Friedrich, my classmate in Berlin, went straight from school into the army. He was born to be, in the family tradition, a soldier. Georg, at first an enthusiastic SS trooper, landed in a concentration camp and then a succession of jails and was released only to serve in the Wehrmacht. He fell at Herpy by the Aisne River in June 1940, and Friedrich followed him into death on the Russian front in July 1941.

I also remember Ernest Jandorf, born in Germany, who emigrated to the United States and died wearing an American khaki uniform. His name is engraved on the plaque in the south wall of the Harvard Memorial Chapel commemorating the 697 Harvard alumni who gave their lives for their country in World War II.

In the following chapters it will be my task to account for the labyrinthine landscape in which I moved, which challenged me, inspired me, and, in the last analysis, shaped me. My youth was in many ways articulated by friendships that were as intense as they were demanding of loyalty. "The essence of friendship," Emerson wrote, "is entireness, a total magnanimity and trust."[1] Yet by the same token, the many friendships I have enjoyed were by no means marked by sameness and unanimity of views and certainly not by political agreement.

My own life experience was distinctly stormy, like that of my friends. The period of my early youth, the 1920s, was characterized by extraordinary cultural creativity and a pronounced sense of crisis and disorientation. For those of us who grew up in Germany, the lost world war and the stringent Treaty of Versailles had repercussions that far exceeded our political awareness. Moreover, in my ancestral country, Austria, where I spent crucial years studying at the University of Vienna, a sense of turmoil was accentuated by the marked disproportion between memories of empire and the reality of the small republic left over after the division of the Habsburg Monarchy. All in all, we felt that we had inherited from our parents a *monde cassé*, or broken world. The very contrasts between past and present, creativity and crisis, hope and dejection gave my youth and that of my friends an ardor that mingled dreams and delusions.

Our values and convictions were formed in the face of the glittering and seductive ideologies that we were exposed to. It would have been easy to succumb to one or another of these, but for reasons that will emerge in this book, we were not swept along by the magnetic and dynamic movements of the 1920s and 1930s. We stood our ground. Our friendships have been conspiracies of sorts, in which we set out to trace a path above the abyss that was opening up around us.

The advent of National Socialism in January 1933 in Germany and in March 1938 in Austria caused a fissure in our lives. In my case it meant emigration, in October 1938, to the United States, which gave me a safe haven and allowed me to start my life all over again. Yet I remained the same young man I had been before. The first book in English that I read crossing the Atlantic, Joseph Conrad's *Lord Jim*, contains a passage that made a deep impression on me. In it, Marlow, the narrator, recalls old Mr. Stein's wise exhortation "to follow the dream, and again to follow the dream—and so—*ewig—usque ad finem.*" Jim, Marlow observes, was a romantic. I too was a romantic, and I suppose I still am—at least my friends tell me so.

During my early years in America, to be sure, the feverish intensity that had haunted me in the old world yielded to a measure of lightheartedness. Certainly, the new shores of America had a powerful attraction for me, and a sense of German heaviness gave way to a liberating pragmatism.

Those of my friends who stayed behind and were drafted into the German army or thrown into prisons and concentration camps and those who joined the German and Austrian Resistance certainly drew the harder lot. This difference, however important, has not permanently separated us. We kept thinking of one another and corresponding as long as this was possible. "Beyond countries and oceans we are friends," Otto wrote me at Christmastime in 1938, when I was already in America. "Our *Heimat* is wide." During the three and a half years that I served in the US Army, I maintained a firm distinction between the foe I was engaged in fighting and those, like my friends, who wanted to cleanse Germany and Austria of the Nazi plague. Once the war was over, I crossed the Atlantic time and again. I will always belong to both continents.

A testimony about one's life, as this book aspires to be, must draw on memory, which is neither complete nor infallible. Memory sometimes has a life of its own, blurring, erasing, embroidering—even inventing. In this endeavor I have been enormously helped by a lifelong habit of keeping documents. I do not mean primarily a diary or journal: that genre has always seemed to me to suggest self-importance. Rather, I mean letters, most of them written to me by family members and friends, some of them written by me and copied before mailing. Some of this material I had long forgotten, including the contents of an old footlocker containing many letters going back to the early 1930s and fragments of a journal dating from August 1939 to October 1941. All this I had somehow held onto through various migrations. My saga will be viewed through the prism of these documents as much as possible.

Inevitably, the voyage through my past could not have been made without pain. Some chapters of my life and those of my family and friends have been sad, and revisiting them now after many years does not make them any easier to bear. Yet doing so impresses on me the fact that although my past has been difficult, it has also been full of challenges. As I reread some of the letters written at a particularly difficult time—when Hitler had seized Austria, and my friends were moved into concentration camps or conscripted into army service and others, including myself, had to leave our country—I hear a persistent note of resolve on our part to clarify and reaffirm our ideas and ideals and, at the same time, to master the new situation. If, then, times were hard for each one of us in his own way, they were formative times—times that, for better or worse, were ours.

Chapter One

Beginnings

If ever there was a group of human beings who had reason to assume that they could launch their descendants into a safe and sheltered world of peace and prosperity, it was the European upper bourgeoisie of the nineteenth century. Although born during World War I in November 1916, I was a beneficiary of that sense of confidence and security. The houses of my youth, solidly built if not massive, were intended to stand forever. My parents' home, a spacious apartment in the very heart of residential Berlin at the corner of Viktoria and Tiergartenstrasse, looked out toward the open Tiergarten (Berlin's Jardin du Luxembourg) and the Siegesallee, that boisterous avenue of marble Hohenzollerns—the "alley of puppets"—which had been a gift of Kaiser Wilhelm II to Berliners to celebrate the decisive German victory against the French in 1871.

My paternal grandparents' house in Dresden, where we often spent Easter, was a grand villa surrounded by a large and well-kept garden at the corner of Wiener and Gellertstrasse in the center of the so-called *Altstadt* of the Saxon capital, where the elegant families lived. Our uncles and aunts and a slew of cousins lived nearby, and the frequent and lively exchanges between us encouraged us to assume that the whole city was ours.

My Viennese maternal grandparents, the Kuffners, a brewers' family from Lundenburg in Moravia,[1] lived in a huge mansion surrounded by an enormous park with old trees in the outer district of the city, the nineteenth (Döbling), which bordered on the Vienna Woods. Residents in the neighborhood used to talk about the "Palais Kuffner." Strolling along the streets of the "Cottage" district of Döbling during spring and summer evenings, people would hear sonatas or chamber music emanating from the open windows of many a villa. Grandfather Wilhelm Kuffner's home resounded with music; he played the piano, and among his quartet partners were the prodigy brothers Emanuel and Sigmund Feuermann.

We spent many of our summer vacations in Döbling, playing often with our Zeissl cousins who lived a block away in the direction of the Türkenschanzpark. In the corner of the estate nearest the inner city was a special cottage without modern conveniences in which the butler Martin lived with his family. In the opposite corner, adjoining the greenhouses and the vegetable garden, there was a similar cottage that housed the gardener Herr Steingress and his wife.

I remember the busy comings and goings of important people in my parents' home: the festive outdoor golden wedding celebration of the Dresden grandparents in July 1925 with all the generations of the family assembled, and then the *grand diner* in the Hotel Bellevue by the Elbe River. Memorable also were the ceremonial Sunday afternoon gatherings—the *Jausen*, as one said in Vienna—of family and friends in Döbling, when delicious home-baked cookies and cakes were served along with coffee and lemonade.

Among the luminaries whom I met at home was the Crown Prince of Sweden, later King Gustav VI. Like Father, he was a collector of Chinese china, and attended early in 1929 Father's major exhibition of Chinese porcelain in the Prussian Academy of the Arts. At the reception in his honor given by my parents, we three boys, properly dressed in sailor suits, were supposed to pay our respects to royalty. I remember distinctly the parental instructions to bow to the tall gentleman in the crowd. Since almost all of the Swedish delegation were tall, I singled out for my bow the Crown Prince's aide-de-camp. But family honor, I learned, survived that breach of protocol.

Then there was the servants' realm. I remember the particular and protective part played by Emilchen, mother's special maid (in those days one spoke of her as a *Jungfer*). In Dresden it was Else who, as if plugged into an emergency telephone number, was at all times at grandmother's disposal; I can still hear, going like a wind through the house, the call for "Ääälsé!" And in Vienna there were the daily morning sessions between my aunt, Tante Jani, and Mirzi, the beloved rotund Viennese cook, about the forthcoming menu, and daily sessions between my aunt and the gardener about his realm.

Despite the Great War's impact on the times into which I was born, I was geared for a life in a gilded world that was thought to be insulated against evil and adversity. Our days and years, indeed our lives, seemed destined to follow an undisturbed course.

But this sense of security was already marred by a troubling experience in my Berlin childhood. It must have occurred early in January 1919, when the left-wing Spartacists threatened to gain control of the November Revolution of 1918. The curtains of the window to the Tiergartenstrasse had been drawn to shield us children from turmoil and harm. When I managed to lift them to have a glimpse outside, I saw a machine gun trained on me. This visual flash was among my earliest memories, and it became deeply ingrained in my mind, perhaps as a portent of the troubled world I would later encounter.

During World War II, the house in Berlin where we had lived was bombed to bits. The Dresden villa was also destroyed by aerial attacks. After my family was evicted upon the Nazi takeover of Austria, the mansion in Vienna became the residence of the Nazi Gauleiter Josef Bürckel. Once he had moved on, it was turned into a Wehrmacht brothel. During the short time that the Russians controlled the whole city, it functioned as a Red Army hospital. And when that part of Vienna came under American control, it became a school. The Kuffner estate was eventually sold to the City of Vienna, which tore down the mansion and in its place erected an International Students City consisting of a number of high-rise dormitory buildings. Nowadays, when I walk along the Lannergasse past what used to be an expanse of garden, I can look through the old fence and recognize one enormous chestnut tree in whose shade I often sat while studying my Latin.[2]

My life has not been uneventful. Quite foolishly, I began by wanting it to be so. I was proud to call myself a "war child," vicariously participating in the glory of the soldiers in the field. A sheltered existence seemed to me and my friends all too "bourgeois," and to our youthful cohort everything bourgeois was suspect. For us, the designation "bourgeois" stood for philistinism and conventionality, and we saw ourselves as belonging to that Nietzschean "first generation of fighters and dragon-slayers" that claims conviction from the "power … that acts and fights, breaks up and destroys; and from an ever heightened feeling of life when the hour strikes." In some measure I eventually got what I desired.

Privileged and happy as my early life was, I had to come to terms with the fact that "going to and fro in the earth" was to be my basic condition. Although baptized a Lutheran Christian, I was descended from a Jewish family. My grandparents on both sides and my parents were wholly secular, and no trace of the Judaic background was apparent in their homes. But when upon the death of our Dresden grandfather in December 1926 I read in the newspaper that at the funeral a "Rabbi" had officiated, I asked Father what kind of person this was, and of course he told me. This was how I learned about my family background. I was then ten years old.

For Jewish families, baptism, Heinrich Heine said, was an "entrance ticket to European culture." This may well have been the reason that all of us—my sister Lily and we three brothers, Franz, Alfred, and myself—had been baptized. But the family ethos was distinctly secular. I had to make my own way in questions pertaining to the religious realm. Religious holidays were observed at home with conventional ceremony, but that was all. We all were confirmed in the Christian faith, very much *comme il faut* in the Berlin Dreifaltigkeitskirche, where, in the early nineteenth century, Friedrich Schleiermacher had preached and, in our time, Pastor Geest, who also was President von Hindenburg's pastor, officiated. Besides preaching Christian doctrine, he occasionally thundered from his pulpit against the wicked Poles.

My sister Lily, undeterred by Geest's harangues, kept going to this old church on Sundays. Whenever I was in Berlin in the mid-1930s, I would deposit her there and proceed along Unter den Linden to the Catholic St. Hedwig's Cathedral, where Provost Bernhard Lichtenberg preached. He excoriated the Nazis' misdeeds and did not hesitate to pray with the assembled worshipers for the persecuted Jews and concentration camp inmates.[3] I shall never forget the spectacle of the congregation departing from the Cathedral after the service and emerging into the open, shouting "Heil Christus." All this seemed to me more relevant than Pastor Geest's diatribes against Poles.

Yet no less complex was my divided—or perhaps I should say double—loyalty to Germany and to Austria, along with my relation to my two hometowns, Berlin and Vienna. Although both sides of my family were Austrian, I was born and raised in Germany. For the average American, this distinction does not mean very much. But in the old world, which the Europe of my youth still was, the concrete identities and distinctions of place mattered very much. The word *Heimat*, meaning homeland or hometown, is a singularly German one, belonging to the German romantic vocabulary with distinct overtones of sentiment. *Heimat* suggests a region where one was born or where one feels at home and is generally accepted without having to prove oneself. Can one, then, have two *Heimaten*, as I had Berlin and Vienna?

My family's double identity presented a problem of sorts to me. My parents and grandparents took it in stride; in fact, they were proud of it. I remember a porcelain statuette, mass-produced during World War I, representing two soldiers, one German and the other Austrian, striding side by side. Proudly displayed in both my Dresden grandparents' and in my parents' homes, the statuette symbolized the wartime "comradeship-in-arms" that, it was assumed, was to foreshadow a new *Mitteleuropa*, which was to emerge from the war.

At the same time, however, I recall that in school my brother Fred and I were teased that Austrian officers carried umbrellas when it rained. The strapping, self-denying Prussian officer was the ideal in Berlin, while Austrians were suspected of being decadent. In the cold North, a special condescending adjective, *schlapp* (meaning flabby), was often applied to anything Austrian.

In time I came to see through these childish prejudices and learned to be proud of my Austrian self. As I shuttled back and forth between Berlin and Vienna, I achieved some distance from the crass hustle and bustle of life in the Prussian capital and came to appreciate the mellowness of everything Austrian. Later, as a student, I found in the work of Hugo von Hofmannsthal, an uncle of mine by marriage, a confirmation of my "conversion" to Austrianness in a "scheme" he had jotted down during the Great War, juxtaposing Prussian and Austrian "characteristic traits."⁴ In this scheme, Austria, rooted in traditional values and in humaneness, was seen as a counterbalance to Prussia and its regimented efficiency. Eventually, I shed my initial ambivalence about my two homelands and allowed my dual allegiance to enrich my life.

The climate of my home was non-political and certainly devoid of any nationalistic taint. My forebears were all men of affairs. Although public-spirited, they stayed out of politics. This may have had something to do with their Jewish background and a certain hesitancy to get involved in public controversies. But my paternal grandfather, Gustav von Klemperer, the Director of the Dresdner Bank, took his public functions and responsibilities seriously. Under his guidance, the bank became an institution of national and worldwide scope. As a *Geheimrat* (Privy Councillor) he was a much respected citizen in the courtly city, distinguished, as the *Dresdner Neueste Nachrichten* noted when he died in December 1926, for "his pronounced sense of justice and his iron sense of duty." He and his wife Charlotte were welcome guests at the Saxon Court, and the story goes that King Friedrich August III, a witty and popular ruler, referred to my grandmother, a person of distinct presence and wit herself, as "la Klempératrice."

As for my grandfather's connection with the House of Habsburg, he was in the early years of the century appointed Consul General of Austria-Hungary in Dresden,⁵ and in 1910, in the eleventh hour of the old empire, was elevated to the hereditary nobility by Emperor Francis Joseph. The latter has in popular parlance been called "der Adler" (meaning both "the Eagle" and "the Ennobler"). I believe that the award came about because the Emperor, making a halt in Dresden, had to reciprocate my grandparents' hospitality with a present. From then on, Gustav Klemperer could call himself Gustav Klemperer Edler von Klemenau, and he did so proudly. The designation Klemenau, I should add, was wholly imaginary.

Grandfather seems also to have had a particular relation to the heir to the throne, the Archduke Francis Ferdinand. My grandparents visited in the Konopischt castle in Bohemia, and the Archduke in turn made a stop in Dresden. I remember the photos on the piano in Dresden of the Princes Max and Ernst von Hohenberg, the sons of Francis Ferdinand and his morganatic wife, the Duchess of Hohenberg. According to a letter from my father, when the Archduke visited Leipzig in 1913 for the inauguration of the monument to the Allied victory over Napoleon I in the 1813 Battle of the Nations, he sent for Grandfather and revealed to him his plans for imperial reform after his accession to the throne. Nobody knew why he confided this to Grandfather, who was a very apolitical person.

In contrast, the lives of my Viennese grandparents, devoted to their brewery and to family, were much more private. The mansion in Döbling was a symbol of success. The family had originally lived in a more modest house on the same grounds. My grandmother, whom we called Granny, was a down-to-earth person who had been raised on a farm in Hungary. She often expressed regrets about living in "that huge *palais*," but Grandfather needed to show the world his new trophy house. It was huge and had virtually no private rooms—only high-ceilinged salons and cavernous halls.

The mansion was spacious enough to shelter bedridden "Tante" Mitzi (and her nurse), who was rumored to be an illegitimate daughter of the Emperor and was, as we learned later, Grandfather's mistress. Although she and Granny had little in common, my grandmother would take her the morning paper after reading it and stay for a brief chat. I never thought much about this until later, after the war, when my cousins enlightened me about the true relation between the two women. Now I must say about Granny, *quelle tenue* (what dignity)! When I visited her after the war in her exile in southern France, I asked her whether she had loved Grandfather. The answer was cryptic but very telling and by no means surprising: "My boy, in my day marriages were arranged."

Life in my parents' home was marked by a decorous harmony. Father and Mother were well matched by background and general outlook; that is, Father was the patriarch, and Mother accepted his rule unquestioningly. By the standards of those days, this was the basis of a good marriage. Father was an important industrialist. After spending his apprenticeship in two of the chief armament factories of the Austro-Hungarian Monarchy, he ended up in Berlin as the head of a locomotive factory. Mother, very much a Viennese by temperament, never quite came to feel at home among the rough-and-tough Berliners. But Father's rather institutional view of life set the tone. He lived a life of service to his profession and, indeed, to his family.

Insofar as he sat on various boards of directors, Father was a public figure and accordingly lived the "high life," associating with ministers and ambassadors, bankers and industrialists. But for personal friendships he seemed to have little time or inclination. Whatever opportunities were available for hobbies and sports went into occasional bridge parties, which we children looked down upon as being a bourgeois waste of time, and golf, which we considered boring. What we needed was parental guidance about the pressing and increasingly perturbing problems out there on the political stage. But on this score we drew a blank.

It was only natural that generational tensions should develop between Father and us children, especially Fred and me, with Mother playing the role of the healing go-between. It is said that if you don't rebel in your youth, you will later become a policeman. We did not turn into policemen. No doubt Father was too stiff and formal and lacked a way of responding to our concerns. We grew up in very troubled and troubling times and faced burning issues, both ideological and political. The less responsive Father was to us, the less able and willing we were to confide in him. We were determined to go our own ways.

At the time we did not sufficiently appreciate how deeply Father cared about us and for us, in his own somewhat unimaginative way. During the Nazi time, when the tides had turned against us, overcoming considerable difficulties and with great imagination, Father patiently shepherded us boys, one by one, toward safety in America. It was only then, days before the outbreak of the war, that he, Mother, and our sister Lily found refuge in England. The captain was the last one to leave the sinking ship.

Looking back on my beginnings, then, I see myself as having been exposed to many competing influences. Nothing in my youth was self-evident. I did not belong to any one place or social group or religious community. I could easily describe myself in my early years as having lived in a state of rootlessness, if not anomie. But I was fortunate enough to discover that the very complex conditions that defined my youth added up to a singular challenge. It did not take long for me to learn that there was no belonging anymore—that we all, my friends and I, had been plunged into a world in which we were all disinherited in various ways. The alternative to my supposed state of anomie was not to try to belong but rather to establish who I was, to find friends and kindred spirits with whom I could connect, and to define my place in a very complicated world to which I could cheerfully and proudly make a meaningful contribution.

Chapter Two

School Years

The Germany of my youth was Prussia, and the Prussia that I encountered most closely was my school, the Französisches Gymnasium, also called by its French name, Collège Français, where I studied from 1924 until 1934. This Prussia, I hasten to add, was a far cry from the stereotype that is generally associated with the name. Law No. 46 of 25 February 1947, issued by the Allied Control Council after the defeat of Hitler's armies, decreed the dissolution of the State of Prussia, which it identified "from early days on as a bearer of militarism and reaction in Germany." This was hardly a fair epitaph for it.

Of course, there were the obdurate Junkers, frantically holding onto the privileges of status and class. There was also the proverbial heel-clicking soldier. But there was another Prussia. Germaine de Staël wrote that Prussia was "Janus-faced," and indeed it was: no mere "vast barrack," it was also the home of enlightenment, of the *esprit* of justice and independence,[1] which Hofmannsthal had alluded to in his "scheme."

My school was part of that "other Prussia." The Französisches Gymnasium, or Collegium Gallicum, as it was called in a document from its founding days, was established in 1689 by the Brandenburg Elector Frederick III, later King Frederick I, for the education of the sons of Berlin's French colony. Established as an elite school with a special mission, the roster of its graduates over the three centuries of its existence is impressive, including the names of distinguished professionals from the French colony, as well as, since the mid-nineteenth century up to the present, some of Germany's leading minds. In the twentieth century it had both Junkers and Jews sitting on its benches, all getting along well with each other.

I found the teachers in the Gymnasium to be without exception highly qualified men; some, in fact, were overqualified for secondary school teaching.

Almost all of our classes were held in French; thus, we had to translate Homer and Thucydides, as well as Cicero and Virgil, into French. The use of German was limited to German, mathematics, and gymnastics. Every 31 October, the whole student body was led in procession to a nearby French cathedral to attend the Reformation Day service commemorating Luther's nailing of his ninety-five theses to the door of the Castle Church in Wittenberg.

These early schooldays of mine carried over into my later American experience. Since 1873, the Gymnasium had been located in a stern and rather forbidding brick structure by the river Spree, adjoining the area occupied by the Reichstag. Later, when I was at Harvard, John H. Finley Jr., the classical scholar who became a friend of mine, liked to remind me that when he was studying in Berlin, he used to walk home from the university along the Dorotheenstrasse adjoining my school's playground, from which he could observe us boys playing in the dusty schoolyard.[2]

Of course, the academic side of things by no means monopolized our attention. We were determined to break out of the confines of bourgeois respectability. After school hours and when our homework was done, some of us would roam through the Tiergarten, splitting up into two harmless gangs. One of them was headed by Friedrich von Schweinitz and the other by Thilo von Plessen. In this make-believe setting, my brother Fred was an "adjutant" of one group and I of the other. Often when making our rounds, we would observe a gaunt, ascetic clergyman pacing along the bicycle path in meditation over his breviary. We knew that he was the Papal Nuntius to Berlin, Eugenio Pacelli, who was later to become Pope Pius XII.

During vacations, we went on expeditions along the great rivers of Germany, the Elbe and Oder, rowing, camping, singing songs such as "Aus grauer Städte Mauern zieh'n wir durch Wald und Feld."[3] We gave ourselves to the unbridled spirit of the German Youth Movement.

But beneath this romantic exuberance, there was a sense of disorientation and a hunger for direction that we thought neither our parents nor the church nor school could give us. As I look back now upon my formative years, I see that they were marked by a political and spiritual void and an absence of any generally accepted tradition. A few of my friends—in particular, the scions of the Prussian nobility—related to the German imperial tradition, that of Hohenzollern Germany, but clearly there was no future in that. Certainly, democracy did not mean much to us. We were citizens of an interregnum, and our reality was an unreality of dreaming, longing, and searching, of conspiratorial friendships dedicated to the architecture of grandiose castles in the air.

The closest to me of my contemporaries, Friedrich, with whose family I am still in touch, was descended from a distinguished line of Prusso-German diplomats and officers. If he had one destiny in life, it was to be a soldier. In school he never managed to pronounce properly those French nasal sounds, which, I thought, he considered degenerate. Once I happened to tell him that I was to play in a doubles tennis match on the grounds of the French Embassy at the Pariser Platz, and his reaction was swift: "I don't set foot in the French Embassy."

When in 1932 Friedrich's father, the Major,[4] died, there were no tears. I accompanied Friedrich to the post office where he dispatched a telegram to Doorn in Holland, where the Kaiser lived in exile, reporting to His Majesty the departure of His obedient servant. And when the year immediately after the Nazi seizure of power I met up with one of my schoolteachers for a walk though the Tiergarten, our path happened to cross Friedrich's. He had proudly donned his father's fancy imperial uniform, and we passed each other like ships in the night. Nevertheless, later, before leaving Germany, I saw Friedrich, who by then had joined the army, and he asked me to turn over to him any forbidden books, which I could not take along with me, since his unit had a special place for them in its library. I never saw Friedrich again. He died in November 1941, fighting on the Russian front. His death was commensurate to his assigned mission in life, as Valentin in Goethe's *Faust* had it, "a soldier and an honest man."[5]

But it is the story of Friedrich's elder brother Georg that particularly grips my imagination and indeed my sense of empathy. His politics were hilariously unsteady, to say the least. He started off as a democrat, that is, he became affiliated with Prince Hubertus zu Löwenstein, a unique figure among German aristocrats, who advocated what he called "militant democracy," and went as far as joining the republican paramilitary Reichsbanner. But for Georg this was a mere way station in his search for a political home. Before long, prior to the Nazi seizure of power in Germany, he became a member of the SS, wearing his black uniform proudly. When during his Nazi phase he attempted to present the Major with a copy of Hitler's *Mein Kampf*, he was rebuffed. For the deeply traditional father, Hitler was plain vulgar, and his gospel was the devil's. This is the way things stood when I graduated from school.

On the night of the Nazi seizure of power in 1933, it was Georg who marched at the head of the Berlin and Brandenburg SS past Hindenburg and Hitler to the overwhelming jubilation of the masses in the Wilhelmstraße. Yet even while he was in school, there had been some mumbling among the higher-ups of the Hitler Youth about Georg's part in power struggles. Indeed, before long Georg found himself behind bars in the notorious Gestapo prison in the Prinz-Albrecht-Straße. This first spell of confinement lasted from October 1936 to March 1937. In the proceedings against him, the ominous Nazi People's Court charged him with "Preparation of High Treason" by maintaining "relations with foreign youth organizations" aiming to "overthrow today's government."[6]

It was between his acquittal, for reasons unknown, on 25 March 1937 and his re-arrest on 8 December that Georg saw a great deal of my family. While planning a trip to Africa, he consulted with Father, who had maintained old connections, about his professional future. Father managed to help him get a position with the private Delbrück, Schickler bank. About the state of my family, Georg had no cheerful news to report to his mother: "Last evening I was *en famille* at Klemperers. The parents send their best regards to you, which I am not to forget to convey to you. The eldest [Franz] has been for some time in America and the second [Alfred] will go over in September. Naturally the mother is very unhappy about this and makes a very depressed impression."[7] Concerning me there is a brief entry in Georg's diary for 14 September: "Farewell with Klemens Klemperer." It was to be our final farewell.[8] Having been reinstated into the army in December 1939, Corporal Georg von Schweinitz fell on 9 June 1940 at Herpy by the Aisne River. Over his temporary gravesite his comrades erected a simple cross topped by his steel helmet. His Battalion Commander wrote to the family that Georg died "faithful to his oath of allegiance to the Fatherland."[9]

As I write this, I ask myself why I am so preoccupied with Georg's odyssey. I shared none of his political oscillations; rather, my preoccupation with Georg and his plight transcends politics. While tempted to attribute it to a common generational experience, I fully realize that a generation can speak with many voices and encompasses a variety of generational units, as Karl Mannheim termed them,[10] defined by differing exposures and responses to common challenges. The paths that lay ahead of Georg and myself were replete with impediments, demanding from each of us forays into unknown territory. Behind us was *le monde cassé*, as the French dramatist Gabriel Marcel called it, the dissolution of a traditional world, and any further steps threatened us with pitfalls. We could not simply follow trodden paths but had to orient and reorient ourselves at every turn of the road. So far, Georg and I were two of a kind. But asking the big questions took Georg into a pact with the devil from which he ultimately could not disengage himself. I was immune to the "temptation" of National Socialism. To begin with, its racial credo excluded me as much as it was abhorrent to me. Moreover, a healthy dose of skepticism made me recoil from its fanaticism.

But back now to my schooldays. There were two spirits especially to whom my friends and I turned for direction: Friedrich Nietzsche and Stefan George. We were inspired by Zarathustra and identified with him as the herald of a Dionysian renewal. My friend and classmate Hans-Lukas Teuber wrote to me that the youths of Langemarck, where in November 1914 German volunteers were hurled into battle and slaughtered, were ready to follow the great iconoclast, but they were left lying in the mass graves of Flanders. "Which other generation, then, but ours," Hans-Lukas asked, had the task bequeathed to it "to proclaim the new faith?" All of us felt that we were Nietzschean missionaries of sorts.

Hans-Lukas was the high priest of intellectuality among us students. A young man with a mission, he wrote poetry and was a serious student of philosophy. He never engaged in small talk and hardly ever laughed. He saw himself as an apostle of a Nietzschean-Georgean creed to which he sought to commit all of us. Hans-Lukas and I met again in the early 1940s at Harvard. He eventually became a distinguished scholar in the fields of neurology and psychology.

The austere and cultic Stefan George was the model in our ventures into poetry. As aspiring poets, we emulated his mannered and archaic German. His somber words, which evoked a spirituality distant from and elevated above greed and glitter, conjured up a revival of long-lost mythical values and the commitment of a new nobility to service for a secret Reich. George was to us more than a mere poet. He saw himself as a seer and prophet, and he was the founder and center of a circle of disciples, wholly under his spell, who guarded his message. They were the elect, and we somehow imagined that we also belonged to them.

I thought that poetry was to be my vocation, and in going over my past I have found a trove of poems, some eighty of them, written in the mid-1930s. While not bad, they are altogether derivative of the Georgean mode. The very subjects are akin to George's: "Circling around Nietzsche," "Secret Germany," "Dreams of the Reich." (I would occasionally follow the poet's lead by not capitalizing the German nouns.)

Here is a sample of my attempts at poetry, indicative less of poetic quality than of my generation's searching turn of mind:

winde ziehen um
und wogen tragen sich weiter—
irgendwo immer ist flut.
die aber sich fügen
um der ebbe erwartung
werden vordem verweht sein.
nur die trotzen,
treu dem beginnen
sind auch sturm
und auch brandung,
sind wie wir fackel und glut.

winds blow over
and waves keep coming—
somewhere there always is flood.
but those who give way
expecting low tide
will be swept along.
only those who resist,
faithful to their calling
are storm

and are surf,
are like us
torch and fire.

Our preoccupation with both Nietzsche and George was cut short by Hitler's fateful seizure of power on 30 January 1933. I still had a good year to go before my baccalaureate. My infatuation with Nietzsche and George posed no particular problem for me. Nietzsche's *Übermensch* clearly was not the Nazi Stormtrooper, and Stefan George's *Führer* definitely was not Hitler, nor was his *Neues Reich* the Third Reich. Yet both Nietzsche and George lacked that "middle register of human experience," as Michael Hamburger put it in reference to Nietzsche.[11] In any case, for the moment at least, the big words, the big dreams were canceled and had to yield to more prosaic concerns. The climate in the school remained humane to the very end, an enclave of decency and humaneness. The story goes that after 30 January 1933, when the swastika flags went up all over the capital, the Französisches Gymnasium hoisted the black-and-white Prussian banner. The school was after all a Prussian foundation, which provided a good excuse not to display the Nazi emblem.[12]

To be sure, upon graduation in 1934, the moving song that hitherto had sent out every graduating class was no longer sung because its melody had been composed by Felix Mendelssohn-Bartholdy, who was Jewish by birth, although the family had later converted to Christianity.[13]

Nun zu guter Letzt geben wir dir jetzt
auf die Wandrung das Geleite ...

Now at the end we extend our hand
to guide you upon your journey ...

Yet as in all previous years, the parting certificate contained the beautiful old motto, "Que Dieu le tienne en sa sainte garde" (May God keep him in His holy protection).

After our *Abitur* we scattered—or *were* scattered, I should say—all over the globe. M.-L. N., a daredevil of sorts, ended up in Kenya, K.E. and R.E. in Australia. My brother Fred, who was by my side all my youth and who shared my dreams and daydreams, left Germany one year before I did, following in the family banking tradition. Heinrich H. H. Remak became a distinguished scholar in the United States, and we have exchanged guest lectures in our respective institutions. Heinz Weyl, the art historian in our class, was always tutoring his friends on the architectural wonders of the medieval past. After graduating he joined the Wehrmacht and was assigned to a motorcycle unit. I remember getting a letter from him in which he reported exultantly about entering France with his unit at breakneck speed. Being of Jewish descent on his father's side, he could not become a commissioned officer; in fact, his officer cautioned him to lie low, lest his racial background be detected. All the while, his father languished in a concentration camp from which he did not return. Some few years ago I visited Heinz in Germany. He had become a city planner in the north of Germany. We sang together, just for kicks, the old songs of earlier days. But his face was marked by torment over an unresolved past.

Klaus von Kardorff and his brother Jürgen, coming from a firmly anti-Nazi family, found some degree of immunity from party chicanery in the army. Their sister Ursula, who wrote a most perceptive and moving diary on life in Berlin from 1942–1945,[14] tells how one morning in November 1942, after having breakfasted with her brothers, she and Klaus took Jürgen to the railroad station to rejoin his tank company. After Jürgen had disappeared into the crowd, Klaus said to his sister: "Believe me, the good Germany will not go under." Jürgen fell early in February 1943 on the Russian front. The death announcement in the papers read that First Lieutenant Jürgen von Kardorff "died the way he had lived, a brave man and believing Christian." There was no mention of "Führer und Vaterland."

In the years preceding the fateful 30 January 1933—and of course even more so thereafter—youngsters like myself and my friends were anxiously in search of direction. We saw a great deal of each other. We had fun together, sang and joked, and often took long walks late into the night. All this was a way of airing our concerns, of encouraging one another and arguing with one another and simply finding in response to the momentous events a direction that we could reconcile with our innermost convictions. The more turbulent the times, the more we drew together and confided in each other. We also widened our circles, opening ourselves up to youths outside our school. I must add here that our initiates were exclusively boys. In this kind of business, especially in a setting that bordered on conspiracy, there was, we foolishly assumed, no room for girls. Yet Ursula was not the only female who came to play a vital part in the conspiracy against Hitler.

From among my wider circle of acquaintances and friends, I must single out Kurt Josten, an extraordinary person. He was my brother Fred's friend to start with, but then I took him over, and the friendship between us lasted until his death in the late 1970s. A few years older than my brother and I, Kurt had something of a gnomish appearance. An oversized head rested on a smallish, altogether non-athletic body. In fact, he detested all sportsmen—soccer players in particular—and he loathed "the rabble." He was a patrician, certainly no democrat, and he left behind a strangely arcane autobiography,[15] which even to the select among his friends remained a puzzle.

If Kurt was no democrat, neither was the man who became his mentor, Diarnos. The word "Diarnos" is an anagram for Herr von Jordans, and once Kurt took me along to visit him. He lived in a rented room in a Berlin pension, where he received a stream of friends and friends of friends, engaging them in Socratic dialogues that often lasted late into the night. Like Kurt, he despised the Nazis, whom he traced, with a magician's virtuosity, to the "blessings" of the French Revolution and the gospel of rationalism. Kurt later told me that Diarnos also collected funds to support those being persecuted by the regime.

It was the German novelist Frank Thiess who coined the phrase "inner emigration." Kurt and Herr von Jordans were part of that emigration. They suffered deeply under what they conceived to be the combined rule of criminality and the rabble. Yet they entertained no thought of leaving their country. They held on stubbornly to their vision of the "venerable old Germany," as Kurt put it, just as Klaus kept believing in the survival of the "good Germany." The existence of their secret society and their mutual support sustained their sense of dignity, purpose, and, indeed, mission.

Here, then, were the options before me, the two prescriptions by which to survive the Nazi menace: inner emigration or outer emigration. Conformity was out of the question for me, and I could not have survived even with inner emigration. But as National Socialism consolidated its hold over Germany, another proposition presented itself: resistance. I cannot claim to have been seriously engaged in this effort. After what amounted to some initial skirmishes with the Nazis in the streets of Vienna, when I was idealistic but wet behind my ears, I left for the United States. My Viennese friends who stayed behind resisted. Their example has remained in my mind, and because of it, I eventually decided to devote years of my scholarly work to the issues of resistance.

Chapter Three

"O du mein Österreich …"

Early in 1983 I was in Oxford to give a lecture in memory of Adam von Trott zu Solz, an outstanding figure in the German Resistance who has had a pivotal place in my work on resistance. The lecture was in Balliol College, where Trott had studied as a Rhodes Scholar from Germany in 1931–1933. One of the dons asked me if I had ever been to Balliol. I answered: "Yes, but I ran away."

In 1934, my dear father used all of his connections to get me admitted to Oxford so that I might continue my studies abroad. I remember some parts of the entrance examination. I remember a dinner at the table of the Master, A. D. Lindsay, on whose right I, as a foreign student, was placed. And I remember our arguing about Nietzsche, with the Master being rather dismissive of his standing as a philosopher and I, in all my ignorance, standing up for him. I was given a tutor, B. H. Sumner, a distinguished historian of the Balkans and Russia, who assigned me heaps of G. M. Trevelyan's British history to read. But then I ran away.

I was a difficult son. Indeed, I was ungrateful for my father's care. But I was a young man with a mission. I felt that I should not be a rat leaving the ship and that I must continue playing my part in the search for that elusive "good Germany." Thus, in the fall of 1934, I left Oxford for Vienna, my ancestral home. Because of my Jewish ancestry, the academic career to which I aspired was, in any case, closed to me in Germany.

Moving to Vienna gave my political searches a new lease on life. After all, Austria, however troubled, was still "free," and to a young and idealistic mind it offered a glimmer of hope of preserving the tradition of that "good Germany" and making it a magnet for all right-minded Germans. I remember that in bidding farewell to some of my Berlin friends, I grandiloquently proclaimed that

I felt a calling to save Austria from what had happened in Germany and thus ultimately to save Germany itself. I added that I envisaged being able to play the part of "savior" and saw no obstacles in my path.

Time seemed to have bypassed the enchanted *palais* in Döbling. Since Grandfather Kuffner's death in the mid-1920s, Granny had resided there with her youngest and maiden daughter Jani. Granny's bearing was as regal as her way of life was simple—to the point of parsimony. She rarely left the premises of house and garden, and when she did, a horse-drawn coach owned by the family brewery would be driven in along the graveled pathway—I can still hear the crunching sound of the wheels—and stop under the *porte cochère* of the *palais* to take her to town, where it would probably hold up traffic in the narrow streets of the inner city. The Kuffners never owned a motor car.

Granny recharged her wit by receiving occasional visits from family and friends and by avidly reading novels and newspapers. I remember sitting in the garden under a large linden tree by the wading pool, studying some Latin text, when an elderly gentleman, a visitor of Granny's, approached and engaged me in conversation. The topic was the French Revolution, about which I spoke with much conviction based on abysmal ignorance. The Tennis Court Oath? the Great Fear? But the visitor's forbearance knew no limits. I later found out that he was none other than the great philosopher Edmund Husserl, a friend of the family.

The daily news was brought into the house through the *Neue Freie Presse*, which every respectable Viennese citizen was supposed to read and which was published twice a day. I generally came home from the university at about 5:00 PM to join Granny for tea—tea with rum and thinly sliced bread and quince bars. By that time she had studied the evening paper and closely interrogated me on the events of the day.

As for Tante Jani, she was the ideal aunt. Having been self-taught herself, she took a great interest in our education, gave us books to read, and went on trips with us to show us the natural and architectural beauty of the Austrian countryside. Being with her was always fun, not least when she played the piano for us.

But the protective circle of my Viennese family could not confine me. My turbulent inner life reached beyond it. I expressed myself by writing poetry and sought the company of like-minded friends. Here, then, is a sample of the frame of mind of the young man who came back to Vienna in order to heal the wounds of the world:

Ihr seid euch so fern
auf einsamen Inseln,
Ihr Großen.
Ihr seid entstellt

und im Innern gezweit—
suchtergeben gestraft.
Wo ihr gescharrt habt
schweigen die Schätze,
und im Aufbau
sind die Jahre vereinzelt.
Ihr habt die Welt geteilt
und verloren,
und ihr Odem erreicht euch nicht mehr.
Lieblos, wirkungsbesessen
treibt euch die Irre,
fahlt die Gesichter
zu Scham und zu Hass.

Oh—hört ihr von den Inseln
den Schlag noch des Wassers
das euch alle beflutet?
So fertigt die Boote,
fahrt aus—ewig aus,
dass die Sonne wieder bräune
und der Wind euch durchfurche,
dass ihr einander—Harfenspieler—
an den Liedern erkennt,
die ihr dem Meer übergebt.

You are so distant
on solitary islands.
You adults
are disfigured
and alien to yourselves—
obsessed and punished.
Where you dug
the treasures don't show,
and all in all
the years are broken up.
You have distributed the world
and lost it,
and its breath no more reaches you.
Loveless and obsessed with effect,
you have gone astray
in shame and in hatred.

Oh, do you hear from the islands
the beat of the water
that engulfs you all?
Get ready the boats,

Row out, always out,
that the sun may shine again
and the wind sweep you all,
that you—harpists—
hear each other by the songs
which you consign to the sea.

* * *

Spring, 1935. A carefree flash. One morning in the spring, lured by the sun rising over the roofs of the city, I went out into the country. Wandering and inhaling the fresh air, I made my way to the open land westward without a particular destination. I was out in the cornfields of Lower Austria, singing to myself, when a peasant in a cart, whipping his horse to go faster, overtook me. Ahead was a fork in the road. I stopped him, hoping for a ride. Without asking my destination, he said that he was "going the other way" and moved on. But I ran after him, caught up, and made him stop after all. Up I climbed next to him, and once again he cracked his whip in the open air. There we were, rolling along, the golden fields bright with red poppies and blue cornflowers dancing in the sun, and a beautiful old song came to my mind. I sang:

Hoch auf dem gelben Wagen
sitz ich beim Schwager vorn.
Vorwärts die Rosse traben,
Lustig schmettert das Horn.

Über die Felder und Auen,
leuchtendes Ährengold.
Möchte so gern ruh'n und schauen—
aber der Wagen der rollt.

High on the yellow wagon
I sit by the coachman up front.
Forward the horses are trotting
To the sound of the horn.

Over the fields and the meadows
And the shining gold of the grain
I want so much to rest and look—
But then, the wagon rolls on.

* * *

The friends I wanted in Vienna had to have a sense of mission that was similar to mine. Soon I met them: Otto, Fritz, Helmut, and a number of others. Our vocabulary was much the same as that of my friends in Berlin. We argued passionately and seriously about eternal problems. We saw ourselves as standard-bearers of the Reich—not, to be sure, the "Third" one but the secret Reich of our dreams, the *sacrum imperium* of the Middle Ages, which was to serve as the model for overcoming the ills of modern materialism. Here is one of the many adolescent aphorisms that I jotted into one of the notebooks I always had with me: "Nonsense: to speak of the Second or Third Reich.... The Bismarck Reich was no doubt only a state, and Hitler's Reich is but materialism and inbreeding. The Reich is the German destiny; it is *the* German mission, and we shall turn towards it, the First one, as it is the only one."

The medieval *Reichsidee* was our model, inasmuch as it had, or so we fantasized, substituted transcendence for power and domination. We spoke of myth and mission, of the heroic and of destiny.[1] One of us, no less high-minded than the rest, stood out by virtue of his sobriety of mind and maturity. I first met Friedl Lehne in the university, where together we functioned as unpaid assistants to our professor, Heinrich Mitteis. Coming from a distinguished civil service background, Friedl had a lucid mind and was much preoccupied with legal and constitutional matters. Somehow he led us all the way into maturity. After the war he became a judge on the Austrian Supreme Administrative Court.

The rest of us, in our youthful exuberance, wore the attire of the German Youth Movement and sang its songs about fire and battle and sacrifice. Testing our courage and our friendships, we went hiking and skiing and climbing in the mountains. We called ourselves the Gray Free Corps. Our models for this designation were the volunteer units going back to the Prussian fight against Napoleon I and the formations that sprang up in Germany late in 1918 to supplement the imperial army, which was then in dissolution. Although we co-opted the mystique of German chivalry that prevailed in the German Free Corps, our aims and ideals were a far cry from those of the German units, which had become a breeding ground for right-wing extremism. We saw ourselves as the nucleus of a movement that would be able to counter Nazism with a populism of our own. Since the Nazis had usurped and corrupted the *Reichsidee*, we were persuaded that it was up to us to be its guardians. We were idealists—youthful, dead serious fools.

Imbued with anti-capitalist longings, we also had our own ideas about the social order. Quite apart from our disdain for everything "bourgeois," we looked on the social divisions prevalent in the capitalist order as odious. Coming from diverse social backgrounds, we considered ourselves comrades, although not in the Marxist sense.

The headquarters, so to speak, for us self-styled guardians of the Holy Grail was Osterleitengasse 7, a typical yellow ocher house of the Maria Theresian period in Döbling, removed from the hubbub of the city. Walking through the archway on the facade of the building, one faced an old garden shaded by majestic chestnut trees. Upstairs was the apartment of the Molden family.

Ernst Molden, the father of my friends Otto and Fritz, was a distinguished man of affairs in Vienna. In the later years of the Austro-Hungarian Monarchy, he had belonged to the so-called Belvedere Circle around the Archduke Francis Ferdinand, and after the war he took over the chief editorship of the *Neue Freie Presse*, Austria's great liberal organ and indeed Central Europe's leading newspaper. When in 1961 President John F. Kennedy was about to meet with Nikita S. Khrushchev for the summit in Vienna, I received a letter from the White House asking me to prepare material on "liberal" Austrians that Kennedy could use for ceremonial talks. There was, alas, not much material to work with. But Ernst Molden was clearly a man I could present. In the Austrian setting, marked since World War I by increasing political frustration and polarization, he was distinguished for his moderation, erudition, and good sense.

Ernst Molden's wife, Paula von Preradović, granddaughter of the Croatian national poet Petar Preradović, was a deeply religious poet and novelist with a radiant humaneness. Today, a plaque by the door to the house in the Osterleitengasse reads: "In this House lived the Poetess Paula von Preradović, Mediator between the Nations." Indeed, she made her home a center of intellectual life where people would come together in openness and friendship. When after the war the second Austrian Republic was in search of a new national anthem, it was Paula von Preradović who carried the day.[2]

Among the friends of the Molden house were Heinrich Mitteis, my teacher at the university, and Karl Rudolf, a prelate at St. Stephan's Cathedral. Like the Molden parents, they watched over us and tried to steer our rather effusive and in many ways immature ideas into constructive channels. Mitteis, a well-known authority on the history of German law, was a dynamic personality and a great teacher, and was therefore very popular among the students in Vienna. But when in the politically overcharged climate of the 1930s he lectured about the leadership principle prevailing in the Germanic pre-feudal warbands, the so-called *comitatus*, he met with a roar of applause from the Nazified students, who twisted Mitteis's altogether scholarly fervor to suit their own political agenda. Nothing was further from Heinrich Mitteis's mind than to endorse the Nazi cause. In 1935 he had left his chair in Munich for Vienna in order to escape the fangs of the Nazis, and I remember distinctly how he impressed upon us youngsters the fact that the word for his vocation, "professor," was derived from the Latin verb *profiteor*, meaning to declare openly one's convictions. Mitteis's beliefs were passionately libertarian, and he left no doubt among those of us who understood him aright as to what he stood for. He assured us that our chosen path was the right one. After the *Anschluss*, he was, to my knowledge, the only teacher at the University of Vienna who refused to take the obligatory oath of loyalty to the new regime. He was removed and banished to the lesser university in Rostock.

I did not know Father Rudolf as well as I did Mitteis. However, one encounter with him is imprinted indelibly in my mind. It took place in the Molden house on Christmas Day of 1934 or 1935. I had prepared a brief composition for the occasion, and when I showed it to Father Rudolf, he remained silent. It contained this passage: "War is the resurrection of the people." Was it not the legend of Langemarck that had made me write this? Father Rudolf merely shook his head, and this taught me a greater lesson than words would have done. Some ten years later, when I was in the United States, I noted in a looseleaf diary a quotation from André Malraux: "May victory be on the side of those who have waged the war without loving it."[3] By then I had learned my lesson.

Boys of strong convictions and of unusual resolve and drive, Otto and Fritz Molden were prepared to carry the ethos of their parents into a world fraught with new challenges and vicissitudes. They embodied the boundless romanticism of the German Youth Movement, although they did not allow it to get lost in thin air. In a *New Yorker* profile of Otto published after the war, Joseph Wechsberg referred to the "somnambulistic certainty"[4] with which Otto sought to realize his wild dreams. A visionary, he pursued his objectives with single-minded determination. After being thrown into jails by the Nazis, he took cover in the Wehrmacht and continued an adventurous life with forged identification papers supposedly belonging to Sergeant Alfred Steiger. Under this alias he met up late in 1944 with Fritz, and together they crossed the Brenner Pass into Italy and thence into Switzerland. There they joined some French and Italian resisters and also Allen Welsh Dulles, who directed American intelligence operations out of Berne as Special Assistant to the American Minister. Making their way back into Austria, the two brothers set out to organize the Austrian resistance, the so-called O5 movement.[5] In the end, in May 1945, Otto was instrumental in carrying out the liberation of Innsbruck.[6]

Fritz, six years younger than Otto and always in tandem with him, was and is a veritable *chevalier sans peur et sans reproche* (knight without fear and beyond reproach). His wartime exploits, like his brother's, were dazzling. Using the names "Luigi Brentini," "Pietro Delago," and "Gerhard Wieser," he outwitted the Nazi war tribunal, which had condemned him to death. Meanwhile, he was at work, meeting with Allen Dulles in Berne, coordinating the movements of the Austrian Resistance with Allied intelligence operations, and, on a larger scale, adjusting the plans of the Austrian Resistance to the projected Allied post-war division of Austria into zones.

Fritz Molden combined his Austrian family heritage with an extraordinary sense of entrepreneurial initiative: he was a robber baron of medieval-American vintage. All of his ventures—journalism, publishing, building a high-rise printing house in Vienna—have been driven by a sort of art for art's sake activism. Taking chances was more important to him than amassing millions; indeed, Fritz repeatedly had to pay a heavy price for his adventurism. "Other printing house owners," he remarked whimsically to a reporter from *Der Spiegel*, "buy themselves houses on the Riviera."[7]

Idealism? Adventurism? Quixotism? The brothers Molden, like myself, were born into a world of transition and uncertainty. There was no way of reconstructing a past that was irretrievably gone. The Vienna of waltzes, of Café Griensteidl[8] and the cult of Empress "Sisi," which even now mesmerizes the city, was not theirs. They had no part in the wrangles and acrimony that marked the political scene of the Austria "left over," as Georges Clemenceau cruelly put it, after the breakup of the old monarchy, and that eventually led to the return of Austria's native son, Adolf Hitler. In a setting of escalating crisis, Otto and Fritz showed a singular levelheadedness and resilience. When the Nazi movement encroached upon their country, there was no path for them but resistance, and it remained so throughout the time when Austria was degraded by being designated the Ostmark, an administrative district of the Third Reich.

* * *

Together with my brother Fred, I spent Christmastime in 1935 high in the mountains. Although geographically part of Bavaria, the village of Mittelberg, an enclave in the Kleines Walsertal pointing in a southeasterly direction into Vorarlberg, was Austrian territory. During the winters, thanks to the masses of snow, it was altogether severed from Austria and was served by the German postal and customs systems. In the outer reaches of the enclave, a village by the name of Baad, adjoining Mittelberg, was accessible in wintertime only after heavy avalanches had come down from the steep slopes on the west and east and the residents could start digging a tunnel to reconnect the two villages.

Skiing on the glittering slopes around Mittelberg was magnificent, and the weather, as it happened, was kind to us that winter. After sunset, the center of sociability was the Gasthaus Krone, where good food and unlimited red wine added to the general cheer of the group, who exchanged tales of the day's skiing adventures. Among the crowd was Karola von Kempis, who hailed from the Rhineland, where, between Cologne and Bonn, she was the lady of a stately moated castle and had a feudal title—Herrin auf Kitzburg. In Hirschegg, a neighboring village farther to the northeast of Mittelberg, Clarita Tiefenbacher from Hamburg was my steady skiing companion. These two women, Karola and Clarita, played an important part in my life when we reconnected after the war.

Christmas in Mittelberg was my first Christmas away from the family and therefore was an adventure of sorts in itself. On Christmas Eve, after a jolly celebration in the Gasthaus spiked with perhaps too much good wine, I made my way back to my room in a peasant house located next to the village church. I fell into my bed at about 11:00 PM, but soon afterward, shortly before midnight, the sonorous pealing of church bells shook me out of my sleep. As I got up and peeped out the window, I saw lights coming down along the opposite snowy slope as people on their skis made their way to the midnight service. It must have been my conscience that made me put on my clothes again and led me to the church. The mass having just begun, I found the priest playing a violin and a child with an angelic voice singing "Stille Nacht, heilige Nacht." This solitary Christmas in the Alpine snowscape turned out to be one of the most memorable Christmases of my life, even more than the many happy celebrations at home in the family circle.

At Christmastime two years later, Otto Molden and I left Vienna for the Tyrol. We landed high in the mountains on the Arlberg in St. Christoph, where there was one solitary hospice guarded by two gigantic St. Bernard dogs. There we were to take a ski teacher's course, which in the end I flunked. But we wanted to get out and have fun and adventure. One night, when a full moon cast its magic over the blue snow, Otto and the others who were taking the course went out skiing, but I stayed behind with my romantic self and was moved to jot down the following incantation:

Ich habe kleine Gebete gehabt und grosse Gebete. Der Mond hatte die Berge bunt gemacht, blau, sonnengrell, tiefblau und schwarz. Ich lebte schon lange da oben, ganz oben am Pass. Aber die Abende blieb ich meist in der Hütte, und wir lasen gemeinsam und sangen—die Freunde und ich.

Aber einmal eben, wie selten sonst im Jahr ... ging ich hinaus zu der Freude die mich draußen einlud.... Und da habe ich kleine Gebete gehabt und grosse Gebete.

Wenn wir sonst alleine gehen suchen wir Ruhe, aber diesmal war ich belacht, begrüsst, und das grosse, unebene und bunte Glitzern fragte mich, ob ich mittun wollte im freudigen Tanz und ob ich auch trunkene Gesichte liebte, die die fernen und nahen Gipfel schnitten und ihre kalten, eiskalten Feuer und Brände...

Und als ich da weiterstieg, als ich geschüttelt wurde und geworfen, und die Kleider waren noch so zerblasen und der Körper müde und starr, da lachte auch mein Gesicht nicht mehr so schön, aber stolz, und da betete ich wieder mein grosses Gebet: "Herr, lass mich so wild, lass mich so trunken bleiben."[9]

I have prayed short prayers and long ones. The moon lent the mountains a blue cast, almost bright, deep blue and black. I have lived up there, way up there on the pass, for a long time. But in the evenings I mostly stayed in the hut, and we read together and sang—my friends and I.

But once I went out to the joy which invited me out.... And there I prayed short prayers and long ones.

When we walk alone, we seek solace, but this time I was cheered and welcomed, and the great uneven glitter asked me to join in the cheerful dance and to celebrate the profiles of the far and near mountain peaks and their cold, ice-cold fires....

And as I kept climbing, as I was shaken by the wind and my clothes were blown and my body was tired and stiff, then my face laughed, not in beauty but in pride, and then once again I prayed my long prayer: "Lord, let me remain so wild, so drunken."

But the time for romantic wonders was over. What awaited me from then on was a storm—a nasty storm. Had my dreams shielded me from it? Or was it that, difficult as the following years were to be, they had lent me the resources to cope with things to come?

* * *

There is no entry in my diary for the 11th and 12th of March 1938; I had blacked these days out with a pencil. More happened during that time—more for me, more for my country, more, I daresay, for the world—than I could ever have forced into the little space of my calendar. At night, from the 11th to the 12th, upon orders of Hermann Göring, German troops prepared to invade the little Austrian Republic. *Finis Austriae*. It was an end to my imperial dreams and the first act of what turned out to be the disastrous World War II.

My friends from the Gray Free Corps and I found ourselves in the middle of it all. We were called together in an old red-brick barracks, evidently with a mission to defend the country. As evening set in, we stood around in the dusk, equally bewildered and excited, until some old factotum arrived to distribute rifles with long bayonets. I had never before so much as handled a rifle, and these might as well have been taken out of storage from the days of the Thirty Years' War. Dumbfounded, I was, so to speak, poking my nose with my bayonet when, at about 7:30 PM, someone turned on the radio so that we could hear the voice of Federal Chancellor Kurt von Schuschnigg. I will never forget this devastatingly sad sentence from his address: "I have been charged by the Federal President to inform the Austrian people that we shall yield to force." At that, the factotum reappeared to collect his rifles and left us to our fate.

We then stumbled into the inner city to encounter a howling mob of people. I have never witnessed such mass hysteria, and I hope I never shall again. As we reached the massive headquarters of the Vaterländische Front, the political organization of the old regime located in the big square Am Hof, I witnessed men climbing the walls of the building like monkeys to tear down the huge brass double eagle, symbolizing the regime, which must have weighed tons. The miserable eagle fell to the street below, not without crushing some of the crowd.

For the rest, we were left to ourselves. The first thing we did was to hide those among us, including Otto, who had been politically most exposed and were therefore most threatened by Nazi reprisals. We hid Otto in the inner city at his aunt's. At about midnight I boarded the number 38 tram back into Döbling. By my side was my friend Rolf. I still remember the stony silence between us. There was nothing to say. Our youthful dreams had been shattered; we were left defeated. Once at home with anxious Tante Jani, I turned on the radio and then turned it off again and on again, in disbelief and in the fading hope that it all might have been a bad dream.

Waking up on the morning of 12 March and looking out of the window, I saw a man who had always gone to work at 8:00 AM. Once again he appeared, neatly dressed, to go on with his routine as if nothing had happened. I was furious. I made haste to board the 38 to take me back into town so I could see Otto in his hideout. There I found his father, sitting with his head down and his hands folded over his head. He said to me: "Now I have lost my fatherland for the second time," the first, of course, having been the breakup of the old monarchy. Otto Molden spent various stretches of time in jail. Fritz was pressured by the Gestapo to give them information about me, whom they suspected of being a remote and behind-the-scenes puller of strings for an active political underground group.[10]

Helmut Jörg, as mentioned earlier, after spending three years in a concentration camp, was finally released to fight on the Russian front. Still a sworn enemy of everything Nazi, he fell in June 1943 in the uniform of the panzer troops, with the obligatory swastika sewn on his uniform. My friend Wilfried, a highly gifted and deeply religious artist, emigrated to London and then on to Canada, where he studied architecture and built churches. In a letter sent from London on 6 April 1939, by which time I was already in America, he reminded me of a sentence I had written in an earlier letter to him: "Wherever I am, the (inner) fatherland accompanies me." Both of us, Wilfried and I, left our fatherland with the resolve not to turn against it.

My friend Kurt v. B. also was guided by a distinct sense of mission. A scion of the Carinthian landed aristocracy, he liked most of all to go hunting on the family estate, preparing himself on the side for a career in law at the University of Vienna. Due to the sizable Slovene minority in Carinthia, there had always been among the Austrians a distinct German—indeed, Pan-German—self-consciousness. Kurt was one of those Pan-Germans. As a matter of fact, he was a Nazi and proudly called himself a National Socialist. Might I say here that he was one of the decent Nazis—and they did exist—whom I have known. In truth, he was my friend, and what brought us together was that he, like myself, had ideas about the reconstruction of a world, our world, which we thought was wanting.

We were always very frank with one another. He found me a "romantic," which I was, and a representative of a kind of liberalism that he felt he must reject. I hasten to add that I have always considered myself conservative in my predisposition to accept a created and traditional order and in my skepticism about man-made constructs. However, I have always seen the liberal as my neighbor and liberalism, in Leopold von Ranke's words, as a "ferment of life" to which I am indebted. While in its early nineteenth-century phase liberalism had a distinctly progressive worldview, in Kurt's opinion it had become retrospective and sectarian, a tool of class interest, and therefore an agent of disunity. Only the *Volksgemeinschaft* as envisaged by the Third Reich, he maintained, could overcome class divisions and lead the way out of the present-day hard times.

When on 15 March 1938—that dreadful day of Hitler's triumphal entry into Vienna—I found Kurt in an improvised gray uniform with a Hitler Youth armband, conducting the traffic in front of the Votivkirche, I walked up to him and said: "Kurt, you are crazy." We did not meet again until after the war, when he managed to trace me through an inquiry to the *New York Times*. In a long letter[11] he reminded me of that macabre farewell, himself in that "pseudo-uniform," enraptured by the events, and me "no longer dreamy, but full of pride in the resistance that you fellows offered in the end." He had not forgotten the encounter in front of the Votivkirche. Kurt proceeded to tell me his whole wartime saga. He had seen action in virtually all phases and theaters of the war[12] and returned "unexpectedly intact and healthy" to his estate in Carinthia. After ten idyllic days at home, he was jailed by the British occupiers and spent three years in an internment camp ("time to think—it did me no harm"), after which he started a family and opened a legal office in Klagenfurt, Carinthia's capital.

Here is an excerpt from one of his last letters to me, written in December 1997:

> After a beautiful—our common—time, you experienced here the worst, namely, to have to flee from this gentle and lovable land into foreign parts, into a land that is unique in welcoming and absorbing men and women.... You know, our fates have not been that divergent: I swept enthusiastically into our Greater German Reich—to find and to learn after all what Austria meant to me. We both have been fortunate enough to survive. Even today, after death and destruction, I must admit that those days of euphoria when we met by chance in Vienna [that is, in front of the Votivkirche] were the most beautiful ones of my life, but the subsequent sobering up was all the more impressive, like the confession after the sin. It will be hard for your children to understand this; here it is rather the grandchildren who want to know and who ask questions.... I have explained to them our different paths—so our friendship does go on!

The reason why I could hold on to our friendship was his honesty with me and with himself. In my response to Kurt's letter, I wrote:

> The letter in which you trace our respective journeys through life has moved me very much. Certainly, we have gone very different ways—and nevertheless

we have remained together. Why? Socrates supposedly said that the unexamined life in not worth living. And I have the distinct impression that your life is an "examined" one, as I hope that mine is too. Mistakes, my God, we all make—how tiresome for God, had he created all of us without mistakes. This way he may have his fun with us sinners. Dietrich Bonhoeffer wrote that God condemned sin but loved the sinner. Thus, we sinners may safely join each other—in friendship.[13]

I have never regretted my decision to spend my student years in Vienna. They were formative years that helped me set my course in a landscape of glittering and in many ways tempting ideologies. I learned to know myself and to be able to rely on myself. In some ways, of course, these were ugly, frustrating years, in view of the wave of the future that my friends and I tried in vain to stem and that, in the last months before the Nazi takeover, had degenerated into nasty street fighting.

But the *fait accompli* of the *Anschluss* of mid-March 1938 sent a clear signal that I must prepare to leave my country, to sever my roots, to leave behind the mission to which I had become committed, and to part from my friends. Moreover, since in those days I thought of myself as a poet, I was much concerned about losing my living tie with the German language. The exiled Thomas Mann, confronted with the prospect of having to leave the German Writers' League (Reichsschrifttumskammer) after it had come under Nazi control, wrote to Hermann Hesse that for him to make do "with the world alone" would not be easy.[14] In my own way, I was up against the same problem. I was in the process of developing my own German language, my own style, and I loved it. Nevertheless, I sensed that I must face the enormous challenge of learning a new language while holding on to the native language that was so much a part of me.

During the first weeks after the nightmarish *Anschluss*, I frequently went out to the country house of the Hofmannsthal family in Rodaun, a village to the south of Vienna, to be with my Tante Gerty. The Fuchsschlössel, as this enchanting place was called,[15] was a miniature baroque castle protected from the outside world by a high wall and a heavy wooden gate. Its garden, shaded by old chestnut and fruit trees, sloped steeply up to a little church and a hut, from whence you could survey a panorama of the Lower Austrian countryside and where my uncle, the poet Hofmannsthal, used to do much of his writing. Although the house was long past its prime, it still conveyed a sense of wonderment. It was springtime; the chestnut trees were in full blossom and the fragrance of the lilacs and the play of the spring flowers gave the garden a feeling of peace and protectiveness. But reality was no longer peaceful or protective, and the occasion of my visits was sad. My uncle had died in 1929, and now it was left to my aunt to close down the house and prepare for emigration to England. I went out to help her, but I do not know how much good I did.[16]

From my diary notes I gather that I leafed at random through manuscripts and books, not out of mere curiosity, but from a sense of the affinity that I have always felt towards Hofmannsthal's devout, religiously rooted traditionalism. "The German people," I then jotted down, perhaps somewhat pompously, "will lose much of their access to the poet once Rodaun is dissolved."

I had to prepare for my own departure to America. This meant a lot of shuttling back and forth between Vienna and Berlin in order to get my papers ready. Once, when returning from Berlin to Vienna, I found a huge red swastika flag hanging from our house in Döbling. I was really not that surprised; anything in those wild days was possible. The Nazis had moved in. Stormtroopers had occupied the villa, and their womenfolk amused themselves in the garden, breaking lilac branches. In the house, quite childishly, I left notes on little slips of paper, saying things like, "You can take our house, yet not our pride." This was the only weapon I had. Then Tante Jani and I were summoned by the occupiers into one of the downstairs salons. Because of her age, Granny was spared this ordeal. Jani and I were told that the Kuffners had been "banished" from Austria. One count against us, apart from the racial one, was that the family, as was generally known, had supported Archduke Otto, the Habsburg pretender to the throne, who lived in exile in Stenockerzeel in Belgium. Granny lost no time departing from the estate. A tall woman, she left majestically, head up, no backward glance, no tears, entering what turned out to be a long and bitter exile of her own. The rest of us had a few more days of respite to wind up our affairs.

In the first letter after the war that I received from Otto Molden's mother, she reminded me of our farewell in the Osterleitengasse, when she made the sign of the cross on my forehead. This gesture, this blessing, the touch of her hand has always stayed with me. It helped me over some very difficult weeks.

> War es nicht immer so,
> Dass die Götter speisten oder stritten
> wenn die Menschen sie riefen?
>
> Wir merken das nicht,
> wir bilden uns manches ein.
>
> Aber dann sind wir nicht alleine in der Welt,
> Aber dann ist sie uns nicht leer.
>
> Was it not always thus,
> that the Gods dined or fought with another
> when men called upon them?
>
> We do not notice it,
> we imagine this and that.
>
> But then we are not alone in the world,
> but then it is not empty to us.[17]

This was no piece of great poetry. But I detect in it, apart from a sense of abandonment and of pain, a degree of irony and playfulness that stood me in good stead after all. Even when my spirits were at their lowest, when I had every reason to grieve over my world, which had been disrupted, as I put it in a letter, by "those winds which out there blow fiercely and maliciously," I was convinced that "some day I shall have overcome."[18]

My last letter to Otto before my great departure was upbeat in tone: "The days of the crossing are approaching, and I want to make our farewell easier. Even if I was silent so long and even though the times were very hard lately, I believe I have learned to subject myself to the trials of life. Thus, I can derive more and more pleasure from the prospect of the big journey into foreign parts, and I am determined to devote all my love to encounters with the limitless world."[19]

Half of myself, then, had already departed for the United States. The preparations for my departure had to be made from Berlin. Of course, they were not easy, and during the process I encountered as many bureaucratic, if not capricious, obstacles as I experienced kindnesses. One almost insuperable problem was that no passport was to be issued without a guaranteed American visa, and vice versa. At one point, when my father's worries had reached the breaking point, he rallied what was left of the family—my brothers were already safely in New York City—and marched us, each carrying a bag with a toothbrush and other gear, to the Swiss Legation to ask for asylum. The minister was an acquaintance of his, but the answer was predictable.

A few weeks before I was to sail, I was summoned, as a result of a bureaucratic mix-up, to attend the medical examination for induction into the armed forces. Although I was not eligible, I followed the instructions, arriving at the appointed barracks and undressing like everybody else. An elderly policeman approached me and said quietly: "I know who you are. I used to stand guard at your father's factory in the Chausseestrasse. You don't belong here. Get dressed before you run into trouble. Go home." This kindness came from an ordinary German whom I had never met before and would never meet again. I did go home—and I have always remembered the policeman with gratitude. In turn, I cannot help recalling the morning after the infamous pogrom, the "crystal night" staged by Joseph Goebbels in Berlin on the night of 9–10 November. I found myself in a bus, going where I cannot remember, dazed by the sight of the shattered store windows all along our path. The conductor, by no means dazed, exclaimed brutally loudly, as though in triumph: "Now we have shown them [the Jews]." This shook me out of my stupor. Both the elderly policeman and the bus conductor were ordinary Germans.

But there were also loyal friends. Thilo von Wilmowsky, an influential executive of the Krupp dynasty, who was unaware, I suppose, of our precarious situation, came to Father to enlist him in plans for a coup against Hitler. Frau von Siemens, who had married into one of Germany's powerful industrial families, visited regularly, just to be with us. And then there was Maimy, faithful Maimy von Achenbach, who lived in Babelsberg in the lake district East of Berlin and owned a canoe. Every so often during the last summer before my departure, Maimy, my sister Lily, and I paddled out through the silent waters of the Havel lakes. Not much was said, and not much had to be said. We all knew what was on each other's minds. But those outings gave us much happiness. My Viennese friends Charlotte Mautner-Markhof and Otto Cornides suddenly appeared in Berlin as I was packing my bags. They never explained why they had come; there was no need to explain.

I packed my suitcases under the supervision of two beady-eyed Gestapo men. When the day had finally come for boarding the liner in Hamburg that was to take me across the ocean, Lily and I stopped for my last meal on land with a cousin who was married to a Hamburg shipowner. Around the lunch table sat a rather lost lot, including our host's two sons from a previous marriage, both in brown Hitler Youth uniforms. Not much that mattered was talked about. On this occasion, silence was the best language.

Chapter Four

America—Coming Down to Earth

The SS *Manhattan* moved past Fire Island along snow-covered Long Island into New York Harbor on Thanksgiving Day, 1938.¹ By the time I disembarked, I had not a penny left in my pocket; the little cash I was allowed to take with me had been lost on board playing poker. My brothers Franz and Fred were waiting for me on the pier, and they gave me a home during my first months in America. It may not have been purely incidental that during the first days of my stay in Manhattan I came down with a high fever. Traveling from one shore to the other had been no easy transition for me. My whole system had undergone a shock, which now manifested itself in the emigrant's purgatory.

Once that ritual fever had subsided, I busied myself with brushing up on my rather rudimentary English and acquainting myself with the history of the United States. Before long I landed my first job, in the Rare Book Department of the Columbia University Library, located in the rotunda of the original King's College. My main task was to carry and sort books, for which I was paid the regal sum of $15 per week. Receiving one's first paycheck, however small, is a great event in one's life. These months of work at Columbia served as a friendly initiation into American academia.

Among the first letters I received in New York was one from Mrs. E. (Franzi's mother): "The love of *Heimat* will remain unchanged in your heart." Later came the first letter from Otto Molden: "Across lands and seas we are friends; our *Heimat* is great." The word *Heimat* featured repeatedly in the correspondence of those days, tending to assume a particular meaning that it no longer necessarily conveyed.

My first letter to Otto from America was not written until February 1939. It was an epistle of sorts, addressed to "dear friends" and rather high-flown in tone, a strange brew of nostalgia and anticipation of things to come: "Vienna, that dear old city, I see strangely transfigured behind me: always my melody, my intuition." In Manhattan I found "no tree far and wide," only "walls, stones, roofs, and everywhere laundry hanging from the lines, even in the rain, which is grainy and black." New York, I pontificated, was "a bad conscience, the city of the expelled, the forgotten ones—of those who are drowning." In turn I fantasized about Indians and wild horses in Texas and "strong, wild, free Americans." And I concluded with rather inflated admonitions to my friends to face up to "danger, grief, and fortune" like heroes, and with my own understanding of "the American experience as work, work, hard work."

Otto's answer to this letter reached me in June 1939, by which time he was already in uniform:

> Days, weeks, months have passed since your wonderful and clear letter to "the friends." And "the friends," although somewhat scattered by work and military service, meeting only irregularly, but firm in their resolution, have read or have been informed of it as the Corinthians were of the letters of St. Paul [oh, blasphemy!]. Thus, this letter has somehow energized life among the friends. And there probably is no better test of a great friendship than this one. But I think we have passed it, having created by means of mutual concern an atmosphere allowing us to feel at home always and everywhere—to be German while remaining true to ourselves.

In April 1939 I learned that I had been awarded a Refugee Scholarship to study at Harvard College. This generous grant made all the difference in my understanding of what America was all about and helped me to make my way in it. It certainly enabled me to get back on track academically and return to the study of history, which by then had become a vocation for me.[2]

Soon I began to feel solid ground under my feet, as expressed in the following letter to Mrs. E.

> By now the first interesting, indeed fascinating months in America are over; I believe that I have survived the whirl of the New and can now survey both the *Heimat* and the new surroundings without sentimentality, the former with a higher love and the latter with a cheerful sense of discovery.... America is an experience, another continent; America throws me.... Vienna was one of those stations in my life that have shaped me, and America is another one. Stations which allow the gentle magnificence of change to guide us and which give us ground under foot amidst this shifting world.

For the summer I accepted a position as a tutor with a family on a farm in Middletown, Rhode Island, overlooking Narragansett Bay. I did not really teach my charges, Greg and Armar, German, as I was supposed to; they taught me horseback riding. Bridge House became a virtual home for me in subsequent years, and the family members, the French governess and the staff, the dogs, the horses, and the goats all became dear friends of mine. Cousins of the family, the v. B.'s, lived nearby in a stately manor house on an enormous estate. As they turned out to have been friends of my father's parents, I was made to feel at home there all the more. After the usual Sunday morning swims on Third Beach, we often gathered for a ceremonial dinner at the Grey Craig manor.

> (J.) Sunday, 3 September [1939]: Little Widdy,[3] instead of saying "Good Morning," reported to me the outbreak of the war.[4] Dinner at Grey Craig. All of the guests seemed more moved and concerned about events in Europe than most of the other more sensation hungry people here.... Miss D., who sat next to me, said in a very nice way that the winter was bound to be difficult for me and that I should not expect everybody to understand me. Opposite me sat a yachtsman, a man with a strong face, evidently a Dane, who quietly lifted his glass to me, and I followed suit.

In the afternoon I drove to the lovely St. Columba's Chapel in Middletown and prayed: "Dear God! Free my German fatherland of the madness of the tyrant and protect the German soldiers! Amen." The shadows of the day were heavy. I thought much of my parents and Lily in London.

* * *

Someone had recently given me a copy of a speech that Harvard President Charles William Eliot[5] made long ago. It afforded me a wonderful introduction to the college and made me all the more eager to begin my American studies in that setting.

> Harvard College is sometimes reproached with being aristocratic. If by aristocracy be meant a stupid and pretentious caste, founded on wealth, and birth and an affectation of European manners, no charge could be more preposterous: the College is intensely American in affection, and intensely democratic in temper. But there is an aristocracy to which the sons of Harvard have belonged, and, let us hope, will ever aspire to belong—the aristocracy which excels in manly sports, carries off the honors and prizes of the learned professions, and bears itself with distinction in all fields of intellectual labor and combat; the aristocracy which in peace stands firmest for the public honor and renown, and in war rides first into the murderous thickets.[6]

Two guidelines accompanied me throughout my initial years of study in America. One came from Robert Ulich, a German-born pedagogue who lived in Dresden before emigrating to the United States, where he became a Professor of Education at Harvard. In that capacity he was a member of the committee that awarded me one of the Refugee Scholarships. When I paid my respects to him upon my arrival in Cambridge, Massachusetts, he reminded me that long ago he had seen me play in my grandparents' garden. This was a very kind welcome for me. He then said something that much impressed me and encouraged me to make the transition to my new surroundings: "Remember, our German idealism will always stand us in good stead over here."

Once I had gotten my bearings at Harvard, I met Hajo Holborn, a German scholar who also had left his country. A distinguished historian who had found a haven at Yale University, Holborn often came up to Cambridge and, in the course of time, became a mentor of my generation of younger historians all over the United States. He was the kind of historian who, by virtue of his commitment to scholarship as well as his political engagement, set an example for us all; his love for his métier was contagious. Once he said to me: "We Germans are having the benefit over here of learning to live in a climate of pragmatism." He was right.

Somehow, these two remarks, one by Robert Ulich and one by Hajo Holborn, defined the parameters of my American experience. Was my German idealism to remain a cherished possession, or would it turn, after all, into a liability? And if I gave in and went along with the casualness of my new environment, would I not betray myself? Maybe this is the kind of quandary many Europeans experienced upon reaching the shores of the new world. Moreover, had I not moved into a culture that was about to lose its easygoing innocence and would itself be overwhelmed by the serious-mindedness, indeed, by the woes of the old world, and not least by the impact of the emigration from Hitler's Europe? While these thoughts did not articulate themselves at the time, they simmered inside me, and I was fortunate enough to be able to work them out and to find a balance with which I could live. It was a challenge to me to keep my roots alive on both sides of the Atlantic Ocean and to hold on to my European ways while becoming part of the American scene.

One of the first dormitories I lived in at Harvard was Divinity Hall, a beautiful building in the classical style, which had been designed by Bulfinch.[7] Its dignified, symmetrical red-brick exterior contained a chapel in which Ralph Waldo Emerson had delivered his Divinity School address, "Acquaint Thyself at First Hand with Deity," of June 1838. I am not sure whether the building successfully imparted this message, but in any case its felicitous architecture was conducive to good work and fellowship among its inhabitants. Each room, although of modest size, had its own fireplace and sleeping alcove. I put up curtains and bought dirty rugs from an Armenian merchant. Over my desk, I hung a print of Mont Saint Michel, over the fireplace, a van Gogh poster. I really enjoyed living there.

For a short time I became a proctor, a sort of resident chaperone, in one of the freshman houses, Mower Hall, in the Yard. This was fun for me. Not much older than the students, I got involved in lots of roughhousing. It was a way of catching up with some of the collegiate life I had missed out on in

Vienna, where, as everywhere else on the European continent, a prospective student moved directly from a *Gymnasium* or its equivalent to a university. In Vienna there were not those four years devoted to studying the liberal arts in a communal setting that existed in the Anglo-Saxon universities. In any case, the situation in Vienna in the 1930s was far too serious to allow the kind of informality and cheer that distinguished English and American colleges.

Before long I was asked to become a resident tutor in Eliot House, one of the seven residential houses that were built in the late 1920s and the 1930s with the goal of breaking down the impersonality of university life and fostering a sense of community among teachers and students. Eliot House had a majestic location opposite the Anderson Bridge over the Charles River, and its House Master was the no less majestic Roger B. Merriman, a gigantic figure who was more responsible than anyone for grafting Harvard's academic establishment onto the English college tradition. The Eliot House students came in disproportionate numbers from private boarding schools, whose graduates were called "white-shoe boys" and were distinguished by a preference for the liberal arts as opposed to the natural sciences—and also, alas, by a certain amount of snobbery. "Frisky," as Merriman was generally called at Harvard, was the lord of the legendary course History 1, a strenuous introduction to European history, all about wars and peace treaties and kings and queens.

The senior tutor of Eliot House was John Milton Potter, a junior historian of the German Reformation who more than anyone paved my way into the new and exciting world of Harvard. He had the build of a football player and an impulsive, volcanic manner, and he took a fatherly interest in me, shepherding me, tutoring me, trying hard to bring my dreamy ways down to earth. Once, after I handed in an essay I had written for him, he said firmly but kindly: "This [my thoughts on the meanings of the Trinitarian concept] is all very interesting. But remember, you are not a poet—you are to be a historian."

I will never forget the tutorial meeting with Jack (as we students called him) the day in June 1940 when the German occupation of Paris was announced over the radio. The scheduled history assignment faded into oblivion, displaced by an apocalyptic monologue—somber but defiant—given by our teacher. What I witnessed that afternoon was living history. Jack Potter may not have been the greatest of scholars: his lectures, although always inspiring, tended to be disjointed, and he did not write the book that was expected of him. In the end, he did not get tenure at Harvard but was appointed President of Hobart and William Smith Colleges in New York State.

My years in Eliot House were particularly enriched by John H. Finley, who succeeded Merriman as House Master. If ever any human being embodied the Greek ideal of the beautiful and the good (*kalon k'agathon*), it was John Finley. Gently bemused by life's dissonances, he followed the prescription of the Aristotelian mean with the greatest of ease. There was fire in John, the fire which he knew was inherent in big ideas. "It seems of first importance," he once wrote to me, "that ideas be clothed early with some majesty, since needs will in any case tend to beat down ideas." No skeptic, however, and certainly no cynic, he imparted to his students and friends the supreme excitement of those big ideas. "Who would easily forsake the company of sparkling generations?" he mused. He recognized inescapable ironies that, rather than detracting from life, enhanced it and made it truly beautiful.

But John Finley's life went beyond Cambridge. A good half of him belonged to New Hampshire. There, in Tamworth, his great-great-grandfather had been, he recalled, "the village doc." There his father, an associate editor of the *New York Times* from 1921 to 1940, had built a late Victorian lodge or country house in sight of the majestic and legend-shrouded Mount Chocorua, New England's Matterhorn. Some 100 yards above the main house was a red-brick one-room schoolhouse in which Finley *père* had taught his son his Greek letters; John made a point of showing it to visitors all intact, just the way it used to be. Thucydides in New Hampshire, then, was not uprooted but invigorated. John's major work turned out to be on Thucydides.

> (J.) Cambridge, 6 September [1939]: In the evening, dinner at the Rosenbergs.[8] Sometimes I long for the deep German discussions and disputations of old. Every remembrance of Germany solicits a sort of reflection in the midst of this restless continent. This evening I felt that I must in these grave hours be with Germany. Germany is after all my life's task. And if I love Germany, the wholly great Germany, I must also concede its great sins, the dangers that every mighty task engenders. I must acknowledge them.

> (J.) 23 September: The dream of that Thousand Year Reich is prematurely over. Nocturnal bull session in Lowell House at Harvard. My argument was that every state that relies on arbitrary domination is doomed. Only concepts like divine right, institutions like kingship, or constitutions guarantee law and order. Thus, in the end I even staged a defense of democracy: representation and constitutionalism are "eternal laws" of sorts. I pointed to the beneficial functions of a patriciate, of tradition, and of grace. But they all questioned such conservative notions. I think that I was not sufficiently persuasive. We parted at half past four in the morning, unfortunately without agreement. But I am more than ever confirmed in my faith.

> (J.) Sunday, 22 October: Another halting step into my Americanization—last night's Coming Out Party in Brookline. The fellows in Lowell House, where I am living for the time being, said that I should go; it would be fun for me. I had no idea what a Coming Out Party was. Anyway, curious as I was, I went, dinner jacket and all, making my way by public transportation via Boston, which took hours, to the country club where the party was held. I knew no soul and danced once with a girl I did not know. Blue laws: end of the party at midnight. I made

my way home again alone and finally fell into bed at five in the morning. After awakening, as was the habit in the old country, I felt that I had to proceed to the home of my hosts of the previous night, whom of course I did not know from Adam, to leave my calling card with them. So I did. I rang the bell. A nonplussed maid opened the door saying: "Yes, yes, I shall call the lady of the house." Whereupon I ran away.

(J.) 14 November: Ex-Chancellor Heinrich Brüning spoke in the History Club about the plans of his government for Mitteleuropa (a customs union between Germany, Poland, Austria, Hungary, and Czechoslovakia), which no one had known about. He dealt elaborately with his concerns over short-term political loans and the disarmament issue. France was the devil: France's security system, France's (Austria's) successor states. The small powers should change their outlook; their mentality should become Central European. Meanwhile, however, they all have developed their own industry. All of us found it significant that Brüning now spoke about his years in office and so elaborately.

(J.) 10 December: Some evenings one can say the Lord's Prayer very slowly, and every word is a conversation with God.

(J.) 12 December: I have presented my seminar paper [on Novalis[9]], and my fellow students seemed very inspired and eager to read more on Romanticism. Professor [Crane] Brinton, however, laughed incomprehensibly—laughed....

A letter from Hans-Lukas (Basle, 10 January 1940) explored the possibility of rallying German exiles to volunteer "at the Finnish front" in the war with Russia and inquired whether in that case I would be willing to join. What a lunatic proposal! "But," he continued, "we who today cannot stand *with* our own people and do not yet want to stand *against* them are caught in a banishment even from ourselves—at the brink of senselessness.... Are you still the same? But I don't know whether I am!" In a postscript Hans-Lukas invoked—in Greek, which we had learned in school—the legendary drinking song about Harmodios and Aristogeiton, the Athenian dragon slayers: "I'll dress my sword in myrtle ... like Harmodios and Aristogeiton."[10]

(J.) Middle of May [1940]: I certainly shall see Germany again—but will I recognize it? America has become my second *Heimat*.

(J.) 16 May: These are sad days for Europe. The young generation, the bravest, fall everywhere—and who survives, who shall resurrect EUROPE again? This faith can be regenerated only by youth. But post-war years are always disappointing, and the cult of the dead is embarrassing. War memorials do not reconcile.

The German troops are only 70 miles from Paris.

(J.) 21 May: History Club dinner. Professor Fay by my side said that this war would awake two souls in my breast. Yes, it tears me to pieces.

(J.) Sunday, 20 October: Letter from Maimy that Georg has died in battle. Good Georg. Only a few bits of news penetrate to us from Europe: that Otto has been decorated, that Georg has fallen. But who knows for what? Who knows whether he aspired to heroism? The soldiers who move along with these senseless hordes are victims of madness.

(J.) Sunday, 6 April [1941]: Tonight, coming home, I sang for myself the German anthem, to find out what it says to me these days. And it still meant something to me, dear old song composed by Haydn. To be sung by a choir of angels. And now *in partibus infidelium*.

(J.) 22 July: At last I met [Hans] Rothfels[11] face to face. Besides much historical talk, he told me stories about my father on the Isle of Man. Papi had refused to be escorted by a guard to a swim and, after giving a number of lectures to the Academia Manxiana on locomotives, had been awarded a degree *honoris causa*.[12] Good for Papi.

(J.) 5 August: Today news from Maimy arrived that Friedrich has died in the Russian war (sometime in the middle of July). So it was not just accidental that I dreamt and talked so often about Friedrich in recent days. Wherever I have lived, in Germany, Austria, here in America, I have found friends to be cornerstones.

Georg died last year; and now Friedrich has gone. But do you [Friedrich] still remember our last talk before I came to the US? We talked about a better, a lovelier, a pious Germany. And when that day will come, I shall not lament your death anymore.

(J.) 8 August: Bobby Sz. invited me for an evening picnic to meet Felix, the brother of Archduke Otto von Habsburg. I was disappointed by the meeting. Felix, my age, was not particularly open to any kind of interesting discussion.

Anyhow, he is the first real prince I have met so far in Newport.

(J.) Saturday, 6 September: Dinner at the v. B.'s. Peggy talked about my family in Dresden, how she "venerated" Grandmother.

(J.) Sunday: At the Bartols' old farm in Milton. Tennis and swimming. Mrs. Bartol told a little of her acquaintance with [George] Santayana and [Alfred North] Whitehead.[13]

(J.) 24 September: I gave my first lecture in Fay's course. First at 9:00 AM at Radcliffe. At 12:00 PM at Harvard. I enjoyed lecturing tremendously; the class seemed responsive.

I had lunch with Alex Böker[14] in Dunster House. Talking about Brüning, he explained to me the background of what is falsely called his "complex for rehabilitation." Alex said that Brüning suffers from the daily news and reproaches himself for not having averted the disaster.

(J.) 11 October: Pray for Jani.[15]

* * *

In January 1943, I requested and received a license to travel, as the text from the documents below explains:

13 January 1943: REQUEST FOR LICENSE TO TRAVEL
(Enemy Aliens)
Alien Registration No. 4833
Purpose of trip; Settlement of private affairs before being drafted.
Destination: New York City …
sgd. Klemens von Klemperer
(Signature of Alien)

Boston, Mass. 1/16/43
License to travel as set forth is granted.
sgd. Edmund J. Brandon
NO GOOD IN PROHIBITED AREA UNITED STATES ATTORNEY

Chapter Five

Going To and Fro upon the Earth— On Being a Soldier

A Preliminary Tale of Uniforms

On 6 June 2001, the fifty-seventh anniversary of D-Day, over the noontime radio I happened to listen to marches by John Philip Sousa, melodies I have always liked. They make me think of the glorious sides of army life as well as the infernal ones, of brass concerts and somber farewells to fallen comrades, of parades and routs, of victories and defeats, and of snappy uniforms. In my youth I had a distinct fascination with uniforms. Now, stimulated by the Sousa marches, I was daydreaming, and my mind turned to episodes in my youth, to myself and uniforms.

At home we children ate from special picturesque plates. Some showed women in fancy dresses and others soldiers in uniforms. We boys, of course, always insisted upon eating from the ones with the uniformed soldiers.

My father, having served a year in the Austrian army prior to World War I, was discharged with a host of colorful uniforms, which were then neatly stored in a trunk in the cellar of our Berlin house. One afternoon, we three boys, having been apprised of their location, decided to raid the trunk and put on the uniforms for dinner. There was, I remember, hilarity all around, prompted by the gorgeous display of colors. No one's attire matched another's, no one's jacket matched his trousers. Perhaps all armies existed to celebrate the pageantry of life.

Shortly after the Nazi seizure of power in 1933, I had encountered my friend Friedrich wearing the splendid imperial uniform borrowed from his father. But by then the charm of uniforms had yielded to an eerie sense of doubt and deception. Still, since virtually everyone else in the streets of Berlin was triumphantly uniformed, and lest I be completely left out, I made a uniform of my own, consisting of a windbreaker, a pair of breeches, and a leather belt.

My army years, of course, put me in khaki. When I was a rookie at Fort Devens in Massachusetts, one of my first assignments was to carry shoeboxes into a storehouse. A nearby sergeant must have detected my lack of enthusiasm. Moreover, in defiance of regulations, I was bareheaded, as I had usually been in my civilian days. My cap was stashed away in one of my pockets. The sergeant shouted: "Hey fellow, them days are over!"—and out came my cap. After all, like my uniform, I was now "government issue," and I was proud to wear the uniform. I still have in my possession a field jacket that was issued to me secondhand. I assume that it must originally have been worn by a GI who had fallen in battle.

Quite some time after my discharge from the army, I thought that the time had come to turn over my uniforms to our son Jamie. Down we went into the cellar, as years before my brothers and I had done in Berlin to put on Father's Austrian uniforms for our family masquerade. However, this cellar was wet, and when we opened the trunk, we found nothing but shreds. Goodbye, then, to military brass bands on village greens, goodbye to fancy parades to the tune of Sousa marches, goodbye to uniforms.

Induction into the Army: Fort Devens and Later

On 17 February 1943, this "enemy alien" became an American soldier, following his two brothers. Franz, the eldest, had signed up in 1942 and landed in a tank unit in France. He liked army life and evidently had a wonderful rapport with his men. Later on it occurred to me that he might have done well to stay in the service after the war. Fred, my other brother, became a soldier a few weeks before I did. In an early letter from California to Franz and me, Fred wrote (Pittsburg, CA, 29 April 1943): "I am in good spirits and quite looking forward to adventure. Don't be scared for me—I am, pardon me for saying it, a damned good soldier and a good shot. I'll be able to take good care of myself."[1] Fred ended up fighting in the Pacific.[2] As for me, I wanted to serve and chose to "volunteer through the draft board," as the procedure was then called.

As is always the case in such situations I got plenty of advice from family and friends.

> Letter from Franz v. K. (5 September 1942): Don't loan out money until ... you know who can be trusted.... Make it a sport for yourself to learn as quickly as possible their words that you don't know as yet. As soon as you know them, do a bit of cursing and swearing yourself. Don't let anyone bully you into anything—except corporals, sergeants, or officers, of course. If anyone bullies you, bully right

back at him. Be, or at least appear, straightforward, honest, and a real "he man." Be wise and careful. Laugh with the drunks, or cry with them if they feel like it. Be patient.... Good luck! Love, Franz

Letter from Hans J. Epstein,[3] Camp Ritchie, MD (13 January 1943): Get tough!!! Nobody but your officers and non-coms are to bully you.... Push and use your elbows. It is ungentlemanly, I know—but this is in the end a question of survival. Be quick!! Learn to curse and swear with the rest of them.... Never take any chances of breaking a rule or command. Watch your accent and try to improve it rapidly.... Free your mind from all idealistic pictures (our idea, for which we fight, burns unseen deep within) and accept a lousy life as your present status.... Ever your Hans

Two of my German-born friends in America went their own ways in facing the war.

Letter from Hans W. Gatzke[4] (18 January 1943): I have considered volunteering; but ... I cannot get myself to *volunteer* for a service that will involve my fighting against friends and my brother. Should I be *drafted*, I should feel somewhat differently, since I am to be a citizen of this country, in whose ideals I believe....

The draft finally caught up with Hans.

Alex Böker, who spent the war years in the United States, was determined to perform a balancing act as a decided foe of Nazism and yet a pronounced German patriot. He would not and could not reconcile his German patriotism with the acquisition of American citizenship, much less service in the American army. While at Harvard, he saw himself, like his mentor Brüning, as a representative of what he called "the other Germany," with the self-imposed mission of paving the way for a democratic, indivisible Germany. Thus, Alex was instrumental in introducing to Brüning one of his former fellow German Rhodes Scholars, Adam von Trott zu Solz, who had come to the United States in the autumn of 1939 as the emissary of a group of German resisters. Trott was executed by the Nazis on 26 August 1944 for his part in the conspiracy against Hitler. In the early 1970s, when I set out to work on the German Resistance (*Widerstand*), Adam was one of the German resisters who made my interest in them more than a purely academic venture.

As for Alex, after leaving Harvard in 1943, he struggled along as a farm worker in Wisconsin, a teacher of German in Chicago, and even a cowboy in Colorado. After the war, he returned to Germany and joined the Foreign Service of the Federal Republic. His last post was that of Ambassador to the Holy See. Alex and I kept in touch by letters and visits, whether in Alex's elegantly appointed apartments in Rome and Munich or our simple and beloved farmhouse in Conway, Massachusetts. Alex died in May 1997. The *Festschrift* intended to celebrate his eighty-fifth birthday, to which I contributed, became a memorial volume.[5]

(J.) 17 February 1943: The first day in Fort Devens is hell.[6]

(J.) 19 February: The past two days count as two months—for me, at least. I am glad they are over. Yet I suppose they were unavoidable, and altogether we were introduced into the army in a most fascinating way. The IQ test with loudspeaker directions, the interview for classification—very well run indeed. And the clothing! Within 15 minutes a staff of tailors threw at me well-fitting pants, jackets, an overcoat, shoes, and a cap!

Everybody now waits to be "shipped out" for basic training. Otherwise the days at Devens are idle....

(J.) 20 February: They tell me that last night in my sleep I gave an oration in German.

(J.) 22 February: My few days in the army have, after all, not been so horrid. I found out two things: that you can keep good company with almost everybody, and that the sergeants, at least deep down in their hearts, are good fellows after all.

I shall be leaving tonight. Destination unknown. I hope it is Maryland.

(J.) 23 February: Night train to New York, farther on to Baltimore. Thank God, it was not a troop train. I was all by myself, really alone, just the way I felt.

(J.) The arrival at Camp Ritchie took place late in the evening when it was already dark. Thus, some anonymity at least concealed the initiation into the new order of things. I became Private K. v. K., US Army, Co. G, 2nd Tn. Bn., Camp Ritchie, MD.

Camp Ritchie, located near Hagerstown, Maryland, was the US Army Intelligence Camp in which soldiers, most of them German-speakers, were subjected to training in intelligence matters, such as the study of German army documents, the German army order of battle, and prisoner of war interrogation. The courses lasted two months, after which graduates were sent to maneuvers and eventually overseas.

(J.) 6 March: From my barracks:

A Russian: He was born in Siberia (Omsk). He says he is used to army life because he fought against the Red Army with the White Russians in 1919. And now he is a soldier again—as though he had waited for this opportunity for 24 years. He likes to be surrounded by others, to ask questions or to hold forth in elaborate fashion. His laughter shakes the structure of our barracks, and his heavy accent weighs like lead, fascinating to some, repulsive to others. I see him gesticulating. Sitting opposite him on the floor I can catch only a tenth of his words.

A Frenchman: Very definitely European, a man with education, as he boasts. An officer really, yet without rank or bars. He says he served in his life in four different armies. In World War I, he deserted the German army to join the French. In this war, two years ago he fought with the French in Europe, and after defeat he joined the American army. He says it is his destiny to fight every war in two armies.

An Italian: At first appearance smart and aristocratic. He has very much a Renaissance profile. And he too has his story to tell: that he has to get even with the Fascists. His fiery eyes roll to give emphasis to his convictions.

An Englishman: He claims to have been a captain in the British army, but is a private now in this one. A man who knows all the languages of the Middle East yet regularly forgets the passwords.

All of these adventurers are short of greatness. They are condemned to start all over again and again. They are desperadoes.

The fellow who has the bunk under me is called "Pufc." He is Danish and cannot master his "th's" at all. A butcher in civilian life, he has been a soldier for two years now and became a sergeant in the Air Force, but they broke him because he returned from a ten-day furlough ten days late. I like Pufc, and he likes me. He calls me "Dutchie" and tests most of his views on me. He asks me to write his letters for him whenever his spelling fails him. Pufc was never admitted to the Intelligence School at camp because he could not write well enough. When the rest of us, having passed our two-month course, were alerted to go overseas and were marched through camp to the accompaniment of trumpets and drums, I noticed a fellow rushing toward us from way up on the hill, swinging a large butcher knife. As he drew nearer, I heard him shout, "Dutchie, Dutchie," and Pufc had tears in his eyes. I never saw Pufc again.

(J.) The motto of our company is elegantly set in Latin: "Fas est ab hoste doceri."[7] And this is to be taken literally. It is no invitation to a picnic.

(J.) 9 March: From the dedication of [Erich Maria] Remarque's *All Quiet on the Western Front*: "This book ... will try simply to tell of a generation of men who, even though they may have escaped its shells, were destroyed by the war."

A prominent personality in our barracks: Francis (formerly Herr Franz Josef) von T., of old Austrian aristocratic lineage. Now, very democratic, he picks his nose for all to see.

(J.) 5 April: Night patrol. Along our route I noticed monuments to the right and left, old guns lined up, piles of bullets, cemeteries. We were in the battlefields of Gettysburg. I wish we could have stopped, looked and looked again. Yet we were on patrol. No more a historian, but a soldier.

On 19 May 1943, I was naturalized in the Circuit Court, County of Washington in Hagerstown, Maryland. It was not the kind of ceremony I had expected. A clerk rattled off some phrases, and I lifted my right hand for the obligatory oath of allegiance. And that was that: no handshake, no little flag, and a most perfunctory performance on the part of that anonymous clerk of a ritual that meant a great deal to me.

From letters to John H. Finley Jr., in the spring of 1943:

> As for my own contribution to adventure and war, it is not much as yet, I admit. I often fancy myself to be a soldier, but it is not so. Today I was sent out on patrol, and through my binoculars I was supposed to observe "the enemy" on a faraway hill. But soon the binoculars turned away from the hill and focused on the cherry blossoms and meadows nearby. I was reminded of some Dürer etchings that I have seen.
>
> I shall be through with my course in one week. And I shall stay here for two more months at least, during which time I shall get my basic training. I am glad about it; perhaps this training will give a last touch to my soldierdom. Besides, the country here is so beautiful.
>
> I have had a good chance, at least so far, to figure out "what remains," or, as you write, "what is inside that does not change." There are two kinds of conservatives: those who hate change—and frankly I do, in spite of my many migrations—but they are fools, and the others who know that there is the inside that does not change. Let us be of the latter kind. This is really our problem at every step of our lives.

After completing the Intelligence Course at Camp Ritchie, our whole class was rushed by air to Great Britain. My first station was an army camp in the Cotswolds northwest of London called Spring Hill, where for at least a week I was put on KP (kitchen police), which meant washing dishes and stirring huge pots of soup. The picturesque countryside of the Cotswolds reintroduced me hospitably to the old world I had been homesick for since I left. Once I had done my day's duty, I would make my way across an extended hillscape to an old pub dating back to the thirteenth century, where I would sip good hard cider into the night.

Before long, however, I was transferred out of that idyllic world to London, which was under constant attack from the Luftwaffe. On one of my first nights in the city, I found myself, during an air raid, near the Marble Arch out in the open of Hyde Park. I noticed that people were pressing their bodies against Cumberland Hotel, facing the monument. I asked one man how to find my way to Hyde Park Corner. The answer was as short as it was swift: "Just follow your bloody nose!" I emerged from the outing intact. Retracing my steps the next day, I found shrapnel wherever I had walked. It must have rained around me. But a kindly fate rewarded my stupidity.

I subsequently found myself assigned to SHAEF (Supreme Headquarters Allied Expeditionary Force) under General Dwight D. Eisenhower. I proudly wore its shoulder patch displaying a flaming sword on a black field. The headquarters themselves were far in the south of London in a place generally referred to as Bushy Park, but I was there only once. My workplace was in midtown, first in the area of Trafalgar Square and later on in Kensington. I lived in various Red Cross Clubs before moving into one of the many emptied, drafty, and unheated houses along Cadogan Place that had been requisitioned by the American army for its servicemen.

My work consisted mainly of evaluating captured German soldiers' paybooks. The paybook was a triumph of German thoroughness. Consisting of some sixteen pages, it contained information on the soldier's unit, field post number, officers, reserve unit, and other details. This invaluable intelligence enabled us to reconstruct the order of battle of the German army. Our offices were stacked with these paybooks. The head of my unit was a British officer, Colonel Eric Birley. Originally an expert on the Roman army, at the outbreak of the war, he had offered his services to the War Office. Working with him was actually quite exciting. In our briefing sessions he explained that German army divisions would generally appear in the field in waves of three. Assuming that we knew the whereabouts of Divisions 1, 2, and 3 and 7, 8, and 9, he would instruct us to try to identify anyone from Divisions 4, 5, or 6, in which case we would know where we were facing all three Divisions 4, 5, and 6. Although often dismissed by the staff offices and in the field, this kind of intelligence work, which today would be done by computer, was of some appreciable use for the war effort.

From a November 1943 letter to Hans W. Gatzke:

> To some extent you can say that England, and London in particular, has come to represent half of Europe just now, as exile governments have their seats right here.
>
> As to my work, it is interesting. I have a fairly important job, and I am glad of it. It fills my day pretty well. By the time I am through every night, I step into the indefiniteness of the blackout, or rather I stumble home. And the days are getting shorter.
>
> Besides, I joined a very nice officers' and soldiers' club [the Churchill Club], which is situated in a historic building near Westminster Abbey and has a very good library, good music, good food.
>
> If you ever have the time, read Churchill's *Great Contemporaries*. When meeting Churchill as a writer and historian, you cannot help but be deeply impressed by his personality, in particular by his historic perspective and statesmanship. In a letter from September, John [H. Finley Jr.] described Churchill's visit to Harvard in eloquent terms. Were you present?

One day—it must have been late in June 1944—I was summoned by the Adjutant General's Office in London to appear at an appointed hour in the Churchill

Club for some special event. When I got there, I found upstairs a contingent of Allied soldiers and officers milling about in uncertain anticipation. Before long we were lined up in two or three rows, and I found myself in the front row. The Queen was approaching. As she proceeded from soldier to soldier in the front row, I noticed that she asked each one: "Where were you born?" Since this was the time of the Second Blitz, when the Nazis were unloading their bombs over London, I thought this was not the right occasion to respond by saying "in Berlin." So I quietly changed places with the Britisher in the row behind me, who, when the Queen approached him and asked the ritual question, answered, "In Yorkshire, Madam." Thus, I did not quite meet the Queen.

One evening at dark I was caught in Trafalgar Square in an air raid. By now I quite instinctively pressed my back against the wall of one of the adjoining buildings, like everybody else, but my eyes popped with excitement. The tracers in the air, the roar of the charging planes, the fall of some of them into the dark abyss made a scene, at once deadly and fascinating, of imminent death and yet of magic and beauty.

At Christmastime in 1943, I got a V-Mail[8] message from "what is left of the Senior Common Room [of Eliot House]. We think of you and shall drink to your health." It was signed by a rogues' gallery of academic dignitaries, T. Spencer, John Finley Jr., Roger B. Merriman, I. A. Richards, Jean Seznec, Arthur D. Nock, I. Bernard Cohen, Michael Karpovich, Werner Jaeger, F. O. Matthiessen, and "Pvt. Hans W. Gatzke, just recently inducted into the army."

In response, I sent a somewhat pompous return message on 20 March 1944:

> To the eminent Scholars and Friends of Eliot House. This is to return your kind Christmas greetings, which reached me "somewhere in England." Our community now more than ever spreads far—and wherever we are, whether as scholars or as soldiers, our task is unaltered. We learn and we serve. If only upon our return, some day soon, I hope, we shall be stronger, our courage harder, our spirit keener.

My feelings for my adopted homeland grew daily more complex, as this letter to Dr. and Mrs. Otto Jeidels[9] shows (14 February 1944):

> Above all I am amazed and thrilled by the way English is spoken over here—and I don't mean the accent. In the States, English has been degraded to a commercial language, very much shortcut and flattened, whereas the Englishman applies and places words in their correct and precise meaning, thus giving way to fine distinctions of thought.
>
> Being in Europe again affects me very strangely. There are those long walks that you want to take over here, walks across plains, along rivers, and there is an unusually strong effect of light and shade on the trees, houses, on water, and then the old sites: churches, houses, stone walls. Otherwise, I find that European ways have become remote beyond measure to me. All sorts of ideas and

conventions have not been forgotten—and yet I have outgrown them and have turned to quite other ways. I am often homesick for the States.

My dreams are little drugstore dreams, but not really: skyscraper dreams, streamlined and infinite. They go back to America, the wide and varied countryside that I have learned to love, to the people, my friends, my work.

I was happy to be close to my family once more (letter to Hans J. Epstein, 22 February 1944):

Every week I have a day off, which I often spend in Oxford. It is always a great boost to my family when I come: Mother is very sick indeed, and if only I can get her to smile, I am very happy. Father is terribly gloomy about life, and I feel that somebody has got to play the fool out there in order to make life bearable for my sister at least. Next weekend in fact I expect her here, and we plan to enjoy it very much. I intend to take her to a concert.

Otherwise, I am very much by myself in my spare time. The blacked-out war is for me an interlude only, and I do not feel like seeing or meeting people. My correspondence has assumed great importance for me. It's a communication to my friends, it's a way of thinking and expressing myself—it takes the place of a diary for me.

My books complement my correspondence. Here is my little war library: the volume of Plato, the Bible, the five tragedies of Shakespeare, Walt Whitman, various Russian books, a manual of heraldry.

On D-Day, 6 June 1944, my unit stayed in London, where the sky was shattered by roaring Allied bombers flying in formation toward Normandy. This became the "doodlebug season": what we called "doodlebugs" were V-1s—Hitler's secret weapons.[10] Launched from Germany, these unmanned, jet-propelled flying bombs were intended to foil the Allied invasion and to wreak havoc on the cities of England, thus assuring the final victory of the Third Reich. They first appeared in the skies of London during the night of 12 June. By chance, I was just then on duty as an air raid warden, standing on the roof of the building in the Kensington area where I was stationed. Suddenly, I detected fiery tracers piercing the sky from an easterly direction. As they approached, I heard loud rattling sounds as though from winged motorcycles. Then, as these mysterious missiles reached their destination not far from where I stood, a few seconds of silence passed before they crashed into the streets. Early the following morning, puzzled, disoriented, and exhausted, I made my way to the nearby mess hall to take my breakfast. I had coffee and some rolls, as usual, but the big jam pots on the tables sparkled strangely. As I reached into one with my knife to help myself, I discovered that it was filled with glass shards. The mess hall, once covered by a huge glass dome, had been hit by one of those flying torpedoes. I was so tired that I was wholly unaware that I was sitting in a sea of deadly fragments. Londoners adjusted valiantly to living with such surprises from on high, and when I walked the city streets and heard those familiar but ominous noises, I thought nothing of throwing myself flat on the sidewalk. Later, when V-1s were succeeded by V-2s, there were no more seconds of grace.

When in mid-September my unit moved to France, I stayed behind in London to face a board that would decide on my becoming a commissioned officer. I eventually made my way alone across the Channel. Landing in Cherbourg, I had to find and rejoin my unit, which I suspected was in the area of Versailles—more I did not know. I had to hitchhike. "Versailles?" "What? Never heard of it." So I proceeded in installments, Bayeux, Caen, etc., and all this mostly on top of trucks loaded with jerrycans, which did not make the best of mattresses. I had to hold on with one hand to my rifle and with the other to my barracks bag, and I sorely needed a third to keep me from falling off when the trucks went around corners. And it was cold. When at one stop I joined a group of GIs by a campfire and told them that I was searching for my unit, I met with unanimous ridicule: "You sucker, why don't you join us? We all are AWOL." I finally reached Versailles and fell, dead tired, onto a Louis XV couch in what turned out to be the American officers' mess. Busy and obsequious waiters were about to set breakfast for "les monsieurs, les officiers Americains." So I was ejected and had to finish the last leg of my odyssey, to Vaucresson, where I found that my unit had taken possession of a sumptuous suburban establishment called Haras-de-Bel-Ebat.[11]

After rejoining my unit as a commissioned officer, and in order to keep me from fraternizing with my friends among the enlisted men, I was sent to Paris, where I stayed for about two months. Following this, I was to reappear in Vaucresson as a different person—one whose authority would be commensurate to that of an officer. In Paris I was billeted very elegantly in the Crillon hotel by the Place de la Concorde, only to be ousted from it when it became the preserve of generals. I was then transferred to the Hôtel des Deux Mondes at the Avenue de l'Opéra, which could hardly compete with my previous quarters. It might as well have been called the Hôtel du Demi-Monde.

After I reappeared in Vaucresson, I kept seeing my enlisted friends. One of my soldiers was Corporal E. of the British army. Once, when my unit was still in Britain, he and I and two others were riding in a jeep when I heard the rattling of a V-1 approach from afar. I ordered the jeep to come to an abrupt halt and shouted: "Get the hell out of here." Three of us instantly ran for cover along the roadside. And Corporal E.? He had hidden underneath the gas tank. How lucky he was that the jeep was not hit.

Later, in Vaucresson, Corporal E. got a pass to spend a weekend with friends of his family in Paris. To get to Paris he had to cross the bridge over the Seine at Saint-Cloud. E. thought of taking along a present, but what was there to bring? At the time, there was not much to be had in the stores. Corporal E. then had a brilliant idea: since our workplace was full of German soldiers' paybooks, why not take along one, only one, to show to his friends, which was against military orders designed to safeguard the confidentiality of the operation. Alas, at the bridge he was stopped by the military police. Then E., speaking with a distinct German accent—like me, he was a refugee from Germany—was searched. And what did the MPs find but a German soldier's paybook. Corporal E. landed in the clink, and it took our commanding officer weeks to get him freed.

At about the same time, four of us in a jeep on our way from Paris to Versailles were stopped by an MP roadblock. It was the time of the Battle of the Bulge, in December 1944, when the Germans under Field Marshal Gerd von Rundstedt launched a last desperate attempt in the Ardennes to break through the Allied front in the West. It was also the time when the daredevil parachutist SS Colonel Otto Skorzeny was rumored—correctly—to be in Paris with the mission to kidnap General Eisenhower, whose headquarters were in Versailles.[12] Paris had every reason to be watchful—jittery, even—and for security to be tighter than usual. As the other occupants of my jeep were being scrutinized by the MPs, I, who still spoke with a German accent, was closely interrogated. "Who won the World Series?" I blush to admit that I had no idea what the World Series was. "How many feet are there in an inch?" Brought up with the metric system, I barely knew how many inches there were in a foot. So I myself would have been a candidate for the clink, had it not been for my GIs in the jeep, who managed to convince the most suspicious MPs that I was "all right."

While stationed in Paris, I received a phone call from the Office of Strategic Services (OSS), the American intelligence agency, asking me to come over to the Champs Elysées, where a friend of mine, Gerhard Wieser, was waiting for me. "I know nobody of that name" was my reply, but I was persuaded to go anyway—and whom did I find there but my old friend Fritz Molden, who was on a short mission from Vienna. Fritz had lived a wild life during the war, traveling virtually all over Europe under assumed names and with fake identity papers on behalf of the Austrian Resistance. At that point, he was Gerhard Wieser. Landing in Caserta in southern Italy, he had undergone a security check by an American officer, Dyno Loewenstein, who happened to be a friend of mine from basic training at Camp Ritchie. When in the course of the interrogation Fritz gave me as a reference, Dyno encouraged him to look me up in Paris. Thus, we met again, Fritz and I.

A short lunch together bridged the seven years that we had not seen each other. Then Fritz left for Berne to confer about secret matters with the American intelligence chief, Allen Dulles, before disappearing again into the fog of the secret service, parachuting back into Austria. Otto Molden's life during the Nazi era was no less brave and adventurous. In and out of jail, he was drafted into the army, which gave him some immunity from Nazi Party control. However, he deserted to organize, under the cover name Alfred Steiger, the Austrian Resistance and in the end helped bring about the liberation of Innsbruck.[13]

In retrospect I am impressed by the fact that the Molden brothers were able to translate their youthful ideals into action, even under the adverse conditions of Nazi tyranny. Unlike that of Otto and Fritz, my life was clearly not one of action. Yet as an American I proposed to translate my early dreams into work as an academic. Had I changed? I kept asking myself the question posed to me early in 1940 by my friend Hans-Lukas: was I still the same?

Opposite our establishment in Vaucresson there were many people who had plenty of reasons for asking themselves the same question. Herded together in a camp of so-called displaced persons (DPs), these Russian refugees had been forced westward from their homes during the course of the war. Now they were awaiting an uncertain future. Even today I hear in my mind the stirring and often sad songs that reached us from across the road. Once, at Christmastime, we Americans were invited to their camp for a special performance of music and dances. Yet we could not escape the sadness of it all. A secret clause in the agreements of the Yalta Conference among the Allies in February 1945 gave the Soviets the right to "repatriate" these DPs—men, women, and children. Some but by no means all of the men were captured in German uniforms. In fact, all those who saw themselves as political dissenters and refugees were considered by the Soviets to be traitors and were condemned to be tried. According to the terms of the Yalta Conference, then, repatriation meant that Britain and the United States had yielded to Stalin's pressure and that these unfortunates were to languish in Soviet labor camps, many of them consigned to certain death.[14]

While I was in France, my mother died. My father wrote to me and my brothers (25 March 1945): "The cremation was just as Mami would have liked it: a psalm, a prayer, the benediction, the 'Ave Maria'—and the curtain closed. Lily and I, Eva [a cousin] and Gerty [Hofmannsthal], and the special nurse. Beautiful sunshine and flowers."

Throughout my overseas service I kept up a lively correspondence with Otto Jeidels. In one letter (March 1945) I shared with him my thoughts on the German defeat and the prospect of general planning for a new Europe and indeed a new world order.

> I have been in France now since September, always with SHAEF, and my work has given me a good chance of viewing the war from the perspective of a historian. I have been over wide stretches of France, from Cherbourg to Strasbourg, witnessing what someday will be described as the Fall and Decline of Europe.
>
> I am much concerned about this problem. The cities all over the Continent are largely in ruins, the resources exhausted, and worse, people are confused. Look at liberated Poland and Bulgaria and Romania, Greece and Belgium: social unrest, atrocity trials in the name of justice, and here in France a shocking revival of nationalism. The "prestige of France," the "Honor of France" are 64-dollar words again. Ever since the Thirty Years' War, the idea of "Europe"

has so completely failed on the Continent, and the French are not aware of it yet. Here lies, it seems to me, the difference between France and the Big Three, as Europe was not liberated by us to establish national sovereignty again. Undoubtedly, we have learned from the mistakes committed in Versailles (I hope). The historical rights of nations, however contradictory, were guaranteed in various secret agreements before even general lines of a basic understanding had been defined.

My thoughts on the reordering of European affairs after the war, which had changed just about everything, were clearly waiting to be sorted out, and Otto Jeidels helped me to do this. In response to my ideas, he wrote a long letter that gave me the benefit of an experienced and mature mind in addressing the problems that mattered so much to me. While concurring with my lamentations over the physical destruction of the cultural monuments during the war, he shifted my perspective by calling my attention to the need for rebuilding Main Street and, in the process, averting its disfigurement by "the chain store and the skyscrapers."

But the burden of Otto's argument was on the question of the survival of the post-war order of national states on the Continent. Europe's "recuperative power," he said, did not lie in the formation of large combines with their "mass solution of problems." These would only constitute a new imperialism that would add up to what Otto called the ill-disguised "patriotism and nationalism of big nations."

* * *

(J.) Frankfurt am Main, July 1945: The first sight of Frankfurt was interesting: the spectacle of a ruined city ... and the constant expectation that some other one may look even worse ... The state of communications, municipal and political life, education, religion, morale—all completely disrupted and altogether exploding my trust in progress.

It is all very tragic; from time to time you feel moved—after all, even this godforsaken German land knows people who give up and resign and others who try to build up again. It has its differences and contrasts within itself, good and bad, white and black, high and low. All these, though, seem to be overshadowed by our stern government, according to which all Germans are bad, very bad.

I see in this morning's paper that the fraternization policy has been modified. I hope that this means that our plans for Germany are, although no less stern and firm in method, more constructive than was evident before. In other words, I hope that we know what we are doing.

Thus, at second sight, if Germany is to be left a land without hope and without a future, our mission here cannot amount to much. It is imperative that the right formula be found, providing for a German effort with wise guidance on our part.

Never, even during wartime, had I made a secret of my rather complex position on the "German problem," combining unqualified condemnation of the policy of oppression and narrow nationalism with a deep affection for "the other Germany" of decency and urbanity, which, I was convinced, had not become extinct. Let me add, though, that while my viewpoint was not easy for most people to understand, let alone share, I never once experienced suspicion or recrimination. A negative attitude towards all things German may have been rampant in the United States during World War I, but during World War II, it was the Japanese, including the so-called Nisei, individuals of Japanese parentage born and educated in the United States, who became the victims of discrimination.

I reflected on these post-war issues in a letter to Fritz T. Epstein (September 1945):

> I have been in Frankfurt since early May. To cover the sightseeing: the facade of the Römer is still standing, the Paulskirche is an empty shell and the Goethehaus on the Grosser Hirschgraben is now a heap of rubble. People placed a bust of Goethe on top of the ruins, and others brought flowers. I overheard a woman saying to her husband, for my consumption, I am sure: "That's what the Americans have done." Still, I cannot understand why the air force had to destroy all areas of the inner city, yet not the outer industrial districts like Hoechst. There will be a lot of arguments among historians…. There must be before long a peace with Germany. We cannot keep this whole people at our mercy indefinitely. At present, the situation is beyond control. The partition of Germany and Berlin, Austria and Vienna just proves to be absurd. Here is a case where history is made and pushed ahead by the halfwitted…. We surely are forcing the Germans into that very state of mind which we propose to kill in them…. Once we eliminate all active Nazis—functionaries, SS men, etc.—we should give self-government to the Germans and support their liberal elements.

I pursued these thoughts further in a letter to A. Tillman Merritt (October 1945):

> I am afraid that, like Woodrow Wilson's Fourteen Points, the Atlantic Charter[15] has been dropped, and we the Allies are resorting to crude power politics and we the Americans are without inner direction. Thus, over Radio Berlin, which I tune in frequently, I hear horror stories about the Junker and bourgeois, and to hell with that reactionary Weimar regime. De Gaulle is flattering the Rhinelanders, appealing to their French traditions, while French soldiers are reportedly soaking their land dry, and General Patton says that the Nazis aren't much worse than the Democrats and Republicans.
>
> The problem of Germany is incomprehensible even to those who know the country; it is a gigantic problem. Last week's *Hessische Nachrichten* carried a reply from Thomas Mann to invitations sent to him by various German groups to return to Germany. Mann declined, saying that he had been estranged from Germany and could not now be her doctor.

Just a miscellaneous item, which is rather symptomatic. Asking a 16-year-old girl, a former member of the Nazi Girls' League (BDM), who Goethe was and Schiller, I got "don't know" answers. She was able to identify Beethoven, though, as the "Führer der Luftwaffe."

Two weeks ago I went to Berlin, driving along the Autobahn. The secretive Russian zone is, of course, inaccessible to us. Russian guards all along the highway flagged my jeep down, to proceed or else to stop and sell them cigarettes, gas, schnapps, or watches. A carton of cigarettes brings $100, an average watch $350. One fellow offered to buy my pants for $50, but I preferred to reach my destination with my pants on.

Next week I shall accompany a friend of mine, Dr. Sinclair W. Armstrong, a historian from Brown University, on a two-week trip through the American zone in order to report back to its commander, General Lucius D. Clay, on conditions there.

During my tour of duty in occupied Germany, my feelings were understandably very mixed. On V-E Day, 8 May 1945, I had found myself in the streets of Paris, surrounded by singing and dancing youths. But now I saw Germany, which had unleashed that terrible war, lying prostrate, with its cities in shambles. In the streets I saw only old men, worn women, frightened children, and veterans in shabby gray uniforms hobbling on canes and crutches, all making their way among the ruins. Under those circumstances, pride in victory yielded to a sense of identification with the country of my birth and upbringing. Was it perverse of me to sympathize with the country that had inflicted so much suffering on the world, including my own family? Was I feeling simple compassion for the people in misery all around me? In any case, I wanted to help.

My first posting was in Frankfurt am Main, where SHAEF had set up its headquarters in the enormous complex of the IG Farben offices. My SHAEF duties involved me in one of the most bizarre archival migrations ever.[16] It seems to me ludicrous that in the aftermath of World War II—when so many population groups had been uprooted and forcibly moved, undergoing untold suffering—the transfer of documentary collections should have assumed any importance and become an object of diplomatic priorities. But it did.

The archival holdings in question were those of German ministries, in particular those from the Auswärtiges Amt (Foreign Office). These were evacuated by the Nazis themselves during the intensified air raids over Berlin in the summer of 1943 and taken to the safety of a number of castles in the Harz Mountains in central northern Germany. This territory was eventually assigned by the European Advisory Commission to the Soviet zone of occupation. But when the American forces advanced into the region ahead of schedule in March and April 1945, the archives were evacuated again. To save them from falling into the Russians' hands, the American army transferred some

425 tons of archives, first to Marburg in the US zone and then to a more spacious former underground ammunition factory in Fürstenhagen to the south of Kassel. This is where I first saw them. Early in October 1945 we were visited by a delegation of Russian officers who were eagerly trying to locate the files of the German Foreign Office. In answering their inquiries, I followed strict orders: "Sorry, they are not here." The French were not treated any better; in accordance with instructions from on high, they too were to be kept from these documents.

The Fürstenhagen Ministerial Collecting Center, as it was called, was but a stopover in a long archival odyssey. In late 1945, orders came from General Clay that the center was to be closed and its precious contents moved to Berlin.[17] There, in Tempelhof, the Berlin Document Center was set up in a huge fenced-in compound with a large German support staff. My responsibilities were the hiring and firing and feeding of this German personnel.

* * *

I shall end this chapter with sundry recollections from my return to Germany as an American soldier:

1. On my way to Frankfurt am Main, I somehow got involved in distributing to a group of German civilians copies of the "Questionnaire" (*Fragebogen*), later so controversial, containing 131 questions that all adult Germans had to fill out as part of the de-Nazification process. When one of the Germans, overeager to help distribute the papers, displayed a mastery of bowing and heel-clicking, a sense of nausea came over me. This was the Germany I had left behind me.

2. While billeted in Frankfurt am Main, I worked in an abandoned red-brick factory, a subsidiary of IG Farben in nearby Höchst. One day, as I was negotiating with one of the German officials, he suddenly emitted a shriek as though in extreme distress. A group of DPs had been loitering there. But now the German, outraged, pointed to a figure speeding away from us on a bicycle so fast that he became smaller and smaller by the second. This was one of the DPs; he had helped himself to the German's bicycle. But who, I thought, had brought the DPs to Germany to begin with?

3. From Frankfurt am Main I occasionally took off on weekends to drive to a nearby castle, Schloss Friedrichshof in Kronberg, which had been built for Empress Viktoria after the death of her husband, Emperor Friedrich III, in 1888. Constructed in a grandiose Tudor style, it was set in the green Taunus hills and surrounded by a huge park with many trails for walking

and horseback riding. An avid horseman since my Newport days, I wanted to go for a ride. Once I got to the stables, I chose the most beautiful of the horses there. But the stable boy waved me off. This horse, he said, was to be ridden by Mrs. Eisenhower that morning. But I had just read in the papers that the general's wife, Mamie, was at a reception in Washington. Was the horse I coveted reserved for Kay Summersby, Eisenhower's attractive Irish WAAC[18] driver, with whom he liked to go out on rides in the hills?

4. Moving into Berlin, I found destruction from the air bombardments staring me in the face, and people laboriously making their way, wherever possible, through a sea of ruins. Naturally, I wanted to revisit the site of my birth. But our house, like all its neighbors, had been leveled to the ground. Indeed, the very corner of Viktoriastraße and Tiergartenstrasse no longer existed. The whole topography of the area was altered beyond recognition. What did this wasteland have to say to me? Did it not after all mirror a world that was mine? Perhaps it was because there was so much destruction around me that I all too quickly made my peace with it, accepted it. What finally shocked me was not the heap of broken images surrounding me, but the sudden sight, as I made my way along what I thought had been the Viktoriastraße, of the same old plane tree that always had stood there, now wearing its yellow October leaves. Had survival triumphed over destruction after all?

5. In the Berlin Document Center, strict security regulations were in force since so many Germans were employed there. No one was to leave the compound without being carefully checked by the MP guards. Along came an old woman with a bundle of firewood in her arms. Ordered to drop it before leaving the compound, she broke out in tears: she needed this wood, she said, to heat water so as to bathe her invalid husband. I ordered the MP to make an about-face while the woman collected her bits of wood and moved on. When after that mini-tragedy the soldier turned around again, I saw a broad grin on his face.

6. I saw our old family friend Maimy on 14 March 1946. Her family's villa was located in Babelsberg by the Griebnitz Lake in the Russian zone. She managed to cross the boundary into the American sector of Berlin, and we had a wonderful afternoon together. Our exchange of memories, information, and photos bridged the few years that appeared to us so much longer and gave us a small but appreciable victory over the general dissolution around us. But my visit with Herr and Frau U., friends of my parents, was very different. Our families had more or less drifted apart during the Nazi time. Since Frau U. was of Jewish descent, they had thought it to be the better part of wisdom to stay away from us. Like Maimy, they had originally lived in Babelsberg,

but for one reason or another they had moved to Berlin. Now they were left in the ruins of the big city in one room with a gaping hole in the ceiling. Herr U. was lying on some sort of bed. He had lost a leg in the war, and neither of their sons had returned from the field. In this encounter there was no bridge to happier times. I went away overwhelmed by sadness and pity.

7. In October 1945, on an inspection trip through the US zone of occupation in Germany with Sinclair W. Armstrong, we had crossed over into Austria and reached Salzburg. Under the pretext of having work to do on his own in the city, Doc, as I called him, freed the jeep for me to take off to Strobl by the Wolfgangsee in search of the family of my friend Franzi E. They had a villa by the lake where I had visited them for a couple of weeks in the mid-1920s. I had become very attached to the idyllic lake under the Schafberg, surrounded by forests and meadows. It was a beautiful, clear autumnal day as I approached the house from the back, wondering whether my memory deceived me, whether what I sought was a mirage after all. Even from the distance, however, walking across the open field through high grass, I spotted an elderly couple sitting on the porch—Franzi's parents. I had always been very fond of them. What a precious surprise, then, was our reunion. But there was no Franzi. He had been conscripted for war service and taken prisoner. He was now a POW in America, awaiting repatriation to Austria to resume his métier as a photographer. Franzi would go back to his Leica after all.

The three Klemperer brothers, about 1918: Fred, Franz, Klemens

The family, about 1926: Fred, Franz, the parents, Lily, Klemens

The Kuffner Palais in Vienna

Klemens at the grave of the Klemperer grandparents in Dresden, about 2001

Helmut Jörg, about 1934

Helmut Jörg—from concentration camp to the soldier's grave in Russia, 1943

The Junker friends: brothers Georg Friedrich von Schweinitz

and Friedrich von Schweinitz

Otto Molden, about 1934

Klemens, Otto Molden, and friends in the Vienna Woods, about 1934

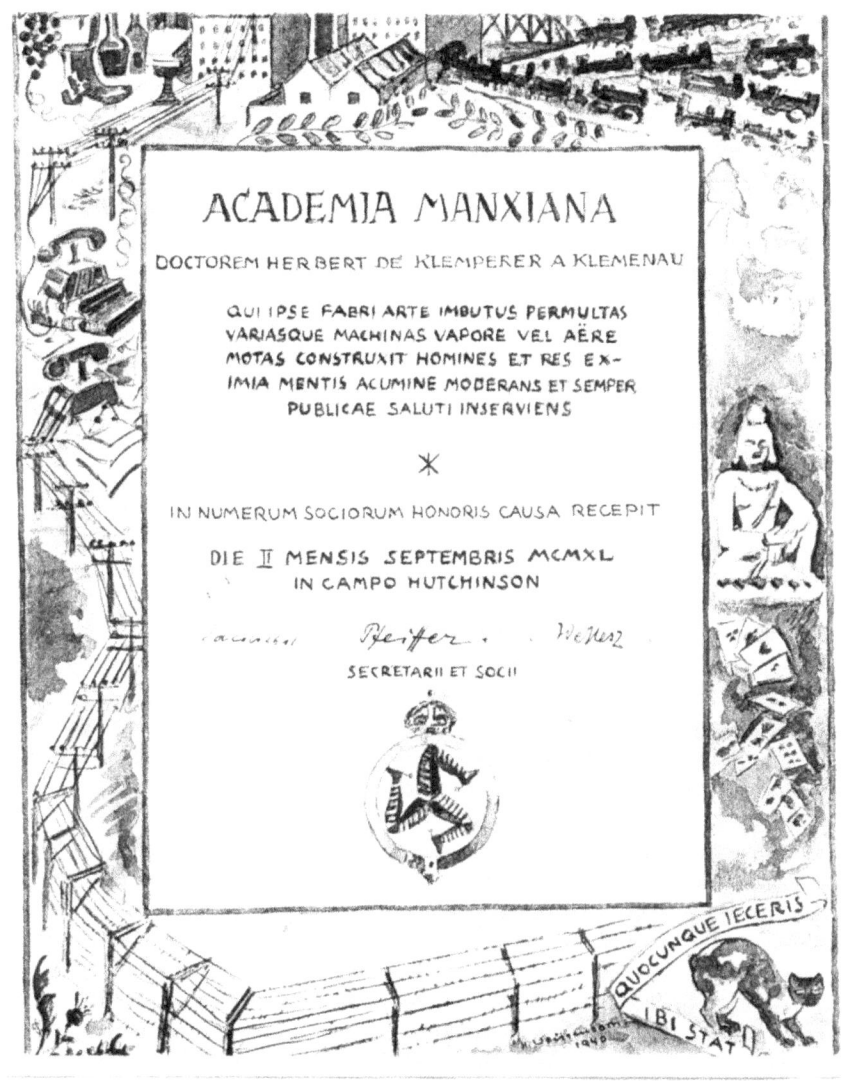

Temporarily interned on the Isle of Man, Father was awarded a degree *honoris causa* by the Academia Manxiana in 1939.

V-mail from Harvard's Eliot House Common Room to Klemens, 1943

Soldier Klemens, 1944

Grandmother Camilla Kuffner in exile,
Beaulieu sur Mer, about 1951

Elizabeth von Klemperer,
about 1955

The children, Catharine and James, about 1960

HINDENBURGSTRASSE 15
8134 PÖCKING b. STARNBERG
(OBERBAYERN)

1. Februar 1988

TELEFON: (08157) XXXX
7015

Sehr geehrter Professor von Klemperer,

vielen herzlichen Dank für Ihren Brief vom 21. Januar. Ich bin sehr glücklich, aus diesem zu entnehmen, wie sehr Sie mit der alten Heimat Ihrer Familie in der neuen Welt verbunden sind. Diese Gefühle zu unserer gemeinsamen Tradition haben mich ganz besonders gefreut.

Mit herzlichsten Grüßen

[signature]

OTTO VON HABSBURG

8134 Pöcking/Starnberg

1 February 1988

Honored Professor von Klemperer

Many thanks for your letter of 21 January. I am very happy to gather from it, how closely you are connected in the New World with the old *Heimat* of your family. These feelings for our common tradition have given me special happiness.

With kind regards

Otto von Habsburg.

Letter from Otto von Habsburg to Klemens, 1 February 1988

And finally a rather unusual letter:

His Holiness, Pope John Paul II   14. January 2000
Vatican City, Rome

Your Holiness,

 About twenty years ago when Poland was still in the grip of the Soviet Empire I had a visit from a young political scientist from Cracow. He told me about a seminar which in those days his Archbishop had convened to study the thoughts of the German theologian Dietrich Bonhoeffer who was executed by the Nazis for his faith and deeds in April 1945.
 Now I have a question and request to you who now are the Pope. Would it be possible at all to to beatify, if not canonize, Dietrich Bonhoeffer for what he stood for? I know of course that he was a Lutheran Protestant clergyman and I could not cite any miracles connected with him. However, he was, as you will be able to attest, a wonderful Christian, a Christian martyr indeed, and I should think that God himself would rejoice in his being recognized by the wide Christian world.
      I write this in all humility

        Yours very sincerely,

        Klemens von Klemperer

Letter from Klemens to Pope John Paul II proposing beatification
of Dietrich Bonhoeffer, 14 January 2000

Chapter Six

"Du bist ein Wanderer …"

The late nineteenth and all the more the motorized twentieth century have transformed *Heimat* people into wandering people.

— Friedrich Meinecke

It took eleven days for the returning troop transport, the SS *Ernie Pyle*, to cross the Atlantic. We were uncomfortably crowded but full of anticipation to get back into civilian life. One by one I learned what had happened to family and friends in Europe. I had known all along that Granny was left alone in exile in southern France, and the disappearance of her two daughters left an open wound in us all. In the summer of 1951, I managed to visit Granny in Beaulieu sur Mer. She lived in a pension, one of those friendly houses with elaborate shutters protecting the windows from the summer heat and the Mediterranean winds. Her room was just above the one where I was lodged. About five o'clock in the morning, I heard a serene voice from above gently humming one melody after another. Granny was singing. The one week I spent with her went by all too quickly, and I never saw Granny again. She was to survive into her ninety-fifth year, in grief but without lament. The funeral service for her was held in St. George's Chapel in Beaulieu looking over the wide, azure Mediterranean.

In 1954, Granny's remains were flown to Vienna to be interred in the family plot of the Döbling cemetery. Our uncle, Hermann Zeissl, gave a funeral oration that wonderfully recaptured this extraordinary woman, who had been born to a life of privilege, was tested by hardship, and emerged from it all with supreme dignity:

She was not granted a peaceful old age. She shared to a considerable measure the unspeakable suffering, the unspeakable sorrow that the past sixteen years have brought to our fatherland and its people. At the age of 81, she was expelled from her beautiful home, which she left with her head up and with the dignity of a queen. She had to go off to foreign parts, two beloved daughters were taken from her forever by a cruel, demonic force, and the third one died abroad of a grave disease. Never did a word of despair or of hatred cross her lips.

Suffering can well reveal human values; some people it embitters, to others it is the way to the purest of humaneness. It is her high humaneness that we want to safeguard in our memories.

She has now returned to her *Heimat* in Döbling. May the native soil protect and keep her.

My family was now scattered over three continents. My father's brothers' families had made their way to South Africa before the outbreak of the war, and my cousins served in its army in various capacities. Father and my sister Lily were awaiting the green light for their emigration from England to the United States. We three youngsters, my brothers and I, returned from our army duties intact. In fact, the years in the service had done each of us a lot of good. For me, the exposure to so many men from all walks of life and to new responsibilities and experiences offered an education that I otherwise could never have had. In short, I became an American of sorts, proudly so, and confident that I could master whatever challenges lay before me.

Little by little, the news about the fate of my Viennese friends came in. That Otto and Fritz Molden survived was a miracle, considering their wild and adventurous wartime exploits. But Helmut Jörg fell in Orel. A letter from Otto reported about other friends:

> Max G., the Free Corps leader of Lower Austria, the cheerful little Doctor of History, lies somewhere in the Caucasus. Rolf Sch. was one of the last ones to fall on African soil, and Sepp G., taken prisoner at Stalingrad, died thereafter of hunger and exhaustion in a Russian POW camp near the Caspian Sea.... Fritz and I are almost alone, and we learn every day anew how bitter it is that the few good people have gone forever. People of our kind hardly exist anymore. It is almost enough to drive you to despair, but we must hold on and bite our lips until we shall again have brought up some who will be like those who were part of our wonderful circle of the years 1936 and 1937.[1]

My Nazi friend Kurt v. B., who had fought on virtually all battlefields of the war, emerged more or less unscathed from his admittedly horrifying but truly soldierly experience. God moves in mysterious ways. Kurt Josten, the conservative aesthete, as unfit for military service as he was disapproving of sports, continued his inner emigration from plebeianism even beyond the Nazi years. He eventually left his country for Oxford University to become curator of its

Ashmolean Museum. Heinz Weyl, who had succeeded in surviving in the anonymity of the Wehrmacht uniform but was deeply troubled by his father's death in a concentration camp, became a distinguished city planner. Hans-Lukas Teuber never did go to fight in Finland. His big dreams of chivalry gave way to scholarly endeavor, and he eventually became a celebrated neurologist and psychologist at the Massachusetts Institute of Technology. Jürgen von Kardorff never returned from the battlefield, while his brother Klaus barely survived the war. Thilo von Plessen was shot down over Sicily in 1943. The worst news came from the family of the Schweinitz brothers. In a letter, their mother related: "I don't know how well you are informed about us. Georg fell in 1940, Friedrich in 1941, Christoph in 1943. One had to bear so much and wonders how one can cope with it all. But life goes on relentlessly."[2]

When I compare my wartime experience with the plight of my friends who stayed behind, I am forced to recognize that they drew a harder lot than I did. Emigration relieved me of having to face the dilemma of loyalty to one's country versus rejection of a regime. Not even service in the American army exposed me to actual combat.

Yet the *vita contemplativa* into which I settled in the United States imposed burdens of its own, forcing me to think through, step by step, who I was and to justify what I stood for and believed in. In other words, the ongoing process of Americanization transcended the dimension of assimilation to a new continent or culture, and was to be essentially a measure of my maturation. In very specific terms, I had to find my way out of a morass of romantic introspection and narcissism and see how I could lead a more casual, pragmatic life without betraying those great dreams that had started my friends and me on our way. Could I find the right balance for being, in Joseph Conrad's words, a romantic "but none the less true"?

By 1946, the so-called Morgenthau Plan, devised by Henry Morgenthau, President Roosevelt's secretary of the treasury, which had provided for a stringent, punitive settlement with the Germans and had initially been supported by the president, yielded to a more constructive approach to the "German problem." On 6 September 1946, US Secretary of State James Byrnes said in a Stuttgart speech that it was the wish of the American people to help the German people win their way back to an honorable place among the free and peace-loving nations of the world. This policy statement confirmed the position that I had taken even during the war years, when it had struck almost everyone as insane.

At just about the same time I had a letter from Otto Jeidels that expressed the feelings I had on the "German problem" and gave me courage:

> The letters from Germany, which I try to answer because a word of encouragement in their misery has assumed such human importance, are documents of exquisite value.... The endurance, strength of character, and supreme decency

of those letters is outstanding and a great hope for the future, if only the ever more strenuous effort at survival succeeds. There is a nation going through the hellfire of punishment and hardship, and it will be a great historic experience to see what kind of man and what sort of nation will arise out of such a trial. There, and not in the attempt of outside re-education, will lie the paths to the return into the comity of nations.³

If at no point in my peripatetic life Otto Jeidels disappeared from my horizon, neither did Maimy. We had had a second reunion in war-ravaged Berlin. She had become a displaced person of sorts, and, like myself a few years earlier, she was thrown back on her basic wits. The ravages of war had left her with a sense of disjunction from her traditional habitat, from her heritage, and from friends who had been dear to her. I, too, had left behind roots, friends, a homeland, and a language. But I was so overwhelmed by the newness of my American impressions and encounters that Europe did not, at least at first, exercise a particular pull on me. There was so much to explore and so much to conquer, and somehow it was left to me to redefine my relation to my old world in new ways.

Comparing my experiences and my transplantation to Maimy's helped me to understand myself and my place in the world of "uprootedness" into which we both, as distinctly conservative people, had been transported. *Heimat*, that German wonder word, was much on Maimy's mind. This important dimension of our lives—defining our identity through inborn familiarity with home—threatened to elude us. But *Heimat* had gained a yet stronger, all the more compelling magnetism for us. It was not the magnetism of a sentimentalized *heile Welt*, or ideal world, that would always grant us refuge and security. Stripped of much of its emotional quality, *Heimat* had become more a rational point of orientation in our lives, and it remained an integral part of us, a challenge to us wanderers, which we would ignore only on penalty of losing our identity. That challenge involved, as Maimy put it so aptly, shuttling to and fro between the two worlds to which we were committed.

On my first return to Germany after the war, I was greeted by some children who said, "Du bist ein Wanderer." In one's migrations through life, one may think that one has left an earlier stage behind and then get mercilessly reminded that one has not really progressed the way one had thought. There was something to what those children said. The more I was ready to put down roots in the new world, the more I felt the need to keep wandering, to continue "going to and fro upon the earth." "Europe of strange tongues," James Joyce wrote, "and valleyed and woodbegirt and citadelled and of entrenched and marshalled races"—it was precisely this Europe that I was determined to keep embracing, even from the faraway shores of America. I had no illusions that this would be an easy task. It would be an exhilarating one, maybe, at times, but then again a deeply puzzling and disconcerting one. At moments I had to ask myself where I really belonged and whether I belonged anywhere at all.

* * *

Clearly, the time had come to settle down and complete my training for my chosen profession. I was no longer the displaced waif or the transient soldier. Left to myself, I was at first restless and disoriented. After such a long absence from academic life, it took some self-persuasion to open scholarly books again and to make sense of them. I may have been ill-advised to plunge into the monumental work by Friedrich Meinecke, the dean of German historians, on cosmopolitanism and the national state.[4] A classic, it was written in the rather convoluted style of the German idealistic tradition. In any case, it taught me that I must pass a formidable hurdle to get back to the essentially solitary and patiently probing ways of scholarship.

Solitary as a scholar's existence might be, to me it never meant monastic seclusion from the world. If scholarship was my chosen language, it was to connect me with the world of affairs that I had never really left, to be instructed by it as much as to be thrust into it. Studying was my way of returning to my commitment to German affairs.

The more the German nation had become an accomplice of atrocious crimes, the more I held onto the conviction that among the many wicked citizens of Sodom, there must have been righteous ones. Some of them, after all, were my friends. I clung to this proposition all the more firmly at a time when the thesis of collective guilt was rampant in American public discourse. Some years later I found in the published correspondence of Friedrich Meinecke a letter in which he observed that he had detected among German refugee scholars in America no resentment; much to the contrary, they played the part of mediators to the scholars in Germany. They were, of course, my elders, and many of them were friends of mine.[5] For me, there was no question but to go the same way as they.

Having been so generously received by Harvard on my arrival in America had freed me from the turbulent ideological struggle that had swept us students along in Germany and Austria. Ideologies tend to engulf one and are accordingly very tempting. In a world of so much incongruity and fragmentation, the grand and cohesive scheme proposed by an ideology such as National Socialism offered great attractions. Although it was not hard for me and my friends to expose it in all its deceptiveness and iniquity, the very effort of battling it was absorbing and channeled much of our energies into politics. Student life at the University of Vienna had less to do with a quest for knowledge and understanding than with declaring one's political loyalties and affiliations. In America, I could leave that climate safely behind me.

There was a great deal of political, if not ideological, agitation at Harvard, but it was freewheeling and allowed for the open exchange of ideas among students and faculty. I found the student body, or its liveliest members, preoccupied with either the Marxist or the Freudian temptation, or both. All rational human constructs seemed exposed as mere rationalizations below which a more compelling underground world—be it the dictates of the means of production or the human subconscious—waited to be recognized and explored. Marxism, which was to redress the ills of an unjust imperialist and capitalist world, and Freudianism, which was to expose as illusions the conventional norms of rationality, had become expressions both of alienation from established canons and of rebellion, and were foremost in the minds of many students. This language was spoken in the 1930s by those in the student body who thought of themselves as avant-garde

But this was not my language, nor that of my friends back in Europe. We were not Marxists or Freudians. At best, Marx and Freud were remote sectarians to us. We knew Marx only as the patron of proletarians, and he was of no concern to us. His early manuscripts,[6] which dealt with the problem of alienation in capitalist society and offered a humanistic reading of communism, were not published until 1932. The *Communist Manifesto* sooner or later fell into our hands, and at best we recognized its masterful stylistic overview of a historical and political universe. Its message, however, did not penetrate to us. Freud we did not think about much except as a figure rejected in Vienna, his home territory.

I learned much from the students of Marx and Freud. Marx the political agitator and apologist of class struggle never had any appeal to me, but Marx the historian and social scientist revealed to me the crucial dimension in social relations and in human conduct of the hard and fast dictates of the means of production. And while the ins and outs of Freud's psychoanalysis and his focus on human sexuality never played a part in my intellectual development, I was deeply impressed by Freud's final synthesis, *Civilization and its Discontents*, which he finished in 1929 in Bavaria "without library," and which I read as one of the really outstanding documents of European pessimism. Freud's dramatic conclusion—that "life, as we find it" was "too hard for us," bringing "too many pains, disappointments and impossible tasks," and that the expectation of "consolation" on the part of both the wildest revolutionaries and pious believers[7] was foolish—did reinforce my inclination to accept a cosmic order and to cope with it as well as possible. Thus, I was somehow able to translate Freud, the rationalist, into religious terms: for me, the cosmic order he invoked was ordained from on high. In any case, when Freud wrote that the happiness of man was not included in the Creator's plan, he both apostrophized and capitalized creation. The capitalization[8] satisfied me and appealed to me.

Which thinker, if not Marx and Freud, was at the center of our student hall of fame back in Europe? I have referred frequently to Friedrich Nietzsche, and no doubt my friends and I were fired by his inchoate thought and his wild, dithyrambic German. The confluence of iconoclasm and poetry in the father of Zarathustra opened up to us new horizons and an escape from parental philistinism and from the deceptive holism and orthodoxies that lurked on the political horizon of the 1920s and 1930s. After all, the era of any Nietzschean fundamentalism had long past. Nietzsche was no longer interpreted, as he had been initially, as a simple and dangerous atheist or as a Teutonic anti-Semite, invented by his tiresome obscurantist sister. He had now become generally acceptable—the German word would be *salonfähig*—and was recognized as a vital agent in the rediscovery of the unconscious. For my fellow Harvard student and friend, H. Stuart Hughes, himself a distinct lefty, Nietzsche had become an inspiration in all areas of the humanities and social thought.[9]

The climate in Cambridge after the war was distinctly less charged ideologically, certainly among us graduate students. There was no room left for playboys; most of us had interrupted our apprenticeship during crucial years of our lives. We veterans had become the GI Bill of Rights generation. As more mature men and women, we were eager to get launched in our professions.

I became a tutor in history and literature, a concentration that analyzed historic problems with the help of largely literary sources. This marvelous discipline, cultural history, brought together a dedicated faculty from virtually all branches of the humanities and social sciences and an eager group of students. At that time, the tutorial staff was led by F. O. Matthiessen, a great scholar and inspiring teacher of literature who attracted a devoted group of disciples. While I always remained somewhat aloof from the circle of the all too magnetic Matty, which was predominantly composed of left-leaning scholars, I learned a lot in this company. I was, I might as well admit, a neophyte in the field of literature, and began to read frantically—Stendhal, Tolstoy, Thomas Mann, Camus—in order to be at least one step ahead of my tutees. One of these, who was working in the field of the Italian Renaissance, knew so much more about the field than I, that before long I turned him over to Matty; his bachelor thesis was eventually published.[10] We kept in touch with each other afterwards and became good friends.

As for Matty, he ended sadly. Coming from a well-to-do family, he was a graduate of Yale, a member of the Skull and Bones secret society, and, at the same time, a socialist and a believing Christian. He was an old-time socialist, deeply concerned about the plight of the common man, while living in the most elegant neighborhood in Boston at 87 Pinkney Street on Beacon Hill overlooking Louisburg Square. Occasionally in the evenings, he would remove his jacket, I was told, so as to proudly show off his proletarian suspenders and go down into the less reputable bars of Boston to mix with the hoi polloi.

In 1947, Matty went to Salzburg to teach in the first session of the Salzburg Seminar in American Studies and at the Charles University in Prague, hoping to find in Central Europe an ideal social order cleansed of both the cruelties of capitalism and the coercions of Bolshevism. But as the Cold War mercilessly took over, Matty's hopes for a "third way" between West and East were shattered. At just about that time, I had arranged for Matty to speak to the members of Eliot House, where we were both tutors, about his Central European experiences. Despite the fact that just a few days before his talk the Communists had staged a successful coup in Czechoslovakia, he frantically held on to his dreams, giving an idealized account of conditions in Prague. We all knew from newspapers what the situation really was, so Matty's tack appeared to us all the more painful. But he soon had to acknowledge the realities and, as a result, came to feel increasingly isolated in the Cold War atmosphere. I remember McGeorge Bundy, who was certainly familiar with decision-making in the upper echelons of American foreign policy, saying that if Matty had applied for a visa for another trip to Central Europe, he would surely have been rebuffed by the State Department. On 1 April 1950, Matty, who had become increasingly subject to bouts of depression, rented a room on the twelfth floor of Boston's Manger Hotel, took off his glasses and his Skull and Bones key, and jumped to his death. He left a note: "As a Christian and socialist believing in international peace, I find myself terribly oppressed by the present tensions."

Those among the faculty to whom I was more attuned were understandably the men in my field. John H. Finley, my friend the classicist, once put me in my place by quipping that all history after the French Revolution was but gossip. All history is more or less gossip—although more or less disciplined gossip—as is also the history of Herodotus and Thucydides. But my field of contemporary history tends to be, in comparison with ancient history, overwhelmed by controversy and thus particularly prone to what Finley described as gossip.

At any rate, my teachers in that field were Sidney B. Fay and William L. Langer. Although very different in temperament, they were masters of historical analysis, and at one time or other I was an assistant to both of them. Fay, who wrote his great work on the origins of World War I[11] while a professor at Smith College in Northampton, Massachusetts, before moving on to Cambridge, was one of the gentlest scholars I have ever met. What made him persuasive was his meticulous use of sources. He emerged from the immediate aftermath of the war with a carefully balanced historization, de-emotionalizing in nature, of the question of war guilt, which he distributed evenly among the principal powers on both sides. That very issue has since been re-examined many times, beginning in the early 1960s with the German historian Fritz Fischer, who has come down heavily on the part played by the German establishments in precipitating the war. The Dutch historian Pieter Geyl, who became a friend of mine when he spent a year in Northampton, wrote that history was "an argument without end," and he was right.

Langer, a leading diplomatic historian, was a challenging teacher and an unsparing taskmaster, which made his methods all the more effective. He held his seminars at his home in Arlington, a Boston suburb. One winter evening, when a report by one student was not of the highest quality, Langer turned on him: "And do you mean to say that all these people came out all this way to listen to that crap?" During the year or two when he directed my PhD thesis, I saw him no more than three times, but those three meetings were crucial. I was struck by his quick and penetrating grasp of the problems under discussion, and the shock treatment he administered helped me treat my subject, the history of German neo-conservatism in the twentieth century,[12] in a rigorous and analytical way. Later during World War II, Langer served in Washington as head of the Research and Analysis Branch of the Office of Strategic Services (OSS), a position for which he was ideally suited. After the war, he returned to Harvard and branched out into altogether new historical fields, becoming a pioneer in psychohistory and the study of the history of climate and population. He left behind a group of students, many of them my friends, who eventually moved into leading positions in the American historical establishment.

Other faculty included Michael Karpovich and Gaetano Salvemini, both political exiles from a troubled Europe. In the Harvard community they stood out as shining examples of political commitment and civil courage. Salvemini I barely knew, but my stall—which is what we called our work desks—in Widener Library was near his office. One day, as I was reading about Italian fascism, I summoned up my courage and knocked on the door of the spirited anti-fascist. What, I asked him, was the theory of fascism? I got a swift answer: "There is no theory of *fascismo*." And that was that.

Karpovich I knew well and loved. He belonged to the rare breed of Russian liberals. In an age when liberalism was on the defensive everywhere and seemed to be waning, he was one of those who upheld its integrity and dignity. He had been a secretary in the Russian embassy in Washington during the short-lived and ill-fated Provisional Government under Alexander Kerensky (July–November 1917), which then was overthrown by the Bolshevik Revolution. But "Karpi," as we called him, stayed in the United States and became a historian. I had come to know him well even before the war, when I was apprentice teaching in the famed History 1 introductory course that Karpi directed, after succeeding "Frisky" Merriman. We teaching fellows considered ourselves privileged to work under Karpi's humane and inspiring guidance.

It must have been in 1947 that my friend John Conway and I set out in my car on a jaunt to Vermont, where Karpi had a dacha in West Wardsboro, a village in the hills of southern Vermont. We came upon him in the village square, accompanied by a tall, thin man, slightly bent to one side, and a smaller man who kept both hands in his bulging pockets throughout our visit. The tall fellow, distinctly aloof, turned out to be none other than Alexander Kerensky, and the small fellow his bodyguard. We then proceeded to the New England farmhouse that Karpi had converted into a dacha—with sagging ceilings and peeling wallpaper, just as I had imagined—where we had good talks. But the great Kerensky stayed in the adjoining dark room, an invisible *éminence grise*. As the conversation between Karpi, John, and me went on, Karpi mentioned in passing the name of a Russian friend of his who had visited recently. Thereupon, a deep, imperious voice came out of the dark: "Nicolai Andreievich was here and did not report to me?"

This interjection from the other room told me something that I believe to be important about Kerensky. In the tragic history of twentieth-century Russia, he has all too often been seen simply as a failure. Of course he failed, having been swept into a position of responsibility for the Russian empire at a time when it was bound to succumb to overwhelming pressures from within and without. But Soviet historiography went on to brand him as a fool and weakling. He was nothing of the sort. As his voice out of the dark told me, he was an authoritative figure who had been thrown into a situation of intractable adversity, which he faced with considerable dignity. Kerensky was, in plain words, a tragic figure—an exile.

At about the same time I met two other well-known political exiles, the German ex-Chancellor Heinrich Brüning and his Austrian counterpart, Kurt von Schuschnigg. I had heard Brüning before the war, addressing the History Club at Harvard. This time around I saw him face to face on the occasion of an interview he gave me while I was at work on my doctoral dissertation. He was living a hermit-like existence in a suite in Lowell House at Harvard, taking no part in the communal life.

Brüning had assumed the chancellorship of the Weimar Republic in March 1930 when its plight was critical and the chances of obtaining parliamentary support for any functioning government coalition had faded. He realized at once that he had taken over a situation that, he admitted, was 90 percent lost, and that for his government to function, he had to look elsewhere for support. Was Brüning the last stalwart defender of Weimar Germany in the emergency of the 1930s, or was his government merely a transition to government by emergency decrees, in other words, to dictatorship?

In the course of our interview, it became evident that I was confronting a man who was as bitter over the past as he was fiercely proud. He had to bear the burden, first, of having been the *Krisenkanzler*, even worse, of being denounced by the hungry masses as the *Hungerkanzler*, and, worst of all, of not having been able to prevent the Nazi catastrophe. Then he found himself rewarded by the Allied bombings of German cities and the demand for and policy of unconditional surrender, both of which he fiercely condemned. Indeed, he gave the distinct impression that he carried over to America the burden and hurt of his misadventures in Germany, even extending this bitterness to the very community—Harvard—that had given him refuge.

Then the talk came to the agenda that had brought me to Brüning in the first place, the question of his public persona in Germany. I had of course known that he had been an officer during World War I, distinguished for his bravery and decorated with the Iron Cross of both classes, and that this was why Field Marshal-President Paul von Hindenburg had called on him to serve as chancellor. But now he asked what I thought had been the shortcomings of the 1919 National Assembly in Weimar. He himself gave the answer—that "so few *Frontkämpfer* [front fighters] were represented in it." Then he asked me in a similarly half-challenging vein what the acronym "SS" meant. I answered, "*Schutz Staffel*," referring to the Nazi elite guard of ill-repute. He shot back triumphantly: "No, *Scharfschützen*." These, he hastened to explain, were special shock troops of the German army in World War I who had distinguished themselves by their bravery. Brüning himself had been a captain of one of those units. I realized then that I was sitting opposite a very conservative gentleman, a man whose instincts were still captivated by the mystique of a war long past and lost.

What was I to make of this encounter? Was I to join the chorus of the many historians who chide Brüning for having been all too cautious and naive in the exercise of power? Theodor Mommsen wrote that a statesman should be no knight; but was not Brüning too much of a knight and too little of a politician? What was I to make of the argument that by virtue of his recourse to emergency decrees he was the "pathfinder for Hitler"? Was I to judge him for holding on stubbornly, even now in America, to the German mystique of the war experience? Late in 1938, the ex-chancellor took to reading two dramas by Euripides, commenting that he had gained a certain understanding from the Greek tragedies: "They offer a particular example of the way one accepts a hard fate in silence and with dignity."[13]

My encounter with Kurt von Schuschnigg took place in the early 1970s at Saint Louis University, a Catholic university where he was teaching. He had found refuge there after having survived harrowing years in a concentration camp following Hitler's entry into Vienna in March 1938. As I was in St. Louis giving a lecture, I took the opportunity to ask for a meeting with him. My interest in Schuschnigg was manifold. In those terrible March days of 1938, had he not been the last protective wall against Hitler's conquering troops? That was the way my friends and I saw things, and that is why we were ready to fight for our country. Or was he, as his critics insist, a "clerico-fascist" or "Austro-fascist" after all, and so another "pathfinder for Hitler"? The Austrian corporative state over which he, like his predecessor Engelbert Dollfuss, presided was indeed a restorative, authoritarian state. After the dissolution of Parliament in March 1933, Austria was no longer a democracy, inasmuch as the government did not shrink from repressive measures. In defense against the German fascism, Schuschnigg saw himself justified in resorting to methods of governing that came close to those characteristic of fascism—all this with the aim of saving the independence of Austria. All of us, my friends and I, were caught in that dilemma, and we did what we did knowingly.

When I met the ex-chancellor, I found him reticent and uncommunicative. I had wanted to interrogate him about the grand old man of his party, Chancellor Ignaz Seipel, who had dominated the Austrian political scene in the 1920s and early 1930s and about whom I was writing a book at the time.[14] Also, since I was thinking of writing a longer biographical sketch of Schuschnigg,[15] I wanted to know more about his own views and memories. All of these matters were evidently too sensitive for a man who may have wanted to put a traumatic past behind him.

My meetings with Alexander Kerensky, Heinrich Brüning, and Kurt von Schuschnigg were for me unusual experiences, from a scholarly as well as a human point of view. Of course, each may have failed. Brüning, perhaps foolishly, insisted all along that he had been within a "hundred meters of his aim"—namely, the successful negotiation to terminate the onerous German reparation payments—when he was let go by the aging president as a result of backstage intrigue in May 1932. Neither Kerensky nor Schuschnigg could conceivably have claimed so much for themselves. In the case of all three—the Russian, the German, and the Austrian—the crisis was too severe to be overcome with a single move by the head of government. In those last phases of its war against the German Reich, Russian tsarism was in its death throes and on the verge of revolutionary upheaval. By mid-1932, the Weimar Republic was virtually ungovernable, with radicalism threatening on both the right and the left in Parliament and in the street. Since its establishment in November 1918, the Austrian Republic had been in a state of creeping civil war most of the time. In 1917, Kerensky's Eastern Europe was hardly a fertile ground for democracy, and in the Central Europe of Brüning and Schuschnigg, representative government was in crisis. In all of these areas, the street was prevailing over the councils of rationality and moderation.

I feel privileged to have met these three statesmen, who were at the helms of their countries in times of extreme crisis. I did not obtain much information about their tenure of office that I had not already gathered through my studies, but I learned a lot from these meetings. I emerged from them with a heightened awareness of the fragility of rationality and moderation in government, especially in those areas of Europe that had little or no native democratic tradition, and, in general, of the preciousness of democracy. I became more aware of the latitude that is available to national leaders in times of war, revolution, and other crises—and the constraints on it. My understanding was confirmed that beyond rationality and moderation in government, however difficult to maintain, lies a terrible abyss. Finally, I learned to respect the statesmen who had to face these odds and who bore their fate with dignity. I learned to appreciate the dignity of defeat.

Harvard had set the pace for supporting refugee students, like myself, through the singular initiative of its students and the encouragement of President Roosevelt. But the university did not go out of its way to welcome established scholars who had been threatened by or expelled from totalitarian regimes. The relatively few foreign scholars who found a haven in Cambridge never quite became part of Harvard's pulsating life. They tended to feel that they deserved a special form of recognition, which did not necessarily come their way. In turn, they were seen as intruders into a perfectly well-functioning academic life. Certainly, the happy-go-lucky undergraduate college set-up, which assigned as much weight to character building in communal life and competition in sports as it did to scholarship, was alien to the German *Herren Professoren*, who were used to barricading themselves behind their books. These newcomers remained more or less strangers in a setting whose academic traditions they did not share. Even the exception proved the rule. The economist Alexander Gerschenkron, an exile from Soviet Russia who eventually landed at Harvard, became an avid Red Sox fan and solitary hunter in New Hampshire while remaining throughout his American sojourn the scholar's scholar, remote from the hustle and bustle of Cambridge society.

The aloofness of some of the professorial émigrés was brought home to me at a reception of sorts attended largely by their own kind. I remember distinctly a spirited conversation among the guests, who included some very distinguished visitors from other universities, comparing German and American university libraries. By general agreement, the service and accessibility of the former were singled out as superior. I had worked in both European and American libraries enough to know that this kind of argument amounted to outright nonsense and old world arrogance. In my books, Widener Library was tops.

I saw a great deal of émigrés Karl Viëtor and Werner Jaeger. Viëtor gave splendid courses on late nineteenth-century and early twentieth-century German literature, most of which I audited. Yet the war had cast a long shadow over everything German, which lasted into the post-war years. The field of German letters did not exactly thrive among students, courses were undersubscribed, and Viëtor, to his chagrin, felt quite isolated in the Harvard setting.

Werner Jaeger had succeeded the great and powerful Ulrich von Wilamowitz-Moellendorff at the University of Berlin and occupied the most prestigious chair among German classicists. He had become an untiring apologist for what he called a "third humanism," which was to recapture for the classics the preeminent position in German intellectual life that he believed was its due, even in a modern setting.[16] Resisting Nazi pressure to part with his wife, who was of Jewish origin, he emigrated to America and left his activism behind. Short of withdrawing from a *vita activa*, he played his part as the gentle, serene teacher, exemplifying his guideline that theory and life should always be one. He lived up to the standards of that *Paideia* to which he had devoted his great three-volume work, but the third humanism that he wanted so much to cultivate hardly took root in American soil.

That third humanism, however, has since come under sharp scrutiny. The concept, initially coined by the philosopher Eduard Spranger, was in the air, so to speak, in the German academic world in the 1920s and 1930s. In a time of unsettled political conditions, the country was gripped by an apocalyptic mood that expressed itself even in such esoteric fields as the classics. The third humanism sought the regeneration of a troubled world through the cultural values of classical antiquity, specifically, the Greek ideal of the good and the beautiful.

Moved by an acute sense of a general cultural crisis, Jaeger sought to make his humanist ideals serviceable for the wider world. He thus championed a traditionalism that, falling back on an anti-modernist vocabulary (e.g., a condemnation of "big-city intellectuality" and of "Americanism"), brought him close to the ubiquitous anti-democratic agitators of the times. The concept of a third humanism as a political message was risky at a time when Hitler's Third Reich was *ante portas* and indeed became political reality. Even if Jaeger had no intention of identifying himself with it,[17] some of his students in Germany made a connection between a high-minded cultural elitism and the National Socialist Third Reich, as though the civilizing humanism of the classical world could have been translated into the vulgarity and barbarity of Stormtroopers.

My encounters with Werner Jaeger had more than the personal significance of meeting up with a kindly, exalted academic whose scholarly integrity and commitment served as an example. Jaeger was a cultural conservative, and I sensed that my instincts and thoughts tended in that direction. The dreams of the Youth Movement, which were my dreams, made me long to recapture lost loyalties (*Bindungen*) and a holistic society and universe. Perhaps this longing was immature, and I should have faced up to the reality of the fragmented world into which I was born. Even a religious view of the universe, which distinctly was mine, should have taught me about the fragility and imperfection of everything this-worldly. But why not dream? Why not hope?

I became keenly aware of Jaeger's problem, that is, the propinquity of the conservative position to the fascist and even National Socialist position. This served as a reminder and a challenge to me to define my path while steering clear of what my friend Fritz Stern called the "temptation" of National Socialism.[18] And it did indeed constitute a temptation—"the great masquerade of evil ... disguised as light, charity, historical necessity, or social justice," as Dietrich Bonhoeffer described it.[19] I had to put my ship on course, to define for myself and for those who would be my readers what a healthy and conservative position was in a democratic society, and to distinguish it clearly from its ugly distortion

Among the older historians who had escaped the Nazi hell, there were two above all who took a particular interest in my generation of novice historians,

Hajo Holborn and Fritz Epstein. Holborn, while having a solid position at Yale, was an itinerant of sorts, shuttling between New Haven and Cambridge and helping us youngsters move into the profession. He had an admirably relaxed and friendly way of communicating with us and bringing us together for an informal exchange of ideas. Holborn was both a teacher-scholar of great stature and a consummate politician, a humanist and at the same time a man of affairs—among academicians, a rare breed.

The seminar that Holborn once gave at Harvard particularly stands out in my memory. The topic was the peace settlement at Versailles after World War I. Leaning back in the chair at the head of the table, with a customary, relaxed grin on his face, he drew us students out with questions that were designed to test our good sense as much as our expertise: "Well, gentlemen, what kind of committees would you appoint to get a peace conference under way?" and "What place in this setting should the vanquished nation occupy?" All of us students had in one way or another been brought up in the aftermath of the Great War and now had to face up to its legacy. The topics of our PhD theses invariably dealt with one or the other subject, reflecting our keen interest in contemporary history. We had to come to terms as scholars with our own experiences, and Hajo Holborn helped us in a masterful way to bring together history and political commitment.

Of all the refugee scholars from whom I learned much, Fritz Epstein was the least established. His promising academic career in Hamburg had been cut short by emigration, and he was now a poor and underpaid bibliographer in Widener Library, struggling to support a wife and two school-age children. Fritz was a saintly character. Unlike Holborn, he was completely apolitical and altogether absorbed by his bookish interests, which he enjoyed sharing with us graduate students. Every so often he would give me an envelope containing references to scholarly articles that he thought were relevant to my work. Taken from journals that were often very old, some were in languages that I could not even read. Then there were those Saturday evenings when we students gathered at the Epsteins' hospitable home by the Charles River for long and spirited bull sessions over many mugs of beer.

At that time, Fritz's son Klaus was still a young boy of whom we took little notice. I remember, though, that in the fall of 1940, little Klaus bicycled to visit the World's Fair without his parents' permission and slept at night in the then much-talked-about General Motors Building before being found and sent home by the authorities. Klaus became a historian and a dear friend of mine. I was then between the generations of father and son. While Epstein *père* was distinguished by scholarly antiquarian gifts, Epstein *fils* excelled due to an unusually powerful comprehension of politics. He would have been the outstanding historian of his generation had his life not been cut short in 1967 by a fatal car accident at an intersection in a residential neighborhood of Bonn.

The Greeks used to say that those whom the gods love die young. Klaus was indeed loved by the gods. I miss him.

The resident tutors with whom I was closeted were a singularly exciting lot of young scholars and friends. As I look back on my European friendships, they depended largely on shared political concerns and preferences. But now, with the war behind us, we could safely dedicate ourselves to the pleasures of intellectual exchange. My friends were McGeorge Bundy, John Conway, Walter Jackson Bate, Hans J. Epstein, Hans Gatzke, Howard Hugo—men with diverse interests who were happy to learn from each other. Late in the evenings, a member of the group would call us to assemble in the Senior Common Room, where we settled down with plenty of red wine for sessions that often lasted past midnight. Unforgettable to me are the occasions when Jack Bate recited by heart, in a quiet, almost rambling voice, long passages from the Bible. Mac, the one indigenous Bostonian among us, took the whole group to a D'Oyly Carte performance of Gilbert and Sullivan's *Iolanthe*. And then we went to the Old Howard in Boston, an old-fashioned burlesque that was marvelously grotesque and vulgar and, in the end, deeply serious.

In 1947 that I lay flat on my back in Stillman Infirmary, recovering from a collapsed lung. I had overexerted myself playing squash in the stuffy air of an indoor court. A group of friends appeared by my bed with conspiratorial grins: "T. S. Eliot is going to read 'The Waste Land' tonight in Saunders Theater, and you must come along to hear him." I was nonplussed: "T. S. Eliot—who? 'The Waste Land'—what?" Anyway, with the doctor's permission they packed me up, and off we went to the theater. There we met a large, expectant crowd awaiting the great man, about whose identity I had been informed. But he did not really read. Without any unctuous emphasis, without the self-dramatization that so often occurs when poetry is read, he sang: "April is the cruelest month...." I did not understand much of the text since my command of English was at the time not really up to it. Nevertheless, the event was memorable for me. Even as I write this, I can hear that almost impassively composed voice reciting the poem that in the meantime has come to mean so very much to me.

After leading a waif's existence for years, in 1953 I took the plunge into marriage. Elizabeth Lee Gallaher—Betty, as she was usually called—had been in the theater when T. S. Eliot gave his memorable reading of "The Waste Land." At that time, though, we had not yet met. Upon becoming my wife, she accompanied me through life with her steadfast good sense and humaneness.

Coming from stock long settled in America, Betty was born in New Hampshire and is proud to be a product of that Granite State. Her mother's forebears had moved from Massachusetts to New Hampshire and Vermont when these states were still part of the frontier. Her father's ancestors had migrated westward from Massachusetts, Vermont, and Pennsylvania, eventually settling in Santa Barbara, California. Hugh Gallaher, Betty's father, came east again to study at Exeter and Harvard. For one generation after another, education mattered more than wealth.

When it came to religion and politics, Betty's maternal ancestors were distinctly liberal. Reacting against the severity of the orthodox Congregational Church, they had become Universalists and Unitarians. Betty's great-grandfather, Hosea Parker, was the first Democrat from the North to be elected to Congress. As for her paternal forebears, their religious affiliations were a mix of Protestant persuasions, and one ancestor, oppressed by having three uncles who were Presbyterian ministers, lost his faith altogether, perhaps handing on to his descendants a strain of agnosticism.

When Betty was a year old, her father's work took the family to Paris for several years, and as a result she first spoke, read, and wrote in French. Schooling in Connecticut and New York followed, then four years at Smith College, two years in the navy, and graduate school at Harvard to obtain a PhD in English. In 1952, she joined the English Department at Smith College. Over the years, her love for and command of the English language and literature offered me a firm bridge to life in America.

Meanwhile, Father and my sister Lily, as the rearguard of our immediate family, had managed to leave their wartime haven in England and arrived in New York. Father, the old-time European gentleman, adjusted astonishingly well to the hustle and bustle of Manhattan. In fact, he took it by storm. Greenwich Village, where he and Lily lived, in those days still had the marks of a friendly neighborhood, and on his shopping rounds Father would exchange pleasantries with the local greengrocer and cobbler. Before long, Lily found a position at the Institute of International Education, launching her on a career that became her lifetime vocation.[20]

One sizzling summer Sunday, all of us—Father, Lily, my brothers, and I—took off together for the cool breezes of Jones Beach on Long Island. We of the younger generation were in bathing suits, ready to plunge into the waves, but Father was still in formal attire, reclining on the hot sand in a stiff, collared shirt and tie. But then I saw him rise from the sand, wave a five-dollar bill, and exclaim, "Get plenty of Coca Cola!" This was the ultimate moment of Father's Americanization.

When by the spring of 1949 I had turned in my PhD thesis and completed all the requirements for the degree, Father and Lily came up to Cambridge to witness the impressive commencement ceremony in Harvard Yard. This was my chance to show them the landmarks in Cambridge that had become so dear to me over the years. Meanwhile, the time had come for me to move on to a regular teaching position in the vast maze of American universities and colleges. I was fortunate to find a position in an institution, Smith College, which promised me a happy and professionally challenging future. My teacher Sidney B. Fay had established his scholarly reputation there, and now my friend Peter Viereck, who had also taught at Smith, recommended it to me as a humane and interesting place.

I could hardly have had a better send-off from Harvard than the one I got from John Finley. He was all too complimentary to me when in September 1949 he wrote: "I shall think of you as [Jacob] Burckhardt—high thought indeed—in your removed Basle somehow storing up a rightness and wisdom which Paris and Berlin didn't realize they lacked."[21] I did indeed move to a New England equivalent of Basle: Northampton, Massachusetts.

Smith College at that time was an extraordinarily friendly and vital center of higher education. By no means a cozy, tweedy place, it fostered a vibrant exchange of ideas among faculty and had an excellent student body—all this in the bucolic landscape of the Connecticut Valley. Before, during, and after World War I, the college had one of the truly outstanding American college presidents, William Allan Neilson, a wise and shrewd Scot who, among other things, had the good sense to attract to Smith a considerable number of distinguished European refugee scholars. The president of a university or college tends to have a national presence and to function as an elder statesman of sorts. William Allan Neilson was one of America's elder statesmen.

Speaking of the terrible Nazi pogrom, the *Kristallnacht* of 9 November 1938, he had said: "I will not stand by and be silent before these terrible things. I will not forget my common humanity, the common element in the whole race. I cannot be contemporary with these events and have it said by my children that I lived through that and did nothing about it—for no reason that I could honestly offer."[22] Although I came to the college years after President Neilson's death, his legacy remained intact.

Part of my own initiation into the college was introducing even newer citizens to the blessings of American citizenship. Early in the 1950s, the President's Office asked me to address the Washington's Birthday convocation of recently naturalized citizens at the home of the Northampton Daughters of the American Revolution. I looked forward to the occasion and prepared a talk in which I hoped to convey to my audience my own experiences and feelings. Assuming that most of those attending the ceremony—some fifteen of them—had left behind one form or another of oppression, I began by invoking the time-honored tradition of the Magna Carta and the Bill of Rights, and proceeded to connect these with phases of their encounter with America. However, right after my talk, so ceremoniously prefaced with references to venerable Anglo-Saxon documents, one man came up to me, looking at once combative and sheepish, and said in a heavy brogue: "But I come from Irrrllland." Had I miscalculated my audience? With him, at least, my panegyric fell flat.

In Northampton I came to appreciate fully the merits of the American liberal arts college system. The University of Vienna, where I started my advanced studies before emigrating to the United States, was a huge, impersonal factory of learning. At Harvard, the large size of the university was more or less mitigated by the residential houses that had been created in the 1930s at the initiative of President Lowell. At Smith, the college was the whole institution, not one of several faculties. Its excellent faculty was a stimulating group, eager to exchange ideas and indifferent to academic rank. It included a number of European scholars, among them several refugees from Nazi Germany. These gave the college a distinctly cosmopolitan tone. What was not European, however, was the faculty's easy accessibility to students.

Teaching at Smith was a challenge for me. The student body was not uniformly brilliant, yet it presented me with first-rate minds, especially in the advanced courses. When I was about to give a seminar, I prepared myself to the teeth, lest my students get the better of me in argument. It never bothered me that Smith was a college for women. It was clearly an elite school, with standards similar to those of Amherst and Yale. At the time, most able young women looked forward not to making a lot of money but to serving on the boards of libraries, hospitals, and museums. Their interests were probably not identical to those of their brothers, but the male students taking part in exchange programs in the 1960s who trickled into Smith classrooms certainly found their match.

In recent decades, Smith College has undergone fundamental changes due to the digital revolution, the women's movement, and the surge of men's colleges that now offer co-education. I am daunted by modern technology and allergic to "-isms." Meanwhile, I have retired and grown old. I now go my own way as a *Privatgelehrter* of sorts. Although I miss my encounters with young minds, I still benefit from the presence of friends on the faculty who continue to make life in Northampton a communal cultural experience.

On 19 May 1951 my father died. We never had been close to each other. He was a shy and rather distant man for whom family life was institutional rather than affective. I had received little advice and guidance from him. During the late 1920s and early 1930s, when I was struggling to find my bearings in the political turbulence of the times and when decisions about what political course to follow assumed a paramount importance for me and my friends, Father was the man of affairs, obeying the dictates of his profession. While he no doubt had his own thoughts about the future, he never discussed them with his children and left us to mull over our concerns with our peers.

Yet even though Father and I were not on the same wavelength, I always had unwavering respect for him, for his integrity as a human being and for his professional rectitude. In his rather undramatic way, he had steered the family ship responsibly through increasingly rough waters. I certainly had not made his task any easier by refusing to go to Oxford, but he never held this against me. The beautiful hymn by J. von Hausmann, sung at his funeral, with the text "So nimm denn meine Hände und führe mich" (Now take my hands and guide me), reverberates in my ears even still.

Now I was on my own. I suppose I had too long coasted through life. My constantly shifting environment had had an existential, almost intoxicating effect on me. Fortunately, perhaps, with all its ups and downs, it left me little occasion for excessive reflection. But since Socrates tells us that the unexamined life is not worth living, I realized that I must now at last move into a stage of self-examination.

The first European trips I took after the war helped me in my progress toward maturity. I first revisited Vienna in the late summer of 1951. Otto Molden met me at the Westbahnhof. At his home in the Osterleitengasse, his father was waiting for Sunday breakfast, which in Vienna is always very special. As I entered the sunny Biedermeier salon, I said "Good morning, Herr Molden." Otto's mother, alas, had died, partly from the hardships she had undergone during the Nazi occupation and wartime. Otto's father always had been for me a *Respektsperson*, a person to be treated with reverence. But in answer to my rather formal salutation, he said firmly and calmly: "Haben wir uns nicht immer 'Du' gesagt?" (Have we not always said *"Du"* to one another?). So we became *Du* to each other.[23] I was proud of that.

Later in the day, Otto took me out to Klosterneuburg, that unfinished but still magnificent Austrian Escorial to the west of Vienna. Being in the Soviet occupation zone, the area was strictly off limits to Americans, and there were plenty of Russian soldiers meandering about, enjoying that sunny Sunday afternoon. But somehow I did not care. This was my Austria, and no one should be able to challenge me there—and no one did. Austria was my sanctuary.

When I made my way to the family *palais* in Döbling, it was still in the hands of the American occupiers. As I approached the sergeant in charge, hoping to look inside the building, he said rather gruffly: "OK. Take five minutes and then report back to me." I seem to remember that he was from Tennessee. Anyway, I took my time walking through the halls of the mansion, emptied of the old furniture and the Kuffner ancestral portraits and other paintings that used to hang there and now filled with bare school desks. Once I reported back, the sergeant produced two cases of beer that, for one reason or another, happened to be my family's beer, the Ottakringer Bräu, and said with a gleam in his eye: "One is for you, the other for me." So we sat down together in the garden and finished the assignment. I cannot remember how I ever got back to the inner city after that binge. But I do remember the sergeant from Tennessee very kindly.

In Munich, my next stop after Vienna, I found quarters at the Hotel Schottenhaml, conveniently located not far from the main railway station. Half bombed out, it still offered friendly lodgings. Yet my old romanticism prompted me to move on into the countryside. Off I went by local train to the Starnbergersee, which promised an idyllic rural setting. Having easily found a room in the attic of a peasant house, I was delighted by the view from my window, which in clear weather would give me a glimpse of the majestic Tyrolean Wetterstein mountain range. Alas, I had to share my bed with a flea. Moreover, I discovered that the much desired countryside was full of nudists and, especially on weekends, of "urban imperialists." When I tried to retreat back to the city, I found my hotel occupied. I was thus condemned to return to my insect companion by the lake. In any case, I was cured, for the moment at least, of my inveterate romanticism.

I rather enjoyed my anonymity in Munich, a city to which I had no real ties. In my attempts to sound out people in the streets, I could plunge naively into bothering my victims, who did not know me from Adam. Interrogating them about their politics, I was not cheered by what I heard. Older people (Hindenburg Germans, I called them) in particular saw themselves as "martyrs" wronged by the American occupiers, who had destroyed their city and moved into their houses. They were all too ready to weigh the evils of Nazism against the irritations of occupation. As for the youngsters, I became keenly aware of their great uncertainty about their future. In Bavaria alone, according to the newspapers, there was a shortage of applicants for some 200,000 openings for apprentices. Yet those of the younger generation, I found, were more open-minded than their elders. The future, then, was theirs.

I was able to write to the Moldens that in Munich I had met two individuals who stood out as men "out of season," as Nietzsche would have had it—men who lived up to my idea of the righteous ones in Sodom, who never conformed to German stereotypes, and who always went their own way, even in the Nazi time. The first of these was Franz Schnabel. One of Germany's most distinguished historians, he had never fit into the mold of the old Borussian orthodoxy that was predominant among German historians. A South German liberal Catholic, he had lived in virtual isolation in German academia and in 1936 was dismissed by the Nazis. Only after the war was he given due recognition as a professor at the University of Munich, where I visited his seminar. The class was virtually mobbed, and after his no-less mobbed *Sprechstunde*, he took me to the Hofgarten restaurant for lunch. I remember how his passions surfaced as he complained about German historians' excessive historicism at the expense of deference to universal values. Our encounter confirmed my faith in a regeneration of Germany.

The second individual was Heinrich Mitteis, who had been my teacher at the University of Vienna. He emerged from his "exile" at the University of Rostock in East Germany and moved to Munich, where he became president of the Academy of the Sciences. My reunion with him and his wife at their country house in Murnau, Bavaria, was moving. With his contagious vitality, he was prepared to regenerate university life. Sadly, he died in 1952.

In the summer of 1956, leaving our one-year-old daughter Cathy with friends, Betty and I went to Europe, and she saw Vienna for the first time. Understandably, I wanted her to see it in the best of lights, but much of the city was still in shambles. Otto Molden had reserved a room for us in the old inner city at the Österreichischer Hof, which, I knew, had always catered to a very select clientele. But when our car drew up to the address Otto had given us, we found ourselves facing a ruin. Nevertheless, I left the car and walked to something resembling an entrance gate on which the words "Österreichischer Hof" were still faintly recognizable. Inside, under a 25-watt bulb, sat a tired old man with sideburns like those worn by Emperor Francis Joseph. Ruins loomed around and above him. Yes, he did have a room reserved for us. Thus began a virtually acrobatic climb up a shaky, circular staircase open to one abyss after the other. We felt as though we had landed in a Piranesi interior. But there was a room high up for us, somehow suspended between heaven and earth. A sign announced that the neighboring doors were not to be used—"Bei Lebensgefahr" (Danger). In the room, a large brass bedstead was a reminder of better times. There was a shiny brass telephone, and in the bathroom a neatly scrubbed tub and a bell pull to ring for the maid.

Dusty from the long trip, often on unpaved country roads, we felt we must bathe before meeting with our friends. But no hot water came out of the faucet. I made my precarious way downward to report this to the porter. To my polite complaint he had a quick response: "Tut mir leid, Herr Graf!" (I am sorry, Sir Count!). Back I climbed to the room, and we decided to make do with cold water. But the cold water faucet yielded nothing. Again I went down to the poor replica of my emperor to report our predicament. I had barely finished uttering my new complaint, when he shot back at me: "Tut mir leid, Herr Baron!" (I am sorry, Sir Baron!). Alas, when we had resigned ourselves to bathing at our friends' home and tried to reach them by phone, we found that it worked no better than the water faucets. I made a last effort to get help from the old man at the desk. This time he shouted, as though in triumph, "Tut mir leid, Herr Professor!" (I am sorry, Professor!). He had put me in my place.

The next day I set my mind on taking Betty for lunch to one of my favorite outdoor restaurants. It was in the courtyard of the *Schotten* monks (who were in fact Irish, not Scottish), shaded by old chestnut trees. In Austria it is customary, when no unoccupied table is available, simply to join someone already seated at a table. So we joined a man who, after short introductions, gave us to understand that he had spent years in a Nazi concentration camp. "Perfect," I thought, "now Betty can meet a good Viennese." But the next thing he said was that Hitler had done one good thing: he had rid Europe of its Jews. Painfully disappointed, I figured that he had probably been thrown into a concentration camp for his religious affiliations. Among Viennese Catholics there had always been a strong strain of anti-Semitism. How and where would I find a "good Viennese"?

Back home in the States our carefree days were over. In July 1957, our second child, Jamie, was born. This new chapter in our lives was sometimes hectic but wonderfully happy. My own family life, while not unhappy, had been marked by a rigid generational distance between father and children. I was resolved to change that. From the very start, Betty and I made a point of doing a lot of things together with the children, at work and at play. I always wanted them to master, apart from reading and writing and poetry, a craft like carpentry. Since I myself had had no training along those lines in my youth, my children and I somehow learned together.

Moreover, I have always believed it important to engage children in activities that expose them to nature and make them contend with the elements. Together we settled cheerfully on mountaineering and skiing. I had done a lot of these back in Austria, and now in New England the mountains of Vermont and New Hampshire welcomed us. On vacations and weekends we prepared our knapsacks to camp, to hike, to hit the slopes, and to cope with situations that were by no means always easy. All this brought us together. I suppose that Betty and I have managed to teach our children a great deal more than skills, and have transmitted to them our values, our ethos. Recently, however, as they have grown older and bolder, they have gradually assumed the burden of teaching us: "Mom, I told you … do this and do that … Dad, don't be silly." And we have come to accept this schooling gratefully.

In the autumn of 1957, I went to Vienna with Betty and our two toddlers to stay for a year on a Fulbright Fellowship. The October day on which we arrived was penetratingly cold and gloomy. The once glorious capital had lost much of its cheer and had barely recovered from the quadruple occupation of which the Russians left the most depressing traces. The so-called State Treaty had been signed two years earlier in May 1955 by the foreign ministers of the four occupying powers and the Austrian government, and the last Allied forces had left in October of that year. The "Third Man" of post-war racketeering was still haunting Vienna's sewers.[24]

The historian's work, I have come to understand, tends to be a fragment, however disciplined, of autobiography. What drew me to spend my sabbatical year in Vienna was a vague sense of wanting to pay tribute to the country of my forebears and also an eagerness to disentangle the story of German-Austrian relations that had been so prominent in shaping my personal life. Thus, I chose as a new project a biography of Ignaz Seipel, the Austrian priest-chancellor who was one of the chief architects of the Austrian Republic after World War I. Indeed, he became the commanding political figure of the new state. What attracted me to the chancellor to begin with was that he was a shrewd and accomplished political strategist, who, although having to resign himself to the confines of a small successor state of the old monarchy, was a statesman of imperial caliber. He skillfully shepherded what was left of the monarchy after the war into the Republic of Austria. But while he entered the arena of politics as a supreme pragmatist, one who downplayed doctrinal considerations and was ready to work with the socialists, in the heat of the increasingly critical climate in truncated Austria—and especially in the course of his head-on disputes with the Austro-Marxists—the prelate allowed himself to drift into confrontations that assumed titanic dimensions. This in turn opened the floodgates for the returning native son, the charismatic Führer with his seductive ideology.

The history of that embattled, implacable chancellor had after all been history through which I myself had lived. My revisiting Austria, especially as I viewed its past through the telescope of its least fortunate years, thus had a paradoxical effect upon me. The mere return to familiar haunts, the high fence around my grandparents' estate, the grandparental *palais* that now was yawningly empty, the old chestnut tree on the northwest corner of the garden, the linden tree by the wading pool under which Mr. Husserl had tested my ignorance, they all evoked memories, happy as well as unhappy ones, but certainly memories to which I clung. Although distant, unreal, and ghostly, they were a part of myself.

Yet my preoccupation with the intensity and tension of the Seipel era, the political and ideological civil war climate that then prevailed in Austria, and the subsequent triumph of ideology had the effect of drawing me away from the turmoil of that world. I learned a lot in writing about the embattled and implacable chancellor, but the political lessons that I could draw from the subject were predominantly negative. I had to leave the world of Seipel behind me even as I wrote about it: goodbye to the baggage of heroism, goodbye to crusading, goodbye to aligning with and hiding behind big causes. From now on, the accountability for what I stood for depended on me.

During our stay in Vienna I found myself in a railway compartment with a woman who pontificated passionately, lamenting the absence of idealism among the youth of the time. They were, she argued, absorbed by merely *materialistische* concerns. I myself had always been, and still am, an idealist. But what had been the benefits of the supposed idealism that she coveted? Where had it taken her model youth but into brutality, genocide, and catastrophe? The encounter with that woman, clearly an unregenerate Nazi, brought home to me that in the past years idealism had been systematically turned against itself, abused, and made to turn people's heads. Reality, it occurred to me, complex as it is, could not be mastered by resorting to borrowed ideological crutches. I was reminded of the reflections on the subject by one of Austria's great writers, Robert Musil (1880–1942), who wrote in his novel *The Man without Qualities*: "The expenditure of muscular energy made by a citizen quietly going about his business all day long is considerably greater than that of an athlete who lifts huge weights once a day. Physiologically this has been established, and so doubtless the sum total of little everyday exertions ... does bring far more energy into the world than the deeds of heroes; indeed, the heroic exertion appears positively minute, like the grain of sand laid, in some act of illusory immensity, upon a mountain top."[25]

My friend Friedl Lehne, always judicious, formulated well the climate for me and my friends who had survived the turmoil of revolution and war. It was not the climate of disenchantment, but was it the climate of maturity? He wrote to me that despite the growing prosperity in post-war Austria, he was concerned that the "necessary integration of the liberal-democratic inheritance with the conservative one" was wanting, and that there were few people friendly to concepts such as human rights and the rule of law as the foundation of the state. The free and democratic order, he added, was considered compromising and unattractive, the concept of service (*Dienen*) seemed "outdated," and freedom was confounded with comforts.[26] Was this letter more than a stock complaint about "today's youth"? It certainly had nothing to do with the nostalgia for a supposed idealism, as with the disenchanted Nazi woman in the train. It confirmed my decision to steer clear of the temptations of ideological fervor and to take the less glamorous but more rewarding path of trying to cope with the challenges of reality. There would be no fuzzy utopias, then, no romantic illusions, no heroic exertions; rather, there would be reliance on the benefits of the "sum total of little everyday exertions."

But was I somehow reading myself out of the mainstream of America? Goethe wrote, "Amerika, du hast es besser" (America, you have it better). Possessed by an indomitable optimism, the United States had all along persisted in seeing itself as the land of infinite possibilities and progress, and this had become an article of faith, bolstered by the vastness and variety of the country and by streams of new immigrants promising a new beginning. I was one of those immigrants. My army years, my Harvard experience, my American wife and children no doubt made it possible for me to join in this song of the open road. But at every turn of the road, I continued to ask myself how far it would take me from my European beginnings.

The academic year 1963–1964 found us in Germany again. At the University of Bonn I was to take the place of Karl Dietrich Bracher, who in turn was to spend the year at an institute in California. Since Betty had to teach in Northampton in the fall term, she and the children did not follow me until Christmas. I spent the first three months by myself in Bracher's house in Bad Godesberg, where we were to live. This arrangement enabled me to devote all my time to familiarizing myself with life in the big university and with the Institute of Political Science, which I was supposed to direct.

The imposing ochre baroque facade of the university offered me an architectural welcome, and the institute, opposite the Hofgarten, a spacious park, turned out to be a beehive of lively and friendly assistants who made my academic work in Bonn very agreeable. I blush to admit that, as I was not a political scientist, I did not really have the formal qualifications to head that institute. But since Bracher covered both related disciplines, political science and contemporary history, by covering the latter field I could slip into my deputizing position without false pretences. In any case, I managed pretty well and learned a lot.

My visits to Germany after the war inevitably became a sort of personal archaeology. Unhappy memories would force themselves to the fore, although I resisted being captured by the past. There were moments when I asked myself, as I did in a letter to my wife, whether I was "still the same." In Berlin I had recognized at the end of the Viktoriastrasse, where we used to live, the old plane tree that had survived the bombing. I was shocked at the very fact of recognizing it, as I was when I saw, amid a landscape of rubble, the old Swiss Legation, where early in 1938 Father and the rest of us had pleaded in vain with the minister for a safe haven. I could not disguise my irritation with the many "men in the street" whom I met; they seemed to me dazed but self-righteous and impenitent. Still, I was keenly on the lookout for the "other Germans," and I found them. "Any reasonable German you meet," I wrote to a friend in the States, "is all the more, by virtue of his very uniqueness, a work of art. But I met some and feel richer now."[27]

My encounter with the students and assistants at the university was certainly most encouraging. Here was a new generation, and I was impressed by their openness and their freedom from prejudice and from compensatory behaviors or inhibitions stemming from the Nazi past. If only they could escape the pressures of "re-education." These students were no doubt preoccupied with the history of the Third Reich and its crimes, a subject that was studied and taught at schools and universities. However, it seemed important to me that these young people should be allowed to grow up without having a sense of guilt hammered into them.

What I remember most vividly from this particular stay in Bonn was the American tragedy of the assassination of President John F. Kennedy. With him, a new generation, my generation, had taken over the helm of the nation, promising to fulfill the American dream—the dream of social and racial justice. His inaugural admonition to his fellow Americans, "ask not what your country can do for you—ask what you can do for your country," reverberated within us. We identified with his vision, and he gave us special pride in our country in whose new dawn we were to take part.

But then, one Saturday morning, on 23 November 1963, as I was leisurely reclining on the sofa in Bracher's living room, the phone rang and the voice of one of my assistants came through: "President Kennedy has been assassinated!" This was one of the moments in my life when I sensed that history had been changed for ever. This is what I wrote to friends in America after the event: "Last Monday I cancelled my seminar. All fifty students had appeared, but it was evident that they had their minds on a torchlight procession that same evening for Kennedy. So I let them go, and in fact went myself. It was an impressive, spontaneous march through the dark, a long line of students, finally forming a circle, throwing their torches together and standing around the fire. No songs, no speeches. This is the image of the new generation, prosaic, skeptical, and not without dignity."[28] In the next few days, pictures of John F. Kennedy and clippings from newspapers went up, one by one, on the walls of my assistants' studies.

But now, looking back from the present-day perspective, I reflect on what happened later in the 1960s, when students rose up all over Europe, including in Germany, to protest against the war in Vietnam, against the so-called military-industrial complex, against their professors, whom the German students called *Fachidioten* (specialist idiots), and against social injustice, imperialism, and everything that smacked of the American establishment. By then, the likes of Rudi Dutschke had assumed the leadership of the radical students, the *enragés*. Although in my seminar we had been hard at work studying the origins and nature of Nazi tyranny, we were now suspected by the radicals of the "inability to mourn."[29]

Back in America, it was during that decade that Betty and I acquired an old farmhouse in the hills of Conway, Massachusetts. Only twenty-five minutes by car to the northwest of Northampton, it took us into an altogether different, remote world of woods and pastures where our neighbors' cows looked at us across the fence.[30] The house, a so-called First Period house, still had a central chimney and three fireplaces, the largest with a crane and Dutch oven. The beams were visible and hand-hewn, but the original parlor had a finely painted wall and corner cupboard. Although simple, it offered us more than shelter. We came to love this retreat from the pressures and twentieth-century noises of Northampton, and for thirty years we spent most of our summers there, working leisurely and welcoming friends. We picked berries from June through October, first strawberries and then mulberries (from the biggest tree of its kind in the area), raspberries, and blueberries. Betty tended the vegetable and flower gardens, while I looked after the bushes and trees. Playing the part of country squire, I tried to clear the surrounding land. But New England, as someone once said, wants to be forest.

Not far from the village there was a swimming pond where we always cooled off in the evenings. There were tennis courts in nearby Deerfield, where we often played family games. And of course the children were free to invite their friends to stay. One summer we had with us a young black boy, Richie, whose mother wanted him to have a healthy vacation away from the noise, violence, and temptations of New York City. Richie was about our Jamie's age, although almost twice as tall. In the crowd at the swimming pond, Richie was unique, wrapped in a towel of many colors. Surrounded by curious and admiring children, he enjoyed playing the part of visiting royalty. However, he was rather less regal when, after having bragged about his riding skills, he somehow got astride a horse and was promptly thrown off. In his new admirers' eyes, he had instantly become a fallen idol. We remember Richie with much affection, but I do not know how long he remembered us. Notwithstanding his mother's hopes, it seems that he joined a gang, as she had feared. Violence and drugs won out in the end. Did we do him any good at all?

In a contrapuntal story, about ten years later, in the summer of 1976, we had a visitor from France. Thierry, who was also about Jamie's age, came from a noble Breton family that had come to know Betty's father and uncle during World War I. Thierry, his mother gave us to understand, was difficult—"Il a besoin d'une bonne secousse" (He needs a good jolt)—and she figured that spending the summer with an American family would do him good.

We brought him along to Washington, DC, where we celebrated the United States Bicentennial on 4 July. As we gathered to watch the festivities from the office of Betty's brother-in-law on the seventh floor of the State Department, we noticed that Thierry and Jamie were missing. It turned out that Thierry had been determined to visit the American Nazi Party headquarters situated by Lafayette Square, and Jamie had felt obliged, as his host, to take him there. But the American Nazi in charge at the time took no interest in Thierry, who left with his tail between his legs. "Of course," Betty said to him afterwards, "they are racists, and they saw you as a Latin, a 'frog.'" Thierry retorted, "But I am not Latin at all. My mother is Breton and my father is Flemish. When I was little, I was very blond."

Throughout the summer we tried to make the best of our troublesome visitor. Since he made no effort to conceal his cluster of offensive prejudices, bringing him together with our friends was clearly out of the question. But we showed him the New England countryside and took him to concerts. Once in a hardware store we found Thierry turning a globe to show South Africa, whose apartheid policy appealed to him. His next discovery in the store was a heavy chain, which he lifted and swung tentatively: "Ca peut faire mal, vous savez" (This can hurt, you know). A visit to Tanglewood was no more successful. Seiji Ozawa was then conducting the Boston Symphony Orchestra, and there was a scattering of Asians in the audience. Thierry commented, "C'est plain de jaunes" (It's full of yellow people).

Thierry was a fascist, a Nazi. I had given courses and seminars on these species, and now I was host to a live specimen. I had previously met his parents at a family gathering in their château northeast of Paris. Suddenly, a man I did not know got up from his chair and announced without preamble, "J'ai appris à haïr" (I have learned to hate). I learned afterwards that he was Thierry's father, one of the many so-called *pieds-noirs*, big French landowners in Algeria whose estates had been confiscated. Had his father's bitterness rubbed off on Thierry? Thierry himself liked to say that in school he had to stand up for classmates harassed by Marxists and Communists and that he and his friends had to protect them. But this was the way he rationalized the predicament that was his.

Over the course of time we lost sight of Thierry, and he is no longer alive. Our information is that he died of a drug overdose.

Finally, two anecdotes about my own children also suggest ethical issues. Early in the winter of 1971, Jamie, then an eighth-grader, came home from school to report that another student, a big bully he barely knew, had said menacingly to him, "Tomorrow after class I'll meet you on the hill," referring to an area where students customarily settled their accounts by fistfights. Over meatloaf and vegetables, the family held a council of war. Must Jamie go? We came to the decision, with which Jamie concurred, that he must hold his own, as he always should in life. The following morning, as we awakened with heavy hearts, we discovered that a heavy snow had fallen, a blizzard, and school was canceled. By the time classes resumed several days later, Jamie's challenger had forgotten about him.

That same winter we had promised Cathy, an inveterate sportswoman, a week at a skiing camp in the Berkshires. Driving conditions were terrible, with falling snow obstructing visibility. Time and again the car stalled and almost got stuck. As we finally approached the snow-covered slopes of Otis, Cathy said, "I won't stay at the camp. I won't let you drive home alone. I'll drive back with you." Stunned but grateful, I accepted her offer, and together we made it home at last.

These years of companionship with our children have defined our relationship for all the decades to come and have accompanied me on my long *Wanderschaft* through life.

Chapter Seven

"Mit dem Gesicht nach Deutschland"

In the late summer of 1973, my family and I resumed our *Wanderschaft*. Much academic research involves wandering from place to place, collecting information in remote repositories or, as in my case, chasing after live witnesses. But to me such traveling had a special significance. Was it another chapter of my story as a refugee? Was my having settled down in New England only an illusion? Would I ever really settle down? The Russian exile poet Joseph Brodsky, observing the unsteady and turbulent climate of our age, remarked that "displacement and misplacement are this century's commonplace."[1] As I spent so many of these years abroad, I could not help feeling like a wanderer again. Maybe those children were right—the ones who, upon my return to Germany after the war, said to me, out of the blue, "Du bist ein Wanderer."

There was a special note, though, to those wanderings of mine. Let me try to explain by citing the plight of a German oppositional politician under Nazi oppression. Otto Wels was the leader of the Social Democratic Party, which was outlawed soon after the Nazi seizure of power in May 1933. He had sounded his last hurrah on the occasion of the Reichstag debate on the passing of the so-called Enabling Act, which was to pave the way for Hitler's dictatorship. His speech before the jeering brown-shirted Nazi delegates was a singular feat of courage. "You can take away our freedom and life," he said, "but not our honor."[2] Soon afterward, he had to go with his party into exile, first to Prague and then to Paris,[3] where he is said to have repeated the expression, "Mit dem Gesicht nach Deutschland" (Always keeping Germany in view).[4] That "long dream of home," which Victor Hugo had held onto in his exile from Emperor Napoleon III, was Wels's too.

I cannot call myself an exile. I was a refugee. I left my country and my home because my livelihood—indeed, my life—was threatened. I had taken to my adopted country, the United States, with alacrity, and I was deeply grateful for the welcome I received there. Yet like Otto Wels, whatever I did, wherever I moved, I still had a distinct connection with my origins. Something inside told me that not all ties with my past had been severed and that, to the contrary, it had become my task as a historian to unearth and identify those strains in the German and Austrian tradition that could serve as a foundation for a proud new beginning.

I was asked to spend a year at Cambridge University, and I was happy to be back in England—doubly so because, silly as I am, I like monarchies, the sense of tradition and repose that they seem to radiate. When we signed in at the police station on our arrival in Cambridge, I noticed on the official's desk blotter the vowels "AEIOU" and could not help but identify them with the motto that the ambitious fifteenth-century Habsburg king, Frederick III, had devised for his dynasty and kingdom.[5] Was the police officer that learned? I was quickly disabused of my lingering monarchist sentimentality when told that the official had jotted down those vowels as an aid to making himself understood in traffic when registering foreigners unfamiliar with the English language.

Churchill College was founded in the mid-1960s at Sir Winston's initiative as a counterpart to the American MIT. I was welcomed most generously, and although a humanist, was never made to feel like an intruder in this science- and technology-based institution. The college is located due north of town, and our flat, number 14, was situated on a rise of land with a broad view to the south of the spires of King's College. From the east the winds blew across the fen country all the way from the Urals, we were told, and mercilessly to our flat. On the other hand, at sunset the western sky often gave us a magnificent red display.

Right next to our flat were the playing fields of the college. One afternoon, two games took place. The players of one were all neatly garbed in white and very silent. This game was, I figured, cricket, mysterious and incomprehensible to me. The other game was unmistakably American baseball. Our son Jamie, who had come with us to England for the year, had recruited a number of other visiting Americans. Dressed in messy blue jeans and dispensing with ceremony, they filled the afternoon air with noise. Later I learned that one of the questions in the tripos, the final honors examination in Cambridge, that year was about the extent to which the differences between cricket and baseball reflected differences in the conduct of British and American foreign policy.

I did enjoy the sense of tradition, the ceremony, and the ritual of the college. My conservative heart was cheered by George Romney's fine portrait in the college library of "The Rt. Hon. Edmund Burke." Sir Jacob Epstein's powerful sculpture of Churchill, guarding the grand staircase leading up to Hall, conveyed the very presence of the prime minister in the college. The veneration of Churchill meant a great deal to me. This was in part a generational matter; to those of my generation he was the supreme leader. Revisionists did not question Churchill's greatness until much later, in the 1990s,[6] and I for one cannot go along with them even today. But while Churchill was the guardian angel of the college, I wondered why not much was ever said about Ludwig Wittgenstein, whose association with Cambridge was with Trinity College. Opposite the gate of Churchill College on Storeys Way, as though under its protection, stands the house of Dr. Edward Bevan, who attended to the great philosopher in his dying days, and a stone's throw away is St. Giles Cemetery, where Wittgenstein is buried. Would attention paid to the war leader and to the philosopher be as unequal today?

After a couple of days, I braved the rather awesome High Table. I even trained myself, on my walk across the college lawns to Hall, to prepare certain topics for conversation with my partners at the dinner table. Jamie, my best critic and jester, reminded me to rehearse a bit for High Table, so as to avoid eating with my knife. Seriously, I much enjoyed the long discussions after dinner in the Senior Combination Room, when we usually stuck to a single topic, turning it over and probing it while sherry and hock, a rather sweet Rhine wine, made the rounds.

I can offer two glimpses into my first evenings in the Combination Room. Before my first dinner in Hall, as I circulated shyly and vaguely, trying to get my bearings in a crowd of awe-inspiring men, bat-like in their black gowns, one of them, elderly and dignified, came up to me and fixed his eyes on my tie. "Where," he asked, "did you get this tie?" All I could say was that I must have bought it in America at Lord & Taylor's. This answer did not satisfy him, and he reappeared after a few minutes: "Do you know what this tie stands for?" "Nothing that I know of," I replied. All I knew about the tie was that I liked its thin diagonal stripes against the black field. When he reappeared for a second time, he whispered into my ear: "The tie you are wearing is the navy tie." My informant was Stephen Roskill, a distinguished navy man, a captain, who during World War II had been deputy director of British Naval Intelligence. In Britain, at least in the higher circles of the establishment, one's loyalty is signified by the tie one wears. From then until we left Britain, I refrained from wearing the handsome tie with stripes.

Soon thereafter I took Betty along for dinner in Hall. By then I had struck up an acquaintance with Stephen Roskill. His wish to make us feel at ease in a crowd of strangers by no means suppressed his curiosity about us. He inquired, among other things, into Betty's background. Betty had been a naval person herself, serving during the war as a naval officer assigned to intelligence work in Washington. Exactly what her duties had been she never divulged to me, and I never asked her about them. Now, when the important British captain questioned her, Betty simply stood her ground, politely maintaining the secrecy she had sworn to years earlier. However, the next time she came to dinner with me, Stephen Roskill walked straight up to her, telling her exactly what arcane matters she had been working on during the war. Three cheers for British intelligence! Stephen and his wife Elizabeth became dear friends of ours.

Naturally, we scouted out frequently to other colleges. On the occasion of a visit to King's College, Betty, seated in Hall next to the Master, asked him about the Apostles, the well-known Cambridge secret society to which literary figures from Tennyson to the Bloomsbury group had belonged and about which Betty had read a good deal. She met with stony silence. This was not to be a topic for conversation: the Master himself was an Apostle.

At Gonville and Caius we were the guests of the Master, Joseph Needham, and his wife, both of them distinguished biochemists. Their magnum opus was a multi-volume work on science and civilization in China. Preparing it, they had lived for several years in China and as left-wing socialists had become enthusiastic supporters of the Chinese revolution and China's Communist Party. While the thirty-odd guests, many of them Asians, partook of a buffet dinner, the Needhams circulated among them separately. The Master engaged me in a brief but interesting discussion of Oswald Spengler, Germany's famous universal historian, and his cyclical theory of history. Later, Mrs. Needham came up to us and explained that the Communist Chinese could make bad people good. Instead of killing dissidents, they put them into special camps to be "re-educated." Our rejoinder that this practice, while safeguarding the functioning of the commonweal, amounted to a violation of the dignity of the individuals involved cut no ice with Mrs. Needham. We left the party not exactly elated.

But all told we had a wonderful time in Cambridge. We made good friends and derived much pleasure from the college gardens during all seasons and from the abundance of music, much of it Elizabethan, performed in various colleges. Evensong at King's was always a special occasion. On Sunday mornings we usually took a long walk to the Iron Age ruins south of the city with our old friends, George and Zara Steiner.

Having bought a little automobile, we traveled farther afield. All of England became history for us, in particular, the abbey of Bury St. Edmunds in Suffolk, where the barons swore in 1214 to compel King John to yield to the demands that became enshrined in the Magna Carta. In the Midlands, Coventry was a reminder of less estimable human actions: its fourteenth-century St. Michael's Cathedral was almost entirely destroyed by German bombs. It was left just as it had been found on the morning after the bombing. In the ruined chancel there was a cross of half-melted nails made by German students belonging to Aktion Sühnezeichen (Action Sign of Atonement), a volunteer group that had been founded after World War II. Under it was an inscription reading simply "Father Forgive."

Our stay in England gave us the chance to revisit the Continent. One of our destinations was the Kitzburg, the little castle belonging to Karola, my friend from the old days in the snowscape of the Kleines Walsertal. The Kitzburg, pale pink and moated, was located on a promontory between Cologne and Bonn near the Dominican monastery of Walberberg, where Konrad Adenauer had stayed while negotiating the founding of the Christian Democratic Union (CDU), Germany's conservative party. Years earlier, Karola had been little more to me than a friendly face, but after the war we became friends and wrote to each other quite regularly. On my trips to Germany, I would often stop at the Kitzburg as a matter of course.

The Kitzburg, whose exterior belied its twelfth-century foundations, was at the center of an estate that included vineyards, cultivated fields, and a forest that hid a Roman ruin. Karola, the chatelaine, was loved and revered throughout the region; peasants would tip their hats whenever she passed. She never married, having broken with a suitor when she discovered, as I understood it, that he had Nazi connections. She was deeply religious—Catholic, like almost everyone in the Rhineland—but in a wholly unconventional manner. Her behavior was refreshingly eccentric. It never occurred to her to calculate the effect of what she said or did. She simply let her generous impulses have their way.

I have kept a letter from her in which she described an evening festivity, organized by the local Red Cross chapter, over which she as patroness presided. Because the monks of the monastery had been invited, Karola had provided for singing and skits but not dancing. But suddenly, she wrote,

> there was the sound of a band—two monks and three civilians. Waltzes. A young monk asked me, under great general applause, to a dance.... Then calls from all sides, "Twist! Twist! Twist! Twist!" and nothing helped us who were uninitiated in the rigmarole. And I whispered to the monk: "I did not know that you were allowed to dance!" He: "I don't know whether or not I am allowed to do so. I did not ask anyone, I simply *had* to dance. And I take all the consequences on me! In any case, I already have a great reprimand coming." Subsequently, I went over to the abbot. I: "He won't have any difficulties, I hope???" He: "No, *one* dance is certainly defensible; dancing with you was a bounden duty." Again the music sounded a waltz, whereupon I spontaneously asked the abbot for the dance, who accepted with some embarrassment. In no time *all* were on their feet, and some 200 persons danced without interruption.... Except for two who were really sick and limping, the whole hall fell in, and my eyes even caught sight of a woman, eight times a great-grandmother, who, carried away by happiness, was dancing along.... It all was indescribably funny.[7]

On a more serious note, I remember one occasion when Karola, who liked to entertain, gave a dinner party to which a number of former Wehrmacht generals were invited. It was my task to fetch them at the railway station. Later in the evening, as the guests milled about, one of the generals, who had ascertained my life story, burst out, "How come you fought during the war against your own fatherland?" Should I have responded to the general in the words of Otto Wels, "always keeping Germany in view"? Would he have understood?

Of course, my chief reason for being in England was work, and it took me a while to settle on a new project. I was very generally thinking of research on the "conservative imagination" and was reading widely in the works of authors such as Edmund Burke, Hugo von Hofmannsthal, T. S. Eliot, and Quintin Hogg. This somewhat undirected reading helped me to clarify my thoughts about the need to hold on to a traditional heritage in a world that seemed relentlessly moving away from it and to continue to make it a living force that would inform the present.

I finally settled on a study of the German Resistance (*Widerstand*). Was this a manifestation of conservatism? I must admit that when I was first attracted by this subject, I was captivated by the courage of those men and women from the old German establishment who had the guts to defy the Nazi tyranny. I was little aware that most of those who stood up and sacrificed themselves for their convictions came from among the proletarians, indeed, from among the Communists.

What particularly engaged me were the efforts of the conspirators, facing formidable risks, to forge links across the front lines with the Allies, notably, the British Foreign Office and the US State Department, and even with the Russians. These attempts met with "absolute silence" (Winston Churchill, January 1941) and the demand for "unconditional surrender" (President Roosevelt, January 1943). Were the distrust and ultimate rebuff encountered by German emissaries justified, or were the Allied intermediaries too unimaginative to respond to a proposition when doing so might not only have shortened the war and saved hundreds of thousands of lives but also have supported the universal human rights of dissidents in a situation of extreme tyranny? Such were my questions as I entered into my investigation.

My ultimate intention was to bear witness to the fact that, whatever the conflicts of interest and misunderstandings on either side, righteous Germans had existed. Even in the Federal Republic of Germany, there had been in the early years after the war a good deal of hesitancy to see the members of the *Widerstand* as other than traitors. All resistance borders on treason insofar as it tends to oppose and aim at toppling an established regime. In Germany particularly, where resistance was not an assertion of national interest directed against oppression by a foreign power, as it was in occupied countries, resistance was perforce out of step with the immediate national interest. The success of the plot might have meant the defeat of the fatherland. In addressing a German public, I would have had it perceive the *Widerstand* in terms of higher loyalties above and beyond the conventional meanings of loyalty and treason.

Moreover, in the Anglo-Saxon world, and particularly in the United States, the assumption has prevailed—and still prevails—that resistance in Germany was, in the words of the London *Times*, "one of the non-events of the Twentieth Century"[8] or at best a "myth."[9] Thus, I had my work cut out for me. It was to be an uphill battle, but I have learned to enjoy a good fight when necessary. My new venture became my life's work and furthermore brought into my orbit a number of survivors, admirable people, many of whom became good friends.

As it happened, I was in the right place for my work. Churchill College had archival holdings of considerable interest to me, and I could start, at least, in situ. But I also needed to make regular pilgrimages to the Public Record Office in London, then still situated in Chancery Lane. Early in the mornings I would walk to the Cambridge railroad station, past grazing sheep and, in the early spring, past friendly daffodils in the meadows of the "backs," and return satisfied though tired late in the evening. For the rest I had to travel yet farther afield—to Oxford, Birmingham, Ireland, and eventually the Continent— looking for documents and also interviewing people. Eventually, a wealth of sources, public and private, printed and oral, was waiting to be explored in the United States. Most of the time I felt as though I were on a treasure hunt.

Soon after our arrival in England, I stumbled onto a discussion in the London *Times* of a book on Adam von Trott zu Solz, the German resister who had been executed by the Nazis for his part in the plot against Hitler. A strikingly colorful figure and much discussed in Britain, Adam was a cousin of my friend Georg von Schweinitz, who had died in 1940 on the battlefield in France. The newspaper piece mentioned in passing that Adam had been married to Clarita Tiefenbacher. So this was my Clarita, my skiing companion from years ago in the Kleines Walsertal. Now that I had found Karola, could I also after so many years renew my ties with my other friend of that magic mountain? I re-established my connection with Clarita, now in Berlin, and our friendship deepened over the years.[10]

In the course of my research, Adam von Trott had moved closer and closer to the center of my field of vision. This Hessian aristocrat, young though he was, had been the most persistent and audacious troubleshooter abroad on behalf of the German *Widerstand*. A proud German patriot, he was a decided foe of the Nazi regime, unyielding in his commitment to the rights and dignity of humankind. This, then, was the "Trott problem" that gripped me: How could love of country be combined with activities abroad that, by all conventional standards, bordered on treason? How could the assertion of German national interests, on which Trott insisted, be reconciled with the satisfaction of Allied expectations and demands?

To the Nazi court that sentenced him to death, he was without question a traitor for his "defeatist view." But even to his Oxford friends, Trott's case was by no means clear-cut, and they found themselves unable to come to terms with the complications of his life as a German resister. While seeking the overthrow of Hitler's regime, he insisted on salvaging the integrity of his country. In the clash between his involvement in conspiracy and his patriotism, Trott naturally drew misunderstanding and distrust abroad. Was he after all playing a "double game"? Even after the defeat of the Third Reich, when his high ideals should have become manifest, if only by virtue of his sacrificial death, the "Trott problem" persisted. It involved the seeming incompatibility of German national interests with the common Allied cause, associated with the call for "unconditional surrender." For this reason he emerged in history as an ambiguous figure, never free from controversy. The Trott saga opened up to me the dilemmas and hazards confronted by the resisters in Germany, unlike those in the countries occupied by the Nazis, and it became a special challenge to try to unravel the mystery, to explain the intricacies of his situation, and thus to contribute to an understanding of Adam's part in history.

My sense of place sent me in February 1977 to Imshausen, where the Trott branch of Adam's family lived in a spacious manor built late in the eighteenth century on the site of the old family castle. The snow-covered hills and the trees of the Trottenwald that surrounded the property spoke of a feudal past that had always been for Adam a source of strength and pride. Now Imshausen was the seat of a religious *Kommunität* of "brothers" and "sisters" who tended the land and its sheep and conducted divine services. I found it to be a friendly group, and its religious tone was, quite in the spirit of Adam, cheerful and unostentatious. Adam's sister Vera, a *grande dame*, lived just beyond the manor in a small baroque structure, and a few miles away in Süss lived his younger brother Heinrich, who attended to the forests and timber. The two, Vera and Heinrich, maintained the Trott tradition after all the upheaval of the Nazi era. With Vera I had a long session over tea. As I paid my respects to Heinrich, his wife Elisabeth pointed to a print of a young man like a Greek God that hung on the wall and said quietly, referring to Adam: "He now prays for us."

At the top of a hill on the highest point in the Trottenwald, overlooking the fields and the forests to which Adam once said he had confided all his thoughts and feelings, his family and friends have erected a wooden cross forty feet high. At its base are inscribed the words: "Adam von Trott zu Solz. Executed with his friends in the struggle against the despoiler of our country. Pray for them. Follow their example."

In September 1977, the pursuit of the Trott saga took me to County Cork in the Republic of Ireland. In Castletownshend on a jagged western coast of many points extending into the Atlantic lived Shiela Grant Duff, one of Adam's old friends from his Oxford days in the early 1930s. Shiela, a cousin of Clementine Churchill, was descended through both her parents from Whig aristocrats. One of England's vociferous foreign correspondents, she had reported to the *Observer* from Prague during the critical years of 1936–1937 and resigned from that paper because of its editor's pro-German and anti-Czech policy. Jealously protective of everything pertaining to the interests of Czechoslovakia and having a direct line to Winston Churchill, she acted as his intimate informer about matters pertaining to Czechoslovakia, which was increasingly threatened by the aggressive plans of its German neighbor. Proud and stubborn, if not cantankerous, she saw herself as waging a resistance of her own against the appeasement policies of Great Britain. She finally faced up to the inevitability of war as a last resort for freeing Europe from the Nazi scourge.

Adam's resistance was of a very different kind. He could not have been less interested in the fate of Czechoslovakia. His one objective was to topple the Nazi regime in Germany, and he envisaged a European war as a calamitous fratricide resembling that of the Greek city-states. Maintaining peace, he came to believe, was a prerequisite for a coup against Hitler. His mode of resistance, being conspiratorial, was necessarily covert, and not only within Germany. It became harder and harder for him to present himself abroad as a "good German" and increasingly difficult for his Anglo-Saxon friends to trust him.

Adam and Shiela, like many at Oxford, had formed an intense friendship. They shared fervent dreams of a new Europe, a world order of social justice and self-rule. Yet their bond did not survive the strains caused by the gathering European crisis and by differences of circumstance and temperament. Shiela came to suspect her friend of supporting the appeasement policy.[11] Particularly after Germany and Britain went to war, she was no longer able to maintain a distinction between Germans and Nazis. Almost inevitably, the two friends parted ways.

The visit in Ireland brought me to the last act of a dramatic struggle over Adam, over his integrity, his reputation. Shiela could not have been more welcoming. We took walks along the rocky coastline with magnificent views over the ocean and had long talks about Europe, past and present. In the evening, unforgettably, Katinka, a friend of Shiela's son Alexander, recited Ophelia's mad song from Shakespeare's *Hamlet* to the crackling of the peat fire on the hearth:

How should I your true love know
From another one?
By his cockle hat and staff
And his sandal shoon.

He is dead and gone, lady,
He is dead and gone;
At his head a grass-green turf
At his heels a stone....

Shiela, a great hostess, was a fascinating woman, at once urbane and fiercely independent. Later, when she turned over to me her whole correspondence with Adam, containing some 350 letters going back to the Oxford days of 1932 and continuing to the eve of World War II, I became fully aware of its historical importance and set my mind on publication.[12] I had no illusions about stepping into a hornet's nest; nevertheless, I made it my task to set the record straight, letting the letters speak for themselves.

Without a doubt, from the start this best friendship was a very difficult one. What would have happened, I once asked Shiela, if the conspirators against Hitler had succeeded? For her there was no question but that the success of Adam and his friends would have furthered hegemonic designs on their part. She held on stubbornly to her jaundiced view of Adam's political profile, going so far as to chide him for the "personal ambition" she saw in his "dangerous patriotism"[13] and dismissing those who stood up for him, including Clarita, David Astor, and their friends, disparaging them as the "Trott committee" or the "Trott industry."

Had Shiela and Adam not been, as they set out to be, "children of a yet unborn civilization"?[14] And what had happened to the dreams of their Oxford days? Had they not been united both in rebellion and in hopes for a "new common Europe"?[15] I did remind Shiela of the two friends' original idea of enacting a twentieth-century version of Alfred de Musset's *La Confession d'un enfant du siècle*. But by then, in 1978, Shiela was no longer able to identify herself with it: "I had no idea of what Musset's *Enfant du siècle* was about and knew nothing about his great love affair with George Sand. I imagined it to be a quasi political-philosophical work, or at least a confession of a young man whose life was as much entwined with the nineteenth century as Adam's and mine were with the age in which we lived. But now, having read it, I am greatly perplexed and rather troubled."[16] But Shiela did admit to me that, as she put it, "I seem to have been very harsh to all Adam's pleading—but then he didn't answer my demand that he condemn the terrible things being planned and perpetrated in Germany's name either."[17] Politics, I wrote to Shiela, has a way of smothering human relations.[18]

But with the letters before me, I had to remind Shiela that late in December 1938 Adam had written his difficult friend a very puzzling but clearly coded letter:

> The attempt to couple the venture with a general overhaul and readjustment of the inner gears of the machine was frustrated by your clever Neville [Chamberlain], and the only alternative is another "venture" or an overhauling in the garage in which many chaps only disguised as mechanics would have to be squeezed out of the door as the engine is neither big nor tough enough to stand all their clumsy hands. At present the door is shut, the engine stinks and puffs the evilest poisons, suffocating all the more sensitive lungs while everybody gets more and more uneasy. Although some will still not believe that the gas is poisonous, all seem to agree that something must happen soon.[19]

Shiela, alas, had not understood.

But later, early in 1979, after having reread all of his letters, she sent me the following message: "I assured both Chris[20] and Clarita that Protagoras[21] probably had the last word to say on the subject and we were probably right from our points of view and anyway Adam was large enough to carry it off. *Dear Adam*. What a joy it is to pass these hours with him again. It gives me a very strange feeling that it is somehow all going on still, that he is very near, that he is smiling and laughing and we are happy together."[22] This message showed Shiela as the great lady that I had always expected her to be.

Nevertheless, the Shiela-Adam drama had a long postlude in which I, alas, as editor of the correspondence, was involved. It began with a letter written to me out of the blue by Shiela's husband, Michael Sokolov Grant, which alleged that I belonged to the "Trott committee" and charged me with having unfairly attacked Shiela. The letter concluded: "I strongly oppose the publication of the Adam-Shiela correspondence which I believe will only cause further pain and enmity to all concerned. Shiela now concurs."[23]

The ensuing roller coaster-like signals that came from Shiela are amusing in retrospect only. At the time they were merely tedious, but I was determined to have these important documents see the light of day. The sticking point became my introduction to the correspondence. It was, and I write this without boasting, a beautiful tribute to both Adam and Shiela, which culminated in my identifying Shiela as the crusader who with admirable self-assurance followed the path she had chosen, and Adam as the pilgrim in search of a way that proved solitary and led him into resistance. In this introduction I cited a moving statement from Shiela's memoirs:

> Our tragedy was that it was just what each of us most valued and most admired in the other that set us so painfully apart. We both felt that we must live our lives for a cause greater than ourselves, that we had an inner purpose to which we owed allegiance, and to which all else must be subordinated. Mine at the moment, as I had made perfectly plain to Adam, was to frustrate Hitler and prevent war. These were exactly the purposes for which Adam gave his life. But because we were born in different countries and reared in different historical perspectives with different philosophical attitudes, we had totally different conceptions of how this could be achieved.[24]

Shiela's initial reaction to my introduction was very gratifying. I thought that she had understood me and my sense of the tragedy in the relations between the two difficult friends: "It [the introduction] was *really splendid....* I was deeply touched and moved by it. So much so that I somehow felt detached from it all as if it really were the story of two struggling young people and the struggle was timeless. It could have happened anywhere and in any century and been the *Enfants du siècle* you always said it was."[25] However, this missive was soon followed by a letter from Shiela to Ivon Asquith of the Oxford University Press, of which I was sent a copy. In it, Shiela described the introduction as a "travesty" and withdrew her permission to publish the letters.[26]

In the meantime, a historian from Oxford, Tim Mason, entered what had become a virtual tragicomedy, offering his services as mediator. Tim and I had met when Betty and I spent a sabbatical at Trinity College, Oxford, in 1982–1983.[27] Tim, in his early forties then, was one of the most gifted and innovative of young British historians. A Marxist, he was refreshingly undogmatic and open-minded, and we struck up a friendship right away. With Shiela, Tim maintained a relationship of affection and genuine admiration. But could he bridge the gap that had opened up between Shiela and me? Making the Shiela-Klemens contretemps his own concern, he threw himself with great ingenuity and angelic patience into the arena, virtually shuttling back and forth between us.

Also entering the arena was Alan Bullock, later Lord Bullock, the well-known Oxford historian and biographer of Adolf Hitler. He had been asked by the press to adjudicate in what had become an impasse. Bullock, a friend of Shiela's since youth, decreed that the introduction was to be stripped of "everything interpretative"; it was to be "impersonal."[28] I then wrote to Tim:

> I have always been truthful to the reality as I perceived it and have honored her [Shiela] as much as I have honored Adam. It was not easy to do both, and I have learnt much from you, Tim. Also let me say this quite candidly: I have, abandoned by Ivon Asquith, muzzled by Bullock, harassed by Shiela, felt—for the first time in my life—virtually blackmailed. But you have lifted that burden from me. You have encouraged me to hold out and to do so without surrendering my integrity. I know the book is an important one, and I do hope that it will mean much to many people, British as well as German, human beings all in all, young and old. THANK YOU, Tim.[29]

In my fencing with Shiela, I may have been too one-sidedly protective of Adam's intricate balancing act as a German patriot and resolute foe of Nazism, which Shiela simply could not comprehend, and too insensitive toward her own deeply grounded principles, to which Adam had no access. Did I all too readily identify with Adam's predicament, acting as an advocate of sorts for him who could no longer defend himself, and in turn was I too rash in making light of Shiela's considered position? From a somewhat greater distance and possibly with greater wisdom, Tim, as though an advocate for Shiela, found the right words to put things into perspective. In a letter to me he emphasized her "intense, moral/political sensibility, combined with an absolutely uncompromising outspokenness" in which "friendships, 'loyalty' take second place when issues of this kind are on the table for her—friends have to prove that they are real friends by discussing such problems on *her* ground." Tim continued:

I detect a deep and clear moral understanding of politics in her, always striving to be crystalline, always struggling, always demanding a level of seriousness which is often surprising and uncomfortable to those near to her, because of her capacity to see familiar problems in the novel light of fundamental principles. She brought this rare attitude to bear in her personal life, and never saw why the public realm of power should not be subjected to the same kind of rational/moral pressure, should not be interrogated in the same way. Political justice for her can be built only upon the same uncompromising honesty and moral commitment as solidarity among friends. Her affectionate joie de vivre often disguises the fact, but this is really a pretty austere and demanding creed, and it does not surprise me that her life is now littered with ex-friendships—people who failed to live at her level.... I'm sure that she was a powerful independent actor in the 30s, *not Trott's foil*, so to speak, and she is anxious to appear as such in the book, not for reasons of self-esteem, but for the peculiar cause of moral reasoning which she developed as her own contribution to politics.

Relevant here is a passage from the same letter in which Tim, quite perceptively I believe, stated the basis of my contretemps with Shiela: "I don't think that you have a trace of her utopianism, and I sometimes wonder whether you realise how big this gulf is, and that it matters somewhat to her. Your Christianity and your tragic, thus conservative, sense of the past are something new, alien and difficult for Shiela."[30]

My engagement in this drama was to me no mere scholarly matter. When Tim asked me why I was so interested in Adam and Shiela, I responded, perhaps too rashly, that all of history writing was after all a form of writing autobiography. Tim's moving explanation of Shiela's motives had helped me to see her stance as more than cantankerousness, and his analysis of my own position was more apposite than I dared admit to myself. In any case, I got so involved in the Adam-Shiela drama because both belonged to the "in-between generation" framed by the two world wars; thus, my interest in them, while they were somewhat older than I, gave me a way of defining and understanding myself. When I insisted that Adam and Shiela now belonged to history and therefore to the public, I could not help but think that they also belonged to my life. Thus, it became doubly imperative to me to have the correspondence see the light of day. It was left to dear Betty to go through the manuscript with scissors, and the volume was finally published with the truncated introduction. It had, no doubt, been thus deprived of its poetry. However, the correspondence itself, as it reached the public, remained intact.

During the time that I was so much preoccupied with the Adam-Shiela correspondence, on one of my research trips to the Continent I paid a visit to a man who had been among the most resolute of the *Widerstand*, but whose profile in history, due to events subsequent to the war, had become enigmatic.

"Mit dem Gesicht nach Deutschland"

It was a memorable visit. Otto John, once an untiring conspirator, had used his position as legal adviser of the Lufthansa as a cover for a strategy to establish connections from Madrid and Lisbon between his fellow conspirators and American and British authorities. His younger brother Hans, also active in the preparations for the plot against Hitler, had been caught, jailed, sentenced to death, and finally shot by the Nazi Special Command when the Russian troops approached Berlin. After the failure of the plot, Otto John managed to escape to Spain and later became head of the West German Federal Agency for the Protection of the Constitution.

Thereon, however, hangs a story. When I visited Otto John in the winter of 1978, he no longer lived in Germany or held an official position. He was an exile living in Austria with his wife in an abandoned *Burg*, the Hohenburg, in a little Tyrolean village called Igls, high above Innsbruck. What had happened to bring this about? On 20 July 1954, the tenth anniversary of the assassination attempt against Hitler, when still in his extremely sensitive official position, Otto John disappeared from West Berlin, crossing the tightly controlled border into the Communist sector of the divided city. Three days later, he sounded off on East Berlin radio in a declaration addressed to "my German fellow citizens." He had defected, he said, because he saw in the German Democratic Republic "the best chance to work for the reunification of Germany and against the threat of war." By December 1954, however, Otto John was back in West Berlin.

The question of whether the security chief had gone over to the East of his own free will or whether he had been drugged and kidnapped by an agent of the Soviet Secret Service has never been resolved. The assumption cannot be altogether dismissed that John, impatient with Chancellor Adenauer's foot-dragging, as he saw it, about reunification and his insistence on the priority of integration with the Western powers, might have decided to take things into his own hands and conduct diplomacy privately. In any case, upon his return to the West, he was sentenced by the somewhat baffled Federal Court in Karlsruhe to three years and eight months in jail.

Otto John's exile in the Hohenburg was a self-exile. While he could have returned to Germany, he chose not to. The name of Otto John had been buried in a residue of rumor and suspicion, and the remote but not too distant Tyrolean mountains afforded him a refuge of sorts. But exile is exile. I certainly became aware of this fact as I spent the day with the Johns. Otto John answered my questions about his part in the *Widerstand*, which had prompted my visit. However, the conversation inevitably shifted to the later chapter of his life. Quite understandably, Otto John was fighting hard for the rehabilitation of his name, but the court could not find sufficient cause to take up his case again. When I brought him and his wife greetings from old-time friends, including Clarita von Trott,[31] they would ask shyly and unbelievingly: "And they *did* send greetings?" Although they once had powerful friends all over the country, they now felt abandoned. Whatever the merits of the case, there was sorrow in their human predicament.

Among all the resisters against Hitler, Otto John had been one of the most resolute and clear-headed. He had never clung to the illusion, as did most of his fellow resisters, that the Allied demand for "unconditional surrender" could be bypassed. But the next chapter of his life found him disoriented. Otto John was at a crossroads between the struggle against the evil empire of the Nazis, in which his part was firm and unambiguous, and the unfolding Cold War, for which as yet he was altogether unprepared.

There were to be sure other judicious and weighty men—politicians and publicists, conservatives and socialists—who argued convincingly that the Western orientation of the Federal Republic would prevent eventual reunification and that therefore some preliminary understanding with the Soviets as a precondition for reunification was imperative. There was, then, little reason to take Otto John to task for his solo action, if it really was that. Excessive judgmentalism makes poor history. I have learned that there are situations in history that are truly indeterminate and that do not lend themselves to precipitate side-taking. Indeed, my encounter with Otto John taught me to respect the tragic element in history as it confounds human designs.

At the time that I was putting the finishing touches on my book on the German Resistance, we were in Berlin. I had been invited to spend the year 1986–1987 as a fellow at the Institute for Advanced Study (Wissenschaftskolleg) in Dahlem, which afforded me an ideal opportunity and environment for work. The institute was located at a historic site, just off the big S-curve of the Königsallee connecting the Grunewald with the center of Berlin, where in the forenoon of 24 June 1922 the German foreign minister, Walther Rathenau, while being driven in an open cabriolet from his suburban mansion at number 65 to the Foreign Office in the Wilhelmstrasse, was assassinated by members of a secret, radical right-wing society. I was barely six years old when this political murder occurred, but it left a distinct impression on me. It somehow shook the prospects of growing up in a secure middle-class world. My family and the Rathenaus belonged to the same upper stratum of Berlin society, and Walther Rathenau was murdered precisely because he was a Jew in the public arena.

As I grew up and became increasingly aware of politics and history, I came to understand that this assassination was a portent of the troubled years of the Weimar Republic. Now, two generations later, I sat near the same site as a historian looking back, and I could not resist trying to reconstruct the chain of events that connected that political murder, which after all was not an isolated event, with my present preoccupation with the Third Reich and the resistance against it. Even had I not presumed to search for a causal link between the two, I could not abandon myself to a "virtual" reading of history. In short, the venue of my writing was historical, and it reinforced in me a sense of history, not as a divinely preordained progression towards liberty, but as a sequence of crises that challenges humankind to cope with them. The historian's task is to piece together the puzzle of crises so as to make some sense of them.

It was a productive time for me and immensely stimulating for us both, given the company of other fellows from virtually all fields of study. True, there was no respite from intellectuality, certainly not during our common meals, but this was all to the good. Among the acquaintances we made there, I particularly cherished the company of Mazzino Montinari, the co-editor of the Nietzsche edition[32] that superseded all earlier and abortive attempts to encompass the work of that great German philosophical troubleshooter. Montinari, who died soon after our encounters, was a quiet, responsible scholar who brought sobriety and learning into an otherwise wildly controversial and sensation-prone field of study. I benefited much from our discussions. Being so stimulated by Nietzsche, I profited all the more from Montinari's dispassionate perspective on his thought.[33]

So I was back in the city of my boyhood. For me, of course, it was full of memories, and not only happy ones. But somehow Berlin does not lend itself to nostalgia. Even in its rubbled condition, it exuded its traditional vitality. Berliners used to say about their city, "in Berlin is immer mal wat los" (something always happens in Berlin), and even now—or especially now—this was the case.

In 1986, Germany was still a divided country and Berlin a divided city. The Berlin Wall separated the Western sectors from the Soviet one, just as the Iron Curtain separated Germany into two zones. Transit into and back out of the Soviet sector and zone was possible, but not easy. I believe it was Clarita's idea that we drive over to Potsdam, the summer residence of the Brandenburgian electors and Prussian kings, with its magnificent baroque castle Sanssouci, located about twenty-five kilometers to the southwest of Berlin in the Soviet zone of Germany. Herr Sch., the curator of castles and parks in the German Democratic Republic (GDR), she was assured, would be happy to guide us.

Passing into the Soviet sector and zone was by no means a simple matter. Betty and I, being American citizens, had to cross over at the now legendary Checkpoint Charlie, heavily guarded by barbed wire and suspicious *Volkspolizisten*—and the female *Volkspolizei* looked especially forbidding. Clarita, being a citizen of the Federal Republic, had to use another crossing point, and thereafter we had to make our way laboriously along an unfamiliar grid of streets to find each other again. Yet our troubles were by no means over: we still had to be elaborately searched at the heavily fortified frontier between the two Germanys in Dreilinden. Political divides have a way of duplicating bureaucracy.

Held up by these security checks, we tried to call Herr Sch. and his wife to tell them that we would be late. But each of the public roadside phones at which we stopped was out of order. When finally we reached our destination, we were told to leave our car at some distance from our hosts' villa. They shared it with another family, and we were made to understand that they would just as soon keep secret the fact that they had visitors from the West—a fact announced by our Western license plates. Meanwhile, the food that we had brought along was hidden under the coats of the ladies, making them look pregnant. We did not want to call attention to ourselves as Westerners bearing gifts.

The villa in which the Sch.'s lived was one of those exquisitely proportioned classical structures in the big Sanssouci park designed by the great Prussian architect Karl Friedrich Schinkel. Now, with much of its elegance faded, it housed East German officials. Herr Sch. was actually an art historian by profession, but he had fallen out of favor with the authorities because, we gathered, he had contributed to an art exhibition in West Germany and so had been relegated to a curatorial position. The family—father, mother, and their two boys of student age—lived downstairs in rather cramped style, but two tables, a larger one and a smaller *Katzentisch* (children's table), were lovingly set for a meal that must have occasioned some patient standing in line—especially for the little beefsteaks.

I sat at the *Katzentisch* together with Hans, the younger son, so that I could give him all my attention instead of getting involved in inevitably distracting general conversation. Since I realized as soon as we entered the house that we were among foes of the Communist regime, I was surprised that Hans protested that the German Democratic Republic was his country. His parents would not have made such a concession, but Hans belonged to a different generation. While he disliked and rejected Marxism and communism, he could not see himself as a citizen of any Germany except the GDR. Almost forty years of separation had, judging by my table companion, given the younger generation a distinct sense of separate national identity. Hans's generation could hardly imagine anything different, and this was only three or four years before the reunification of Germany.

In the course of the evening, Betty talked at some length with the elder of the two sons, Martin, who was particularly interested in English and American literature, especially the works of Emily Dickinson. He hoped eventually to study these fields at the university, but he had run into trouble. During his obligatory military service in the Nationale Volksarmee, he had kept a diary that included cartoons and texts making fun of military rigmarole. A snoopy sergeant searched his footlocker and found it. As a result, Martin's admission to university was blocked, and he had to support himself with menial work—mopping the floors of a nearby castle instead of guiding visitors. As they talked, Betty promised to send him a copy of Emily Dickinson's poems, which she did on our return to America. She soon received from Martin the following letter:

Potsdam, 10.10.86

Dear Mrs. Klemperer!

I should like to thank you, not only for Emily Dickinson, but also for your (and the others') company when that evening I returned unsuspecting from work and burst into that cheerful party—finding the wide world around the coffee table at home, and furthermore finding everyone getting along so well from the very start! I remember with particular pleasure the language difficulties, since they made me aware of the fact that by agreeing on essentials we could right away proceed to discussing subtleties.

But now imagine the pleasure when the longed-for book arrived so quickly. I had been away in the evening with friends: we had made bold plans, and I—in an exuberant mood—had felt very independent and, having escaped the parental protectiveness, came home late at night in a state of inebriation (the parents were already asleep)—I find something new next to the stack of letters, *A Selection of Emily Dickinson's Verse*!

I rushed to the dictionary and tried, late at night and somewhat befuddled, to start translating. Of course, nothing came of this. The whole next workday I carried the little thing around with me and stroked it and tried now and then to decipher one line or simply to listen to the melody.

Meanwhile, I have started, systematically and calmly, to translate at least those poems that seemed to me especially interesting. The ultimate proof of this volume of poetry is still to come: if it keeps me long under its spell.

I thank you for the challenge that came my way through you. Yours, M.S.

A few days after this visit to a German family, virtually imprisoned in the fading glory of Sanssouci and savoring their fleeting encounter with us Westerners, I crossed Checkpoint Charlie again. A West German diplomat's wife, who cultivated acquaintances among the East German intelligentsia, wanted me to meet a certain poet, one of the leading personages in the Communist establishment. Making our way past the dilapidation of East Berlin, we stopped in front of a luxurious villa in Niederschönhausen, the gold coast of the regime's functionaries. Here lived the much celebrated Stephan Hermlin, an old German Communist who, after spending years in exile during the time of the Third Reich, had returned to settle in the German Democratic Republic. While not always toeing the line of party orthodoxy, he had supported the regime's suppression of the workers' uprising in East Germany on 17 June 1953, dismissing them as no better than former Nazis and common criminals. I cannot say that the conversation with him and his Russian wife ever warmed up. When it came to the foolish exercise of balancing American and Soviet evil deeds, he brazenly denied the existence in the Nazi-Soviet pact of August 1939 of a once-secret protocol, now common knowledge, in which the Nazis and the Russians agreed to divide Eastern Europe between them. I insisted on its existence, so that when we parted, we were hardly soul mates.

In a short time, I witnessed two very different experiences of the GDR prison. Inner emigration here and compliance there; dignity here and dishonor there. I had no desire to see Hermlin again. As for the Sch.'s, in the course of time we unfortunately lost touch with them. I would like very much to know what happened to the family. Could the father and the boys eventually follow their vocations? Has "the melody" of Emily Dickinson's poetry kept Martin under its spell? Has Hans, as I would suspect, in the end accepted the Berlin Republic as his fatherland?

My brief ventures into East Berlin were a sort of déjà vu for me. When walking along its streets, Betty and I would pass a couple deep in conversation, and I would notice a sudden pause in their talk, accompanied by an anxious look. I remember the same behavior in Nazi Berlin: gestures that were not accidental reflexes but were indicative of life under oppression. Although a terrible world war had put an end to Nazi horrors, whenever thereafter I passed from West to East Berlin, I felt that the present horror would prevail forever. The GDR, it seemed, had gained legitimacy not only in its own territory but even among the European and world powers.[34] And now that this horror is over, now that the "evil Soviet empire" and with it the satellite GDR have vanished, I still find it hard to realize the fact. Yet this is also a chapter of my life, the life of my generation, a chapter signaling hope and confidence in the survival of freedom and decency.

Upon my return to the United States, I had a strange encounter with Germany's "unmasterable past," as historian Charles S. Maier has called it.[35] Everyone concerned with Germany must come to terms with the legacy of unspeakable crimes committed during the Nazi time, and historians like me are duty-bound to try at least to explain it. Whether or not it can be explained satisfactorily, this legacy cannot be forgotten or suppressed. We come up against it whenever we deal with any aspect of Germany's past, present, or future.

Late in the winter of 1987, after I had lectured at the local Holyoke Community College on the problems of the Third Reich, commenting on the horrors committed by the SS, the Nazi elite formation, three rather perplexed students stayed behind to question me about what I had said. One of them prided himself on having a collection of Nazi insignia—and what was wrong with that? Another reported to me that during the past summer he had visited the German Federal Republic with a fellow student whose father, a "nice man," had been a member of the SS and had decorated the walls of his house with Nazi regalia. The third outright challenged my connecting Germany with the Nazis and their emblem, the swastika. "When I think of Germany," he said, as though paraphrasing Heinrich Heine, "I think of Mercedes-Benz's three-pronged star, and not of the swastika."[36] For a moment, this student's unawareness of his country's disturbing past seemed to lift its burden—but only for a fleeting moment.

Now that I survey my wanderings of the past decades, I cannot really fit them into Joseph Brodsky's categories of "displacement and misplacement." I might say that I have been plain lucky, inasmuch as "displacement" turned out to be an enormous challenge. When I came over to these shores, I wanted to leave behind a difficult past, and I was young enough to seize my new experience and discover my adoptive country. America exhilarated me and offered me opportunities to study and pursue my professional objectives—opportunities that, even under the best of circumstances, I could hardly have expected in the world from whence I had come. Of "misplacement," then, there was no question. I found a welcome, and I accepted it with alacrity.

Yet I would not turn my back on my European past. It has remained and will remain part of myself. It would be trite for me to say that I have seen my function as one of building bridges between my two worlds. If I have shuttled back and forth, I have done so to assure myself of continuousness in my life. The very personal encounters in the course of my work have often brought me into contact with people and families who had been friends of my family. Moreover, something in me was resolved to prove to myself that the dreams of my youth were not to be written off, that they still had a validity that fed into my new experiences. In the course of my work, I often felt like an archeologist, digging beneath the surface to uncover treasures and bring them back to light and life, thus giving me, the digger, a wonderful sense of both continuity and discovery. In this way, then, I found fulfillment in identifying my sense of purpose, in interpreting for myself Otto Wels's "Mit dem Gesicht nach Deutschland."

Chapter Eight

Living in a "World Come of Age"

In the mid-winter of 1978, I received a letter from our son Jamie, then a junior at Harvard, which made me think. He assured me that he was happy with his friends, sports, and classes, and yet he found his "lack of belief," as he put it, troubling:

> As a child I had high aspirations—I assumed that, as an adult, I would be able to devote myself to something which had direction, a cause and a purpose. These expectations have become such a part of my outlook that I cannot erase them from my mind. But my mind also has a strong skeptical, one might say nihilistic, penchant which is indelible. I think that my predicament is not entirely due to my peculiar disposition. The modern social and intellectual climate is, as [Robert] Musil[1] pointed out, conducive to the loss of direction. Also, I think that the experience of my generation is problematic. We have not suffered through economic hardship or the international cataclysm which shaped your generation. We look at the political activism of the 60's as starry-eyed impracticability. Idealism is at a nadir in American youth of my sub-generation. And it is the lack of ideals which troubles me. Forgive me for this digression, but these are thoughts which are important for me.[2]

This was an honest statement by a young man for whom I have enormous respect. I wrote back:

> You would disappoint me if you did not give thought to these matters. Many people have a way of repressing them by doing, doing; there is something deceptive, if relieving, about our day by day activities. But it occurs to me that all ... meaningfulness, such as it exists, is predicated on basic meaninglessness.

Assume a basic meaningfulness: there would be no purpose for action, search, creation, philosophy. Our achievements, however modest, are grand attempts at meaningfulness. As such they are but reflections of the divine (or say if you wish "Platonic") perfection. But I feel we must try, we must keep searching. The human accomplishments, poetry, philosophy, good institutions, a good piece of art or craftsmanship, are all the more impressive since they are made by persons imperfect and mortal.... Don't they speak the language of the attempt to recapture meaning in a world of the perceived meaninglessness?... I just want you to know how much I admire you for facing up to these thoughts; just don't let them drive you nuts.[3]

The key word of Jamie's message to me I took to be "skeptical," if not "nihilistic." Skepticism I have come to understand as a position of doubting the truth of generally accepted beliefs and assumptions and, in particular, of all forms of idealism. On balance it is a healthy quality, concomitant with asking questions and with the readiness to face a reality that yields no easy and certain explanation. At first sight an insistence on nothingness, nihilism amounts to more than this, as it is a breeding ground for overcoming a perceived meaninglessness and a vehicle for radical renewal.

Was Jamie's experience and the evolution of his thinking that much different from mine? Certainly, the idealism that had marked his beginnings has been mine as well. If anything, it was in my case accentuated by my identification with the boundless idealism of the Youth Movement. We had big dreams. In our blessed youthful immaturity we were an enchanted conspiracy of sorts, unwilling to put up with the contours of a world that would not yield to our fantasies. We thought that we could defy the modern reality of cold rationality, technology, and impersonal big cities.

The lesson I took from the exchange with my son prompted me to review and reassess the road I have taken since I began my journey to set the world afire. Was it simply growing up and maturing that made me wake up to the realities of life? Was it my reading that added new dimensions to my awareness of the world around me? Was it, God forbid, resignation that had clipped my wings?

In school I was captivated by Plato's *Republic*. The proposition of the ideal state in which the philosopher-king set the tone, and to whom the citizens responded as though by acclamation, was enormously attractive to me and my friends. We were intoxicated by Socrates' Symposium and participated in his forthright Apology before the accusatory jury of his fellow Athenians. We were all, as Karl Popper said, under "the spell" of the "divine philosopher."[4]

Having grown up in a time of crisis, when things seemed to fall apart all around me and people could barely relate to one another, I was all the more attracted by the ideal vision of the *Republic*. Since virtue is knowledge and knowledge is virtue, it would follow that honoring these qualities would make the Republic a perfect one. What was more gratifying than to envisage the state as a supra-individual organism in which the philosopher-king was supreme and in which virtue was rewarded and justice rendered? The prospect that a good and happy life was possible in a just order particularly appealed to me. The Republic, then, could function as the individual citizen writ large.

My acquaintance with Plato's works was admittedly a rather limited one, and I had not studied his later *Statesman* and the *Laws* in which he came down from his speculative heights. But it was in part my encounter with the totalitarian regimes of the twentieth century that alerted me to the pitfalls of the formula projected in the *Republic*. Had not the Nazi regime banked on a similar unison of ruler and ruled, based on acclamation in the form of the *Volksgemeinschaft*, which was a gross distortion of the *Gemeinschaft* that it claimed to be? The acclamation turned out to have been devoid of substance, a myth that was instead a pretext for oppression. The ideal, which Nazism purported to be, was in fact a nightmare.

Karl Popper, a harsh critic of Plato, devised the formula of the "closed society" that lives in a "charmed circle of unchanging taboos, of laws and customs, which are felt to be as inevitable as the rising of the sun, or the cycle of the seasons, or similar obvious regularities of nature."[5] Even if I hesitate to conclude with Popper that Plato's political program is fundamentally identical with twentieth-century totalitarianism, I have come to share his skepticism about the possibility of establishing a perfect society. "The essence of being human," George Orwell wrote, "is that one does not seek perfection, that one is sometimes willing to commit sins for the sake of loyalty ... that one is prepared in the end to be defeated and broken by life."[6]

The spell of Plato had begun to wear off as I matured and as I discovered Aristotle, Plato's disciple. On my archival trips to Europe I had made it a practice to take one book along for evening reading. Once it was Blaise Pascal's *Pensées*, another time Plato's dialogues, and, some twenty years ago, Aristotle's *Politics*. I understand that in classical antiquity the prescriptive pathos of Plato's *Republic* outshone the sober style of Aristotle's *Politics*. To me, however, taking up Aristotle was a revelation. The very sobriety of his thinking process appealed to me. His probing method and prosaic balancing of evidence showed me the liberating quality of inductive thinking. Although the Platonic dialogue had built-in elements of tentativeness, the ambitious horizons of the ideal philosopher-king and the design of the ideal society made Plato, at least when he wrote the *Republic*, an advocate of a closed society whose design was radical, even communistic. By contrast, the questions that Aristotle asked were less ambitious, devoid of the idealistic baggage that was Plato's. They were genuine questions that awaited answers.

What I have come to admire in Aristotle's argumentation is the openness of his thought processes. I am all the more impressed by it now, when a plethora of intellectuals bring to bear on the academic community agendas that veer far from their purported scholarly intent and serve merely to reinforce thinly disguised prejudices. Scholarship thus runs the danger of being perverted into pamphleteering. Aristotle's "usual analytical method,"[7] as he referred to it, draws a clear line at the temptation to excessive preaching and advocacy of causes. His high-minded self-restraint has come to strike me as an exemplary guideline for the search for the always elusive truth.

The Aristotelian prescription has particular relevance to the study and writing of history, which is a distinctly "soft" discipline that lends itself to interpretations closely linked to our value systems. Contemporary history, which is my métier, is especially controversial and vulnerable to the expression of emotions, if not prejudices. There is a grain of truth, after all, in John Finley's witticism that all history following the French Revolution is but "gossip." In that case, to keep scholarship from degenerating into gossip, Aristotle's guidelines remain relevant.

The Sense of the Tragic

As I ponder the question of what has defined my mental outlook over the years, I must fall back on my pervasive awareness of the realm of the tragic in life. If we humans were altogether at liberty in conducting and determining the course of our existence, if men and women were perfect and altogether in concert with the divine, or to say it more prosaically, with the laws of the universe, if there were no sickness and no death, the very notion of tragedy would be unnecessary, if not inconceivable. But who can question the evidence of the dependence of human beings on "the other," on forces not of their own making? The sovereignty of the human being as the highest of living specimens is a noble notion, but clearly it is hubris for us to claim infallibility and omniscience.

If I cannot and do not want to believe in worldly perfection and perfectibility, I recognize the tragic element in the human condition and in human affairs, which is predicated upon the conviction that we are not the masters of our destiny. As I observe life in general and moreover as I survey the course of history, I cannot see humankind as sovereign. We may try to master nature, but we can hardly claim absolute control over it. In society and politics we will always encounter adversity, and there will always be disagreement, conflict, and evil to contend with. The very dependence of human beings, their inadequacies and vulnerability, and the way that they contend with these limitations—sometimes by overreaching themselves—all this is stuff for tragedy. The disproportion between what we aspire to and what is possible to achieve is a major source of the tragic.

I accept the notion that, as Karl W. Deutsch wrote, tragedy is "fundamental and inevitable in human life."[8] Predicated upon human imperfection, incertitude, and misunderstandings and upon the existence in us and around us of evil, the tragic is the basic condition that defines human existence. I have learned to adopt this view as a fundamental guideline in my life, perhaps reflecting my belief in the existence of original sin, not as a rigid theological proposition, but, as I once wrote to my friend Tim Mason, as "a day by day reality on this earth."[9] I hasten to add that this does not mean that I have been tempted to embrace the somber vision expressed in Albert Camus' *The Plague* by Father Paneloux, who saw life as a scourge of God against the wickedness of man. I have never felt that I was being punished by God for my sins. At the same time, I have come to perceive our fallen state as a challenge, an opening into the dramatic landscape of our frailty and sin and struggle and, not least, redemption. Thus, history has come to mean to me a theological argument, that is, a derivative of the drama of creation, fall, and redemption. Call it an inverted theology, and then that supposed "vale of tears" opens up vistas of what Søren Kierkegaard called "the unending pageantry of life with its motley play of colors and its infinite variety."[10]

It is my sense of the tragic that made me realize, welcomed as I felt when I reached these shores, that I had moved to a continent where progressivism was the order of the day. Despite the Depression of the 1930s, and especially in the intellectually vibrant New Deal-oriented atmosphere at Harvard, there prevailed a forward-looking political climate with which I always felt slightly out of tune, even among my friends. A decade ago, Carl Schorske, undoubtedly alluding to this matter, reminded me of the "differences in politics" between us,[11] which I imagine went back to his having been raised in the tradition of the Enlightenment as opposed to my residual romanticism. In response, I suggest that Carl's vision was essentially utopian, wedded to assumptions that society, indeed, humankind, can be reformed and perfected, given the proper social conditions. At any rate, Tim Mason's profile of me written in 1984, and from which I have already quoted, refers to my "Christian stoicism" and my "tragic, thus conservative" sense of the past. It allowed me to look in a mirror and explain myself to myself in order to understand better my relation to my environment and, of course, to my peers.

Tory Men and Whig Measures

It is the conservative frame of mind, I am increasingly aware, that has always defined my habits and my self-understanding, as well as my relation to the world around me. My outlook on life and most of my work have somehow converged on the question of conservatism, and it strikes me therefore as being particularly important to pursue this here, since my generation, in Europe as well as in America, has had to cope with the vexing and delicate proximity of various modern neo-conservative, if not pseudo-conservative, currents of fascism.

I detect in myself a naive, almost blasphemous tendency to regard everything on first encounter, whether it be the garden post or the chair in the corner of the living room, as immovable—indeed, as having been placed there by a providential god. The environment I live in I perceive not as man-made but as "given" in trust, so to speak. This disposition, referred to by Lord Hugh Cecil, the doyen of all sorts of studies on conservatism, as "traditionalism" or "natural conservatism,"[12] goes along with a preference for the familiar over the unfamiliar. This psychological trait has had a way of translating itself into my more conscious worldview and also into my politics. If I had any models on which to train my theoretical and political self-consciousness, they were European, albeit British rather than Continental.

In Britain, conservatism was deeply embedded in the whole culture and guided all of its political manifestations. It was furthered by the eloquent voice of Edmund Burke, the father of modern conservatism. What attracted me to Burke was his down-to-earth vigor and the pungent style with which he pursued the principles of liberty and justice.[13] His guide for political action was not "geometrical exactness," but, as he put it magisterially, "the spirit of practicability, of moderation, and mutual convenience." Burke, who incidentally never used the term "conservatism," was neither a theoretician nor an ideologist; rather, he bargained within the framework of the created order for the latitude of pragmatic policies. "Conservation and correction"[14] was his prescription for statesmanship.

Benjamin Disraeli echoed these sentiments, and what always interested me about him was no romantic notion but his idea of "Tory democracy," which would bring the working-class masses into the fold of the monarchy. Altogether, the combination of tradition and experience, of principle and expediency, of past wisdom and innovation, and in particular the Disraelian ethos of noblesse oblige have always impressed me in my encounters with British conservatism.

It would be a gross simplification, if not falsification, to overlook the distinct conservative strain in the American tradition. The pessimism about human frailty that impelled the authors of the Federalist Papers to devise political institutions that would compensate for it makes a wonderful guidepost to the conservative vision of the Founding Fathers. And it is not far-fetched to see the roots of FDR's New Deal, as did my friend Peter Viereck, in the noblesse oblige of Disraeli's "Tory democracy."[15]

As I have always had a way of projecting my own political self-consciousness on Anglo-Saxon models, I have been cheered by Metternich's assertion in his letter of June 1847 to the French statesman and historian Guizot that conservative principles were "applicable to the most diverse situations."[16] But of course the question remains: how applicable were they to German and Austrian conservatism? Practically all phases of conservatism in the nineteenth- and twentieth-century German orbit were marked by crisis and overshadowed by nationalism and its ideological intensity. The most persistent challenge to the integrity of the conservative imagination and polity in my century came from fascism, and it was in Germany that the divide between conservatism, which had shaky foundations, and the German version of fascism, National Socialism, became increasingly blurred under the impact of the great European crisis after World War I.

This consideration makes me think of the by now well-known address, "Letters as the Spiritual Voice of the Nation," delivered in 1927 by Hugo von Hofmannsthal in the auditorium maximum of the University of Munich.[17] Evoking for the assembled students a "legion of seekers" throughout the country who were striving for the re-establishment of faith and tradition and whose aim was not freedom but "allegiance," he announced the coming of a "conservative revolution" on a scale that the history of Europe had never known. The very paradox inherent in this term conjured up the dangerous possibility of a displacement of the conservative agenda by Jacobin radicalism, less conservative than revolutionary. Unsuspectingly and carelessly, the Austrian poet thus gave encouragement to a radicalized student body all too readily disposed to misunderstand him.[18]

Here I must candidly acknowledge that much of my own intellectual development and work has revolved around the *Lebensgefühl* (mentality) that was innate in the longing for a "conservative revolution." I experienced the world into which I was born as a broken one, which called out for a restoration of communal bonds, for an affirmation of certainties. My friends and I, disoriented and unsettled, yearned for a new faith. Our quasi-religious mood allowed us to hope for a renaissance of values and purpose.

Did my friends and I not move on a very slippery slope? As I think of Georg von Schweinitz's and Kurt v. B.'s involvement with Nazism, I cannot help but answer that question in the affirmative. But to myself and to friends like Helmut Jörg and the Molden brothers, we were all knights of the Grail of sorts, dreamers, idealists. Those Viennese years were not merely a period of high-minded discussions and wanderings in the countryside. For us these were decisive, formative years. We thought that we could clearly define the divide between ourselves and the Nazis' heathen ideology and dictatorial aspirations, and believed ourselves to be guided by the loftiest tenets of patriotism and humaneness.[19]

In view of the Nazi menace, we were not simply opting for a lesser evil in supporting the Austrian chancellorship, but choosing a course of action that seemed to us, however risky under the circumstances, the only one that would be responsible and justified by our ideals. We were ready to pay the price for failing to succeed, and my friends who went into the German Resistance certainly did so. I had been ready to fight for the regime on that terrible night of 11 March 1938 when Hitler was set to occupy Austria. The Marxist Austrian

Social Democrats were not an acceptable alternative, and therefore the Dollfuss-Schuschnigg regime appeared to me and my friends as the last viable defense against the storm tide of Nazism.

Revisiting Nietzsche

> You say you believe in Zarathustra? But what matters Zarathustra? You are my believers—but what matter all believers?... Now I bid you to lose me and find yourselves; and only when you all have denied me, I will return to you ... that I may celebrate the high noon with you.
>
> — Friedrich Nietzsche, *Thus Spoke Zarathustra*[20]

No name, it occurs to me, has figured in the past chapters as insistently as that of Friedrich Nietzsche, and I owe myself as well as my readers some account of his place in my thinking. Clearly, the encounter with Nietzsche's work was decisive for me as it was for most of my friends. In a fashion, we all fancied ourselves as Nietzscheans. But then the first precept for all Nietzscheans, I have learned in the course of time, is to lose him, to get away from him. Only then will his volcanic and perplexing message penetrate to his would-be disciples as well as to his detractors. Thomas Mann certainly was right when he wrote that "whoever takes Nietzsche for gospel, word for word, whoever believes him, is lost."[21]

In any case, Nietzsche is, as Michael Hamburger wrote, "with us, whether we read him or not."[22] To my knowledge, there is no other thinker who, quarreling with himself and others, has sent out signals in so many directions and has accordingly been so variously scrutinized, so passionately fought about. Nietzsche was bound to be for his readers "a *personal* experience."[23] My friends and I related to him with emotional intensity from the beginning. We may not have been "the first generation of fighters and dragon-slayers" that was to enjoy "the right of brave unthinking honesty, and the consolation of an inspiring hope"[24] to whom Nietzsche appealed, but his writings encouraged us to question everything bequeathed to us and to seek new authenticity in our lives.

For me, the initial challenge from Nietzsche was launched by an early essay, part of his "Thoughts Out of Season" on "The Use and Abuse of History for Life" (1874). History was to be my vocation, and yet this piece was a head-on assault on my chosen métier. It is the "excess of history," that "malignant historical fever," which is the confining Hegelian notion of a "world-process,"[25] Nietzsche protested, that destroys vital strength and the ecstasy that lifts humans into the highest spheres of existence. At the same time, Nietzsche, while the perfect iconoclast, inserted into his argument a wonderfully constructive note. It was not the "unhistorical" dimension, the power and art of forgetting, which was to be the corrective to the stultifying historical one, but rather the super-historical dimension, which allows human beings to overcome the confinement of historicist relativism and "gives existence an eternal and stable character—to art and religion."[26] Was I understanding Nietzsche correctly when my reading of him seemed to support my thoughts on history as a disguised, inverted theology?

This train of thought led me to a passage in Nietzsche's *The Gay Science*, which has meant more and more to me as I have become aware of the complexities of his thought. It is the passage about the "madman":

> Have you not heard of that madman who lit a lantern in the bright morning hours, ran to the market place and cried incessantly, "I seek God! I seek God!" As many of those who do not believe in God were standing around just then, he provoked much laughter. Why did he get lost? said one. Did he lose his way like a child? said another. Or is he hiding? Is he afraid of us? Has he gone on a voyage? Or emigrated? Thus they yelled and laughed. The madman jumped into their midst and pierced them with his glances
>
> "Whither is God," he cried. "I shall tell you. We have killed him—you and I. All of us are his murderers.... God is dead. God remains dead. And we have killed him. How shall we, the murderers of all murderers, comfort ourselves? What was holiest and most powerful of all that the world has yet owned has bled to death under our knives...."
>
> Here the madman fell silent and looked again at his listeners; and they too were silent and stared at him in astonishment. At last he threw the lantern on the ground, and it broke and went out. "I came too early," he said then; "my time has not come yet...."
>
> It has been related further that on that same day the madman entered divers churches and there sang his *requiem aeternam deo*.[27]

If the madman proclaimed that "God is dead"—indeed, that "God remains dead"—he made sure to add "We have killed him"; and then he entered various churches where he sang his *requiem aeternam deo*. The premise to the incantation was his incessant cry, "I seek God! I seek God!" My reading of this moving passage tells me that when Nietzsche wrote this, he was rehearsing his compulsive "quarrel with himself,"[28] shocking, violent, prayerful. The self-styled Antichrist did sing his requiem after all.

I am no philosopher, but what always drew me to Nietzsche were the flashes of fascinating insight offered by his always suggestive and increasingly plausible paradoxes. Here were his jagged and tortured aphorisms, a signature of his thinking processes, and there was his acknowledgment of the "higher" dimension, "the need for cohesion."[29] The tension between the recognition of aphorism and fragmentariness and the never-abating search for cohesion was continuous.

In this labyrinth of demonstrative self-contradictions, I was bound to scan Nietzsche's thoughts about his fellow Germans. My own life experience—my deep roots in German life and culture, my close friends in both Germany and Austria, my witnessing of the Nazi madness—had left me with a strange double vision and ambivalence about everything German. Nietzsche, the self-styled "good European," had a lot to say about the various European cultures and nations. He was consistent and unambiguous in his derision of all "atavistic attacks of patriotism and soil attachment";[30] for the rest, he let sarcasm reign supreme.

Germany and the Germans were, of course, his chief concern, and about them he was harsh to the point of vituperation, yet at the same time tender. Germany was "Europe's flatland,"[31] and it was German obscurantism[32]—a composite of German sentimentality,[33] German nationalism ("Deutschland, Deutschland über alles"),[34] and anti-Semitism—that made life in Germany "altogether unbearable"[35] for him. Yet he did not allow his obsessive disdain for the "flatland" and his harsh words for his countrymen to destroy a basic compassion for his *Heimat*. Even shortly after the German victory over France in the war of 1870, "that wild war game," as he called it, in which he had served as a medic, he wrote to his friend Carl von Gersdorff, "Our *German* mission is not yet over."[36] It was not ambivalence on his part that made him contradict himself. The German mission that Nietzsche referred to was still alive—in Goethe. "[H]is voice and his example," Nietzsche recalled, "indicate that the German *should be more* than a German" and that he should "endeavor to grow above and beyond himself."[37] The seeming ambivalence was resolved in the expectation of what Nietzsche's biographer Walter Kaufmann called "self-overcoming."[38]

This, then, is my reading of Nietzsche and the Germans. Undoubtedly, this ambivalence was mine too. In an article about me published a few years ago, in which I found considerable empathy, the author wrote that I had in my life remained faithful to the "*deutschen Geist*," which I "loved" and yet from which I was "suffering."[39] Could not the same have been said about Nietzsche? I could at least understand my own situation in his light.

Even after I had become a mature scholar and could deal with Nietzsche more dispassionately, my fascination with him and his work never quite left me. A revisiting took place that was more scholarly, more sober and critical. It was not that I now aspired to enter into a systematic study of Nietzsche, but as a historian I could hardly escape being aware of and trying to explain to myself the pervasive and variegated, almost universal, impact that he had on modern thought and politics. Nietzsche's influence was particularly pervasive in the German orbit, where, as has rightly been remarked, he "was turned into a persistent and vital part of the fabric of national life."[40] The range of individual thinkers and groups in Germany influenced by or claiming the parentage of Nietzsche extended widely, encompassing dispensations and orientations from anarchism to Nazism, which on their own merits had nothing in common and, in fact, were often diametrically opposed. On one score, though, all admirers as well as detractors of the philosopher might well agree, namely, that he was the prism which brought together all the dissonances of a life that, as he himself put it, "no longer resides in the whole." Nietzsche's aphoristic style of thinking and writing is both an expression of these dissonances and an identification with them.

Let me trace my revisiting of Nietzsche by means of the interpretations of his thought with which I have been most closely connected in the course of my studies. I referred earlier to Crane Brinton, a teacher of mine in graduate school, who in 1941 came out with a work on Nietzsche.[41] Brinton was no friend of anything German, and the passions aroused by the war spilled over into his judgment as a scholar. Begun prior to the Munich Agreement of September 1938, which marked the high tide of the British and French policy of appeasement of Hitler, and finished after the defeat of France, Brinton's study bore the marks of these dramatic events. The specter of Hitler's ascendancy over the European continent was a trauma for all those who could recognize the fallacies of the appeasement policy and were concerned about the survival of freedom and democracy in the West. Brinton, putting himself forward as a Nietzsche scholar in an atmosphere charged with political passions, moved from presenting Nietzsche's thought to translating his eccentricities into political terms.

Nietzsche's imagery was no doubt wild, shocking, irresponsible, especially for anyone who was willing to take it at face value. Expressions such as "superman," "master race," "blond beast," "slave morality," even the "will to power," which were designed to challenge unheroic "bourgeois" discontents and frustrations, suggested a savagery that at first sight might have jibed with Hitler's. The "middle register of human experience,"[42] for which Nietzsche's work lacked metaphors, might have made him easier to understand and protected him from misrepresentation and from being commandeered and straightjacketed by Nazi orthodoxy.

There is no denying that the Nazis did their best to appropriate Nietzsche. The photograph showing Adolf Hitler gazing at the bust of Nietzsche in the Weimar Nietzsche Archive and the active part that the philosopher's sister, Elisabeth Förster-Nietzsche, played by running the archive, producing the first Nietzsche edition, and Nazifying her brother's work certainly indicate a malleability in Nietzsche's thought that called for selective readings. But if Elisabeth Förster-Nietzsche Nazified her brother's legacy, so did Crane Brinton—the former out of familial partisanship, the latter out of impatience with Nietzsche's eccentricities, which seemed out of place at a time when Europe was in the grip of a conqueror whose followers looked up to him as a liberating "superman."

Brinton labeled a philosopher who least of all invited labeling. Nietzsche had praise for neither liberalism nor democracy. The word "liberal" was to him merely a euphemism for mediocrity, and democracy was equivalent to decay. However, these categories were to be understood in juxtaposition to their opposites, which did not spell autocracy, let alone oppression or tyranny.

Brinton went so far as to assert that "Nietzsche wrote a whole platform for totalitarianism of the Right a generation before it came to power."[43] Totalitarianism means total domination. Yet in Nietzsche's view, to dominate meant "to help the highest thought to victory";[44] it did not mean domination of the other, but rather domination—namely, overcoming—of the self. It was through self-overcoming that man was to become truly free.[45] To clarify this thought, Walter Kaufmann has wisely translated Nietzsche's controversial term *Übermensch* not as "Superman" but as "Overman."[46]

Brinton himself first made the distinction between "gentle" and "tough" Nietzscheans.[47] Nietzsche's sister was the toughest of the "tough" ones, who took for gospel even the philosopher's unguarded fancies and provocations. But to the "gentle" ones, to whom I suppose my friends and I belonged, Nietzsche was first and foremost a liberating agent who shook up European bourgeois conventionality and, despite his eccentricities, had to be reckoned with as a major figure in the pantheon of modern philosophers.

My thoughts about Nietzsche were furthered by my encounter with the person and work of the historian-philosopher Ernst Nolte.[48] Nolte's *Nietzsche und der Nietzscheanismus*[49] altogether evades the hazardous game of Nietzsche's political impact on posterity. His legacy, at least as Nolte wants to see it, was primarily an intellectual one. Freud's indebtedness to Nietzsche for opening up our understanding of the thought processes of the unconscious has been generally acknowledged, last but not least by Freud himself.[50] But Nolte's unique correlation of Marx and Nietzsche especially fascinated me.[51] We must sort out the most glaring contrasts between the two. On the one hand, there is Marx's heavy dependence on the overall Hegelian historical scheme, even though turned upside down, and his prophecy of the proletarian revolution and a final synthesis in the form of a classless society of ultimate equality and freedom. On the other hand, there is Nietzsche's "aristocratic radicalism," as Georg Brandes called it in his 1888 lectures in Copenhagen, his Dionysian impulsiveness and intoxication with paradox—not synthesis—and the absurdity in human existence.

Yet the view of Marx and Nietzsche as diametrical opposites is altogether too simplistic, if not misleading. My reading of Nolte has confirmed my interest in the affinities between the two. The psychological awareness of both was quickened by the problem of alienation, that is, the increasing complexity and anonymity of the social order in which we live. The early Marx in particular accentuated human alienation in a capitalistic society and projected "the advent of theoretical humanism, and communism" to mean "the vindication of real human life as man's possession and thus the advent of practical humanism."[52] Nietzsche, the young classical scholar, would struggle with and be tortured by the same issue, albeit from a very different perspective. He would of course speak not the language of "dismal science" but that of enchanted Greek mythology:

Under the charm of the Dionysian not only is the union between man and man reaffirmed, but nature which has become estranged, hostile, or subjugated, celebrates once more her reconciliation with her prodigal son, man. Freely earth proffers her gifts, and peacefully the beasts of prey approach from desert and mountain. The chariot of Dionysus is bedecked with flowers and garlands.... Now the slave is free, now all the stubborn, hostile barriers ... between man and man are broken down.... Now, with the gospel of universal harmony, each one feels himself not only united, reconciled, blended with his neighbor, but as one with him.[53]

The affinity between Marx and Nietzsche was more than a surface phenomenon. These two supposed antagonists were one in their unrelenting pugnacity and more than stylistic directness. However their political legacy was later interpreted, whether in the direction of communism or fascism, both had a dream, both took on the task of facing up to the problem of the fragmentation of Western society and knowledge. Alas, the Marxist dream, tested in the real world, turned out to be a nightmare, and the Nietzschean Dionysian intoxication ended in madness.

My subsequent revisiting of Nietzsche took place in the late 1980s when I was asked to participate in a colloquium at Yale University on Martin Heidegger.[54] Heidegger, a giant among twentieth-century philosophers, was most controversial because of his Nazi affiliations. It was, I suppose, because of his political involvement that I was invited to give a historian's view on Heidegger's "life and times." Since he had been one of the leading interpreters of Nietzsche, it became my task to disentangle the *homo philosophicus* and the *homo politicus* in him.

In an open letter to his friend, the German adventurer-essayist Ernst Jünger, Heidegger wrote years after World War II that it was Nietzsche "in whose light and shadow all of us today, with our 'pro-Nietzsche' or 'contra-Nietzsche,' are thinking and writing."[55] Heidegger was virtually obsessed by Nietzsche, who was to him, whether in agreement or disagreement, the beacon pointing to the rediscovery of an authenticity that Western civilization had lost. Since the time of the pre-Socratics and Sophocles, Heidegger argued, Western thought had gone astray and undergone a long process of decline. In his special language, the "crisis of *Sein*" (Being), marked by self-conscious analytic thinking, had submerged the mystery of Being. Accordingly, Heidegger's rediscovery of Nietzsche was, he explained, a feast that "implies pride, exuberance, frivolity; mockery of all earnestness and respectability; a divine affirmation of oneself, out of animal plenitude and perfection—all obvious states to which the Christian may not honestly say Yes."[56]

What business did I have, I now ask myself, to enter the sphere of eminent Heidegger scholars to disentangle the affairs of that "secret king of thought," as Hannah Arendt called him? By no stretch of the imagination could I present myself as a philosopher, let alone as a Heidegger scholar. Moreover, what possessed me, once I received and accepted the invitation to speak in New Haven, to plunge into the master's great work *Sein und Zeit*, into what appeared to me painfully convoluted language, weighed down by archaic and arcane *Ur* words?

It was evidently my preoccupation with the German cultural scene that qualified me to enter into that arena in which Heidegger faced Nietzsche. Crisis and awareness of crisis have been pervasive in modern Europe, particularly since the Great War. Nietzsche was the trailblazer into that crisis, the great iconoclast among philosophers who challenged the canons of Western civilization, religious and rational, leaving men and women to face the summits and precipices of life, caught in the turmoil of pain and exhilaration and ultimately in triumphant affirmation of the absurdity of human life. While he exposed German "barbarism," he made a point of distinguishing the barbarism "of the depths"—by which he meant the Germans—and the "*other kind of barbarians* who come from the heights: a sort of conquering and dominating creatures."[57] Nietzsche's nihilism was thus as much an indictment of barbarism as it was a celebration of it, a prescription to purge that "slave morality" as much as to conjure up the pristine and uncorrupted values of authenticity. In the landscape in which people had come close to the perception of the Western void, the void itself, however troubling, took on a liberating function, pointing towards a new Table of Ethics beyond good and evil.

But was Heidegger a fitting transmitter of Nietzsche's *Lebensphilosophie*? Making the connection was not at all facilitated by my first exposure to Heidegger's style, which was plain torture: "Ge-stell"? "Geworfenheit"? "das Man"?[58] I remember spending two sleepless nights over the formidable volume *Sein und Zeit*, virtually forcing my way into that tortured "Heideggerese,"[59] as it has been called, which would outdo even the worst excesses of German philosophical idealism.

While I did not for a moment succumb to the verbal charms of the great philosopher, I persuaded myself that in his work was something that I could not lightly dismiss as gibberish. To begin with, Heidegger's teacher in Freiburg, Edmund Husserl, had launched the liberating motto "to the things themselves," urging his fellow philosophers to liberate themselves from the discourse *about* philosophy and philosophers and to live philosophy itself and actually argue it out. Now my encounter with Heidegger took me full circle, back to Nietzsche's reminder of the existential function of thought and scholarship. Nietzsche had stressed the "use and abuse of history for life," and now I was reminded of the advantages of philosophy "for life." In my reading of Heidegger, I was clearly caught in a quagmire. While his semantic juggling required infinite forbearance and made his texts all but inaccessible, the main thrust of his message, that is, the demand for philosophical accessibility in the name of a rediscovery of "authenticity" (*Eigentlichkeit*), hit home.

Heidegger seemed to point the way across the great void that was left to humankind after the fall from the "mystery of Being," and "Being-in-the-world" became a convincing formula for me: "[N]ot until we understand Being-in-the-world as an essential structure of Dasein can we have any insight into Dasein's *existential speciality*."⁶⁰ The Nietzschean vitality was resuscitated, and the unselfconscious directness of the pre-Socratic Greek philosophers, to whom both Nietzsche and Heidegger were beholden, seemed to celebrate a triumphant revival after the "fallness" (*Verfall*) of Western thought under the impact of Plato and Christianity.

Where, then, did my scouting expeditions into Nietzscheana lead me? I found wanting my teacher Crane Brinton's one-dimensionally presentist reading; certainly, it has not stood the test of time. If anything, Ernst Nolte's point of departure, the comparison of Marx and Nietzsche, limited as it is, has been distinctly suggestive to me. Of course, the two were not actually aware of each other, and the differences between Marx's vision from "below" and Nietzsche's from "the heights" are manifest. Yet it seemed to me particularly relevant to see the two united in their attempt to recapture the "whole man," freed from the menace of the machine and the iniquities of capital and the state. As for my reading of Heidegger, his stress on authenticity found resonance in me once I had jumped the hurdles of his language.

Max Weber and the "Ethic of Responsibility"

In "Zarathustra's Prologue," Nietzsche subjected the "last man" who invented happiness to fierce scrutiny.⁶¹ The well-being that he enjoys, while mitigating hardships in life, deprives him of the capacity for passion, love, and longing. He, "the most despicable man," is "no longer able to despise himself." Max Weber, Germany's great sociologist, took over Nietzsche's indictment of that "last man." In his *Protestant Ethic* he turned against "modern man," as he called him, who is, as he elaborated, "unable to give religious ideas a significance for culture and national character which they deserve."⁶²

To begin with, it was the attention that Weber paid to German youth that particularly captivated me. In the spring and late summer of 1917, he attended two conferences at Lauenstein Castle in the Franconian forest that were designed to stimulate an exchange of ideas between the generations "about the meaning and the mission of the age," as Weber's wife put it grandiloquently.⁶³ But it was precisely on this same occasion that Weber came to perceive what separated him from all the idealism that marked the meetings of the group. Ironically, he dismissed Lauenstein as a "department store for *Weltanschauungen*."⁶⁴

Following up on this critique of the romantic mood of the young, he delivered two memorable lectures—"Science as a Vocation" (November 1917) and "Politics as a Vocation" (January 1919)—in Munich.⁶⁵ Addressing the students of the university, he admonished them to abjure their unthinking idealism and adopt "trained relentlessness in viewing the realities of life."⁶⁶ He dismissed as illusory the search for "religious experiences" and the approach to science as the "way to true being," the "way to true nature," the "way to the true God," the way to "true happiness."[67] "No summer's bloom lies ahead of us," he thundered, "but rather a polar night of icy darkness and hardness, no matter which group might triumph externally now."[68] The magic and holistic universe of ancient Greece and the age of Goethe were past, and the "fate" of the modern world had become rationalization and intellectualization and, above all, "disenchantment of the world."[69] In the last analysis, it was a matter of "maturity" (*Reife*) for modern man to face up to an irrevocably fragmented reality. These lectures by Weber, classic statements of philosophical skepticism, were appeals to German youths to cast off an illusory unreality and to rethink honestly the predicament of living in a disenchanted universe.

In this connection, Weber used with special emphasis the term "mature man," the human being who, whether old or young in years, has lifted the veil of enchantment and is prepared to assume responsibility for the consequences of his or her conduct. Politics, he argued, is a matter of accounting for the consequences of one's actions. Engaging in politics thus involves an "ethic of responsibility."[70] This means that the man of action must make allowances for having to maneuver in a world that is imperfect. He is answerable for the exigencies of his actions, even if asserting himself may require force and may therefore have dubious and possibly evil ramifications. The ethically good purpose may not yield good results and may necessarily be subject to the antinomy between means and ends. The good purpose may thus have to justify dubious means and even violence.

With his admonishments to the students in Munich, Max Weber took it upon himself to bring boundless idealism down to earth. My exposure to him confirmed in me the need to navigate in the world as it really is. Recognizing such a world heightened my awareness of the realm of politics as a legitimate means of achieving one's objectives. In this view, politics is not a ticket to perfection but a hazardous venture in an inhospitable landscape, which demands ingenuity and perseverance. The perfect political animal, Weber helped me to understand, is one who is learning to maneuver in an imperfect world and to face it with healthy skepticism.

I now return to my son's avowal of his skepticism. Jamie's predicament brought to my attention the fragility of our personal certitudes, the place or function in our lives of questioning ourselves and our norms and values, and an appreciation of living in a society that is open, with all the attendant tensions resulting from diversity and inevitable conflicts. Its ever-changing reality requires us to recognize the ephemeral transience of every moment and our own limitations in mastering it. In that world, the skeptic assumes a central place. Burdened by the awareness of living in an imperfect world, he will, by the same token, benefit from and be vitalized by the renewing qualities of questioning. An excess of self-assurance and, in Jamie's words, of "ideals" and even "direction" is out of tune with the natural limitations of our vision. Doubt, as voiced by my son, is the seedbed of renewal.

It has been a long journey for me to take a cautionary position on idealism and to arrive at an understanding of the positive features and the function of skepticism, and I see now that my exchange of views with Jamie helped me towards it. My recognition of the virtues of skepticism was a liberating experience. Looking back at that "journey" of mine, I like to say that I progressed by an incessant to-ing and fro-ing between enchantment and disenchantment. I always kept following my dreams—but then I kept guarding against getting lost in them. That "mystic flight from reality"[71] about which Max Weber spoke was not to be my plight.

Dietrich Bonhoeffer and "Responsible Action"

I have no regrets about having allowed my own thoughts and preferences and ideals to meld with those of the resisters against Hitler. As I have come to be so deeply involved in the problems and intricacies of resistance, I was bound to face its "multiple ambivalence,"[72] which accounts for the vagaries, indecisions, and all-too-human mistakes that contribute to what Dietrich Bonhoeffer termed "responsible action." My awareness in the course of my work of that "multiple ambivalence" of resistance, which defies any easy equation with political righteousness, did make me go one step further to explore a question I could not avoid, namely, that of absurdity in resistance.

According to *Webster's Dictionary*, the noun "absurd" denotes the "ridiculously unreasonable, unsound," in other words, an altogether negative condition that deserves nothing more than a sneer. But there is another, higher meaning of the absurd that shifts focus from the personal to the universal, to the irrational and meaningless universe, separated from religious and metaphysical certitudes. Was it not Tertullian, the early Christian author, whose *credo quia absurdum* (I believe because of absurdity) launched the absurd as a philosophical and indeed theological concept? He was referring to the mystery of Christ's resurrection, which was beyond rational understanding. Correspondingly, Søren Kierkegaard came to identify the Incarnation as the absurd, since it could become history only in strict contrast to rational understanding and therefore can be grasped only by faith. In the last analysis, God's entry into human affairs, via the Incarnation, legitimizes the assumption of absurdity. By virtue of the absurd, then, "God has come into being, has been born, has grown up …, has come into being precisely like any other individual human being."[73]

Albert Camus, the prince of writers of my generation and prince among the French *Résistance* fighters, helped me translate my understanding of the absurd into the terms of resistance and to accept its cruel ambivalences. Observing life through the troubled prism of his century, Camus had the courage to give expression to the absurdity of all human endeavors in a bewildering universe that responds to questioning and searching humans only with silence. Writing in memory of his friend René Leynaud, a journalist arrested by the Vichy militia while carrying secret documents for the *Résistance* and then shot by the Germans, Camus remarked on "the absurd tragedy of Resistance."[74]

When I started my studies of resistance several decades ago, I was moved primarily by an eagerness to bear witness to courageous men and women, to their heroism. My vision of that heroism has remained unaltered. At the same time, I have been overwhelmed by the complexity and ambiguity of almost all resistance against Nazism. The virtually unprecedented terror made even those who knew their own minds confront the absurdity of thinking and doing at all. A motivating factor in resistance was a perception of absurdity.

What attracted me to Dietrich Bonhoeffer was the part he had played in the German Resistance. It was through my encounter with Bonhoeffer that I found access to theology. Among all the resisters, he was one of the most unwavering. It was not politics and certainly not ideology that motivated him; rather, it was the self-awareness of a Christian having to act responsibly in a world in which God becomes man and man abandons himself to God's grace and depends on it. Bonhoeffer's entanglement in the "worldly sector" did not involve any concession to it. On the contrary, it meant an acceptance of a fallen and fragmentary reality in the frame of divine providence.

Bonhoeffer was certainly caught up in a secularized world, yet he seldom used the word "secularization" and did not lament this phenomenon. It constituted a reality, the reality that he referred to as the world "come of age." Here I have hit upon the most challenging, revolutionary feature of Bonhoeffer's theology. "We are moving towards a completely religionless time," he wrote.[75] He posed questions to the Christendom of his times: "Who is Christ for us today? What does He ask of us today?"[76] The world "come of age"[77] meant an insistent search for the *deus absconditus* (the hidden God): "[W]e cannot be honest unless we recognize that we have to live in the world *etsi deus non daretur*" (as though God did not exist).[78]

Bonhoeffer was deeply impressed by the figure of Cervantes' Don Quixote, that obsessed knight-errant who became for him the "symbol of resistance" carried, he said, "to the point of absurdity, even lunacy."[79] By contrast, he came to see in Sancho Panza, the obsessed knight's philistine companion, a type of complacent accommodator to things as they are. But Don Quixote, insisting on his rights, put himself in the wrong.[80]

Bonhoeffer's understanding of "absurdity" did not mean disillusionment. Much to the contrary, his perception of the absurd indicated his awareness of a world beyond rationality, as it did in Kierkegaard's case. And as for me, my encounter with the absurd by no means diminished my horizons; rather, it widened them. My very awareness of the realm of the absurd challenged me to find my way in the moral jungles of life.

Bonhoeffer's theology moved, as his friend Eberhard Bethge acknowledged, "to the brink of heresy."[81] It was precisely this feature that spoke to me. When it came to "ultimate questions," a term Bonhoeffer frequently used, nothing but utter candor with oneself and others would do. Here it is not far-fetched to fall back on Max Weber, whose "enormous matter-of-factness" impressed Bonhoeffer.[82] Weber's "trained relentlessness in viewing the realities of life" was Bonhoeffer's too. Just as Weber's admonition to the German students had resounded in me, so did Bonhoeffer's unsparing honesty about these ultimate questions. For me, the proposition of grappling with theology meant asking ultimate questions, nothing more and nothing less.

A letter of mine to Clarita von Trott touches on these matters (2 November 1980):

> I should tell you that I find myself in a strangely paradoxical situation: I am more certain than ever in my faith, and therefore I all the more understand the necessity to face positively the diverse, indeed secular world in which I live day by day. Any holistic ideology that wanted to conceal the fragmentary and imperfect nature of public life would be condemnable. The very dream of "Christendom or Europe" [a prose poem by the eighteenth-century German Romantic poet Friedrich von Hardenberg (Novalis)] is illusory. There never has existed such unity and wholeness, not in the Middle Ages, never. It would mean to misunderstand Christ's mission on earth ever to hope for a perfect order, and this consideration would apply also to Christian society. Therefore, I have to confront the sinful world positively, and I shall have to arrange myself in it cheerfully. Christ after all has come into this world not to judge but to redeem. Thus arises the paradox of my pleasure in the imperfect, yes, in the sinful world, which in turn connects Christian faith with God's grace. Do you understand me? It is so hard to speak, let alone to write, about these matters. In my next life I want to study theology, and then perhaps I shall be able better to express such thoughts. But anyway I might burn to death in hell.

This letter reflects a tension that had been in me all along between a stoic acceptance of an imperfect reality and the temptation to re-enchant my world. Acceptance won the day. I can hardly think of any other generation of young men and women of whom so much decision-making was expected and who carried such a heavy burden concerning the perceived meaninglessness of their world. In a letter of July 1944, Camus observed that the Germans had chosen to turn their "despair into intoxication."[83] Despair? Yes, they despaired over the meaninglessness of the world and responded to political ideologies as tempting ways out of that despair. And it was the Nazi ideology that had become the height of intoxication.

* * *

The years of my youth, when I was forming my ideas about where I stood in life, constituted the high tide of ideologies that were designed to construct a twentieth-century myth of holistic intuitionism, which aspired to bring the Kingdom of God down to earth. It was the hubris of the holistic system builders and their bent toward tyranny that set me on my course into resistance studies. I have come to see the motivation of the German Resistance on which I have worked so long as essentially a revolt against ideology.[84] While it would be foolish for me to insist on a predominantly religious view of the *Widerstand*, I believe that I can maintain the centrality in it of a revulsion against the ideology—the political religion that in fact was but a "pseudo-religion"[85]—that aimed for total control by state and party and suppression of all dissent. Bonhoeffer thus came to oppose "responsible action" to ideology: "The man who acts ideologically sees himself justified in his idea; the responsible man," he added, "commits his action into the hands of God and lives by God's grace and favor."[86] My "pleasure in the imperfect" therefore amounted to liberation from the temptations of all forms of holism and opened up to me in all its fragmentariness a vision of wholeness and fullness in the realm of the beyond.

All my reading, I have found, has led back to some of the questions that had been with me all along, although I had been less self-conscious and articulate about them. Thrown into a world of incertitude and doubt, I was left in a quandary between acceptance of the state of disinheritedness and a compulsive striving to recapture and repair the lost wholeness.

In his inimitable way, Nietzsche himself addressed this problem. He thought that he could dismiss the believers and their need to believe. Their desire for certitudes was to him but a symptom of tiredness, fatalism, disillusionment, and fear of disillusionment. He persisted in arguing that even the "belief in the disbelief," what he called the "nihilism of the Petersburg variety," betrayed a lack of will.[87]

But one should beware of Nietzsche's *pronunciamentos*. He did not abide by them himself. He was unwilling even to stick to his unbelief. Once all was said, he insisted that there was a "hidden *yes*" that was "stronger than all nos and perhaps," and, he continued, "if you emigrants needed to go to sea, it will be—a *faith* which will force you to do so,"[88] a faith after all. But Nietzsche-Zarathustra's faith would have to be faith in a God "who knew how to dance,"[89] that is, "to dance over precipices." The spirit to do that would be the "*free spirit* par excellence."[90]

This final chapter of my voyage has taken me all the way from accounting for the place of skepticism in my life (as in my son's) through the subsequent phases of my thinking. No doubt, the spell of Friedrich Nietzsche's fiery provocations was as decisive for me, especially in my student days, as were my later encounters with the sobering political thought of Max Weber and then the unsparingly honest theology of Dietrich Bonhoeffer. I have found this journey of the mind as exciting and stimulating as my actual journeys to continents and countries have been.

Like Ulysses, I am a part of all that I have met. The various stations of my mental journey were more coherent than they seemed at first, and now in retrospect I see the connections between them that I overlooked when I was actually on my way. In my reading of Nietzsche, the "madman's" message that God is dead was always overshadowed by his accusation that "we have killed God"—that is, as Dietrich Bonhoeffer put it, that God has been "pushed more and more out of life" and that this accounts for "the great defection from God."[91] This means that Nietzsche's apostasy could be understood not as simple atheism but as monastic self-scrutiny. In the course of my self-education, I would neither fall for Nietzsche's invectives against the Christian God as the god who fostered "slave morality" nor engage in a refutation of the philosopher's iconoclasm. But it impressed me deeply that the madman should in the end have entered "divers churches" and there sung his *requiem aeternam deo*. Nietzsche came to mean for me the inveterate challenger and questioner of traditional values and conventions—and the renewer. "Zarathustra," Nietzsche wrote, "is a skeptic," and "strength, *freedom* which is born of the strength and overstrength of the spirit, proves itself by skepticism."[92] What ultimately stayed with me in my infatuation with Nietzsche was his courage to confront the dissonances in life that would be resolved in Dionysian intoxication. The ultimate mystery of life resided in the one word that Nietzsche inexplicably never mentioned, namely, "paradox," the paradoxicality inherent in all life. Once Zarathustra's disciples had denied him, he would celebrate the high noon with them. And if truth could not be found in the here and now, there would in the end be that madman and his singing of the requiem.

It was no mere accident that led me from Nietzsche to Max Weber. Reverberating in Weber I found Nietzsche's unsparing vehemence of expression. What drew me to Weber was his careful, responsible weighing between the exigencies of power and ethics. While the Nietzschean lack of the "middle register," seductive though it was, had too readily gotten lost in overstatements, Weber's guidelines were perspective and balance. True, he thundered against the Sermon on the Mount as the way not to eternal peace but to failure, and he extolled violence as "the decisive means of politics." Yet he made sure to condemn power as an end in itself. Hard-hitting though he was, Weber insisted on balance and responsibility as marks of statesmanship. These qualities were finally a matter of control and "maturity," which the Dionysian genius had disregarded. It was the union of passion and responsibility and a sense of proportion in Weber's thought that in the end won me over and cured me of Nietzsche's still lingering spell.

I came to Dietrich Bonhoeffer by way of my preoccupation with the German Resistance. It was Bonhoeffer who opened my eyes to the spiritual, indeed religious dimensions of the *Widerstand*. But without Nietzsche there would have been no Bonhoeffer. Eberhard Bethge, Bonhoeffer's friend and biographer, attests that young Bonhoeffer was an avid reader of Nietzsche. As early as 1929, while a visiting pastor in Barcelona, Bonhoeffer said that the Christian, like Nietzsche's Overman, creates new Decalogues, setting his standards for good and evil for himself.[93] This distinctly Nietzschean position then encouraged him to argue that, while the knowledge of good and evil seemed to be the aim of all intellectual reflection, "the first task of Christian ethics is to invalidate this knowledge."[94] Christianity and ethics thus were for Bonhoeffer "disparate and divergent entities."[95] Ethics, he argued, are man-made and speak of righteousness. The Christian message ultimately demands that man deny himself and his ethical constructs and that he accept the "merciful love of God for unrighteous men and sinners."[96] Hence derives Bonhoeffer's insistence that the Christian message stands "beyond good and evil," and hence his tribute to Friedrich Nietzsche. But the discovery of what is beyond good and evil was not, he continued, made by Nietzsche as he uttered polemics against the hypocrisies of Christianity. "It belongs," so Bonhoeffer argued, "to the original material of the Christian message."[97] From this followed also his bold and shocking assertion that "there are no actions which are bad in themselves" and that "even murder can be justified."[98]

The youthful flights of boundless idealism that seemed to allow my friends and me to remake the world in our image yielded to a more sober mood. I have learned in the course of time to control my susceptibility to enchantment—not that I have yielded to disenchantment. But what sustained me in those turbulent times was my perception—middle-aged, perhaps—of the benefits of the renewing quality of skepticism. Moreover, in the process of self-analysis I have gone one step further. I have found comfort not only in skepticism but also in making my peace with the perception of the absurd as a dimension determining human life, a perception that has served as a concomitant of a maturing process, however painful.

What, then, about all the dreams, all the flights of fancy of my youth? I can now, as I look back, be certain of one thing: I am still the same. My ideals are still with me, although they have in no way come even close to realization. I may have been rash when I wrote earlier to Clarita that the dream of Novalis in his "Christendom or Europe" was "illusory." Dreams are not illusory. They have a prehistory, as Freud and Jung have told us, each in his own way, and they have survival quality. Dreams lie like perennials deep in the soil, waiting to push into the light, when they acquire a reality of their own.

My journey, despite all the changes I have witnessed, has not really changed my basic disposition. I have learned a lot on the way, I hope, and I certainly have, for better or worse, learned to live more consciously. In the course of my voyage through the century, following Faust's prescription, I have at least aspired to learn what "deep within it, binds the universe together."[99] I had to follow the great herald of the death of God singing his requiem; I had to accept the down-to-earth secularist's self-image of being not "*a-religious*" after all;[100] and I had to follow the saintly pastor's shocking assertion that in the world "come of age," as he put it, "we cannot be honest unless we recognize that we have to live in the world *etsi deus non daretur* [as if God did not exist]."[101] In sum, I have learned to live with paradoxes. I have learned that they are life.

Afterthoughts

I hope that in these chapters I have lived up to the counsel of Søren Kierkegaard that life must be lived forwards but can only be understood backwards. Writing my memoirs has brought home to me time and again the wisdom of John Donne's meditation, "No man is an island, entire of itself." I see myself as part of a certain cultural tradition and of a changing human environment: both have shaped my thinking and doing. From my family I derived, while not much intellectual inspiration, an ethos that has guided me throughout my life. My paternal grandmother left in her own handwriting for each one of us twelve grandchildren a neatly framed directive that included the words "Denke mit Ehrfurcht stets an Gott, an die Menschen mit Liebe! Und mit Ernst an die Pflicht!"[1] And this exhortation is still with me on my desk.

The *Gymnasium* I attended provided me with an education that was possibly too one-sidedly academic, yet also with companionships and friendships that remained with me throughout my life. These ties were as intense as they were demanding of loyalty. We boys educated each other—and that is the way it should have been. No less formative for me was the impact of the Youth Movement, which gave me and my friends a distinctly generational sense of solidarity. But on second thought, without that involvement, might we not have been more restrained in our Nietzschean infatuation and more attentive to Max Weber's stoic admonition to confront that "trained relentlessness in viewing the realities of life"?

Of course we, my friends and myself, constituted but a very small enclave within Berlin's whirl of activity. Some of us were more attuned to the apocalyptic temper that prevailed in the city in the early 1930s, while others were more appreciative of its cultural opportunities. Some were more politically engaged, while others were preparing for a life of "inner emigration" even before the Nazi seizure of power. But all of us had set out for a journey of self-realization. There was a bond between us that surmounted all differences, and whatever separate ways we have gone, we still hold together, even in memory.

Life in Berlin was a continuous challenge. The German capital has always been a nervous city, certainly since the so-called *Gründerjahre* (Founders' Years) of the 1870s, after the victorious Prussian war against France spelled wild economic expansion and exploding cultural prosperity. Bertolt Brecht's Mahagonny—that is, Berlin—was the city in which everything was allowed to be allowed. While I did benefit from the enrichment and enticement it had to offer, I never felt that I was part of that harsh world of sprawling activity.

Although Berlin was my native city, it was Vienna to which all my emotions belonged. Was it because, despite being born in the German capital, my roots were in the Austrian one? Remembering Austria, I find words of affection that betray a singular intimacy. My passage from Berlin to Vienna turned out to be a momentous step for me, just as afterwards my displacement from Europe to America was a similarly pivotal experience.

Here I fall back on some passages from a talk that I gave in October 1997 on the occasion of a ceremony at the Austrian Consulate General in New York City. It started with my quoting the first lines of the new Austrian anthem, composed after World War II by the mother of my Molden friends: "Land of mountains/Land by the river." I continued:

> I am thinking of the Schneeberg in Lower Austria, the Hochschwab in Styria, the Schafsberg in Salzburg—all mountains that I climbed when I was young.
>
> I am thinking of the majestic Danube—which once I crossed swimming, to my great surprise finding myself landing on the other shore a few kilometers farther downstream, although not quite as far as Budapest; I am thinking, too, of the roaring Salzach; I am thinking of the fields, the golden fields, which in those days of my youth were bright with red poppies and blue cornflowers.
>
> I am thinking of the dark and mysterious—as it was then—Stephansdom, and of Salzburg Cathedral, which during the summer festivals was the backdrop for the performance of Hofmannsthal's *Jedermann*.
>
> One never leaves such landmarks behind ...
>
> As I have thought things over, I have come to see the relatedness of Austria and the United States. This is no mere mental acrobatics. Austria, once the heart of a big empire, is nowadays a small—and I understand happy—country. But as I have studied and taught the history of Central Europe, I have become cognizant of the deeper affinity between Austria, its legacy, and America—that is, the challenge that is America. Old Austria was everything but a *Völkerkerker* (prison of peoples), a description that circulated in the early decades of the twentieth century. To the very end, it held together its many nationalities, not as a prison but as a bridge between nationalities. That is the Austrian heritage, as I see it, that survived the end of empire. When I think of Austria, I am always

reminded of this legacy. And is not the American challenge a very similar one—to enable various ethnic groups and different races to co-exist peacefully?

I am now reminded of the question that my friend Hans-Lukas asked of me early in 1940: "Are you still the same?" To be sure, by all indications my life has been marked by discontinuities and incongruities. Naturally, I miss the mountains, the rivers, the fields, the cathedrals so familiar to me. Yet America, as I have found out, has its own hallmarks, which at first sight seem very different: the megacities, the skyscrapers, constant change. Distance has its rewards.

One of the distinctly traditional parts of the United States, New England, where I have now lived for many decades, has become a bridge between my homes old and new. My wife Betty is a native of New Hampshire, and my children and grandchildren were born in New England. The gentle hills of Massachusetts and Vermont and the granite mountains of New Hampshire take me back to the old country after all. I suppose that I have been plain fortunate in being able to bring my two lives, so to speak, in Europe and America into one focus.

I have been able to translate the calamities, evildoings, and suffering that I have witnessed in my lifetime into challenges from which I have learned a great deal. Furthermore, I have had good fortune in my personal as well as my professional life: family, friends, and colleagues have been wonderful companions to me throughout.

It would be pretentious for me to claim to have had a special "mission" to fulfill. But I have always worked hard, and for me work has meant much more than simply "doing a job." I felt the need to achieve my life's goals through my vocation, and then I could feel pride in my accomplishments. My "duty," then, was not something imposed upon me from without; rather, it was what an inner voice told me that I needed to do. If there was tyranny in my world, it was my own tyranny over myself—my altogether happy paradox.

I add here that my deepening awareness of the beyond, that is, the religious sphere, has sustained me more and more. The saying "No man is an island, entire of itself" pertains to the transcendental realm as well as the social one, and the call for service holds for the relation with our fellow human beings as well as with the distant God. In my understanding, being religious means accepting a higher order that is not of our making, but this acceptance must always be tempered by skepticism and doubt. This dialectic between acceptance and questioning has sustained me and has made me free. And it was the very honesty of Dietrich Bonhoeffer's theology—his insistence that "the church stands, not at the boundaries where human powers give out, but in the middle of the village"[2]—that has helped me navigate the perplexing realm between heaven and earth.

Looking back on my life, I must now ask myself what regrets I have about my past actions. For the most part, I do not torture myself with regrets and feel committed to the decisions I have made—as I must, for I want to live with them. My failings, if they have been such, are part of myself. When years ago I let Father down and, despite all his efforts to have me admitted, did not go to Oxford, was I justified to exchange that promised paradise at Balliol College for my Viennese escapade, which turned out to be, however troubled, a very important station in my maturing process? When just before departing for America I encountered Gestapo agents taking Father away for an interrogation, should I have screamed and shouted? I sensed—rightly—that at that instant Father did not want to implicate me in any way.

There is one matter pertaining to my adult years that I must account for and explain to myself and no doubt to my readers as well—that is, the place of the Holocaust in my scholarly career. As I look back on my work, I cannot help noticing that, having written and lectured over the past half-century about topics that have fully engaged me, that I have deemed important—the nature of conservatism in an ever-changing universe, the mandate for resistance in a dictatorial state—I have not addressed head-on the issue of the Shoah or Holocaust. Have I, at least unconsciously, steered away from focusing directly on the very topic that has come, certainly in the past forty years, to be considered the crucial landmark in modern history? It is a trauma that haunts not only the Jews, the immediate victims, and the Germans, the chief perpetrators of the crimes, but all of mankind, which has lost its innocence.

The trauma of the Holocaust is unending. Indeed, it is ever present, an inescapable reality of the world we have been condemned to live in. Günter Grass's novella *Im Krebsgang* (Crablike), a commentary on the agonizing process of Germans coming to terms with their difficult past, ends with the haunting words: "Das hört nicht auf. Nie hört das auf" (There is no end to it. There never will be).

Was Theodor Adorno justified in his belief that to write poetry after Auschwitz was "barbaric"? And did his disciple in the Frankfurt School of social scientists, Jürgen Habermas, go too far in maintaining that the legacy of Auschwitz still affected German generations born long after the event, that they had grown up in the "context of life" (*Lebensform*) that made Auschwitz possible—a milieu, he argued, that they could not escape?[3]

Certainly, Chancellor Helmut Kohl got out of the predicament of everything German the easy way with the phrase "die Gnade der späten Geburt" (the grace of late birth). This will not do. In this grave matter there can be no statute of limitations, and Kohl's easy formulation suggests a lack of understanding—indeed, evasion—of the inescapable reality, ugly as it is, of the difficult world we have been condemned to live in.

The Israeli philosopher Yehuda Elkana, a survivor of Auschwitz, may have been too extreme in advocating the "need to forget."[4] Forgetting cannot be the answer to those horrendous crimes and terrible sufferings. All history after Auschwitz must, directly or indirectly, relate to it, and all "normalcy" after

Auschwitz is elusive. Yet Elkana also urges politicians and teachers "to take their stand on the side of life" and to dedicate themselves to creating their future. Such has been my course.

Involving risk and martyrdom, acts of resistance were a dangerous yet positive response to the suffering and indignities caused by Nazi domination. The "masquerade of evil" was a phrase of Dietrich Bonhoeffer, who had the courage to stand up against the tide of Nazism. I became resolved to record that there had been ten just men, Bonhoeffer and his friends in the German Resistance, in Sodom; that there had been courage and decency in Germany; that there had been people who were willing to act against the ugly consensus generally identified with the national interest. If even in the direst chapters of history there are glimmers of hope and survival, there is cause to celebrate the human spirit.

My voyage through the twentieth century, as I have reviewed it in this memoir, has not been an escape from solidarity with my generation. That generation, which has lived with a passionate thirst for knowledge and an intense sense of commitment to ideas, has not been spared participation in the ups and downs of a violent reality. For better and worse, the turbulence of our century was inescapable for me and my friends. We cared and were eager to give free rein to our dreams of the future. Our passions were dear to us, and yet these very passions placed us into an arena in which we were bound to collide with terrible forces and from which there was—and is—no escape. As for my own work, I have moved in this sphere in the course of my concerns with resistance, and I certainly am aware of the fact that I have to accept at least a metaphysical sense of identification with the horrors that have occurred during my lifetime. Understanding backward, then, is my responsibility, and even if I will not claim to have been an active resister myself, I have been able to bear witness to those who stayed on to fight against evil. They have inspired my life's work on resistance, which, however modest it may have been, is one of affirmation—the recording of courage and hope.

Before I close this memoir, I want to reiterate that I am a part of all that I have met during *my* twentieth century, as I may call it now. In its course, and in the new century that has begun, I have met with much kindness and cheer, and much good will and courage. These high virtues have always lit my path. The spirit of my friends who stood for them should have the last word here. It has helped me to "live forward."

Notes

Introduction

1. Ralph Waldo Emerson, "Friendship," *The Complete Essays and Other Writings of Ralph Waldo Emerson*, ed. Brooks Atkinson (New York, 1940), 236.

Chapter 1: Beginnings

1. An elaborate genealogical document tracing the Kuffner family back to the early eighteenth century relates the founding of the family brewery. It tells the story of Löbl Kuffner, a Jewish ancestor of mine in Lundenburg who was a tenant of the distillery on the estate of Prince Joseph Wenzel von und zu Liechtenstein. The Prince was a devoted chess player, and my ancestor was known in the area as an expert player. Once, in his Viennese Palais, the Prince played chess with the French ambassador, a Marquis, for a considerable sum of money. When the game was about to come to a draw, the two parties agreed to call in the Lundenburg tenant, who immediately made his way to Vienna and helped the Prince win the match—much to the anger of the Marquis. In gratitude for his tenant's service, the Prince had a house built for him on his estate. It came to be the headquarters of the Ignaz und Jacob Kuffner Brauhaus, which later moved to Ottakring, the sixteenth district of Vienna, where it came to be well-known as Ottakringer Brauerei. See also Hermann Edler von Kuffner, *Geschichtliche Daten über die Familie Kuffner vom Beginn des XVIII. Jahrhunderts bis zur Gegenwart* (Brünn, 1902), 4–9.

2. The one surviving testimony of the part that the Kuffner family played in Vienna is the Kuffner Observatory in Vienna-Ottakring, which was endowed by my Uncle Moriz and erected between 1884 and 1886. A painfully silent person, he was a passionate mountaineer and a patron of the arts and sciences. In his and his wife's honor, the Moriz and Elsa von Kuffner Foundation was established in 1970 in Switzerland by their son Stefan. See Werner W. Weiss, *Die Kuffner-Sternwarte* (Vienna, 1984).

3. Father Lichtenberg was arrested in October 1941. After spending two years in jail, he was relegated to the Dachau concentration camp but died while being transported there. He was beatified in 1996 by Pope John Paul II.

4. Hugo von Hofmannsthal, "Preusse und Österreicher: Ein Schema," *Gesammelte Werke*, Prosa III (Frankfurt am Main, 1952), 407–409.

5. Earlier Grandfather served as Honorary Consul of the United States of America. To my knowledge, this was the first connection between my family and the United States.

Chapter 2: School Years

1. See Madame de Staël, *De l'Allemagne* (Paris, 1813), 89.

2. A game that we often played, called *Schlagball*, was a cousin of sorts of American baseball. But I am struck by one difference between the two games. In baseball, in order to put out a runner, you have to catch the ball before he reaches the base; in *Schlagball*, you have to hit the runner before he reaches safety. The reddish-brown ball was made of hard leather, and when you were hit, you heard the angels trumpeting.

3. "Aus grauer Städte Mauern zieh'n wir durch Wald und Feld/Wer bleibt, der mag versauern, wir fahren in die Welt./Heidi heido wir fahren, wir fahren in die Welt" (Away from gray city walls we roam through woods and fields./Who stays behind may get sour, we move into the world./Heyho we wander, we wander into the world).

4. Meaning in this case a retired Major in the Kaiser's army.

5. "Ich gehe durch den Todesschlaf/zu Gott hin als Soldat und brav" (Now I shall cross death's sleeping span/To God, a soldier and an honest man).

6. *Handakten des Oberreichsanwalts b. Volksgerichtshof in der Strafsache gegen Georg Hans Hermann von Schweinitz aus Berlin wegen Vorbereitung zum Hochverrat*, Berlin Document Center, 1940.

7. Letter of Georg to Mama, 13 July 1937, Berlin.

8. Re-arrested in December 1937, Georg was incarcerated in the Sachsenhausen concentration camp to the north of Berlin and subsequently in an array of jails for another twenty-two months. Still, he persisted in seeing his plight as "ordained from on high" and kept searching for "meaning in every stroke of fate, however hard" (letter of Georg to Mama, 10 December 1937). He was eventually transferred to the fortress Landsberg am Leach in Upper Bavaria, where Hitler had sat in 1923–1924. Pursuant to the amnesty decree for the Wehrmacht of the *Führer und Reichskanzler* of 1 September 1939, he was released from captivity soon after. If only for his own protection, Georg hastened to join up, emerging as a Corporal in the Reserve Battalion of the renowned Infantry Regiment 9, a crack unit stationed in Potsdam, which carried on an old Prussian Junker tradition. He was now, according to his testimony, made to feel as though he had "always been there" and was "among soldiers and comrades" (letters of Georg to Mama, 15 November 1939; Georg to his brother-in-law Udo Klausa, 16 November 1939). The details derived from Georg's diaries and letters correspond to the information that I have obtained from his nephews, brothers Michael and Ekkehard Klausa.

9. This phrasing is significant since after President Paul von Hindenburg's death in 1934, all officers and enlisted men had to take the oath of allegiance to Hitler personally

instead of to "Nation and Fatherland." The Battalion Commander chose the older, traditional version of the oath.

10. Karl Mannheim, *Essays on the Sociology of Knowledge*, ed. and trans. Paul Kecskemeti (London, 1952), 24, 306ff.

11. Michael Hamburger, "A Craving for Hell: Nietzsche and the Nietzscheans," *Encounter* 19 (1962): 40.

12. See Christian Velder, *300 Jahre Französisches Gymnasium* (Berlin, 1989), 534.

13. The text to the song was written by August Heinrich Hoffmann von Fallersleben, who also authored the text of the song "Deutschland, Deutschland über alles," which in 1922 became the German national anthem.

14. Ursula von Kardorff, *Berliner Aufzeichnungen aus den Jahren 1942 bis 1945* (Munich, 1962).

15. Anton Cordes, *Löse und Binde: Auf der Fährte der verborgenen Qualität* (Zurich, 1971).

Chapter 3: "O du mein Österreich ..."

1. Considerably later, my friend and former classmate Henry H. H. Remak returned some of my old letters from that period to me, commenting that they were "very characteristic of the idealistic-philosophical-abstract tendencies of our generation. We must have been a very serious bunch" (Henry H. H. Remak to K. v. K., 20 December 1958). He was entirely right.

2. The new anthem, "Land of Mountains, Land by the River," sung to the melody of Mozart's Masonic Cantata, was adopted in 1947. By contrast, the Germans had no luck with the creation of a new anthem. Clearly, the old one, "Deutschland, Deutschland über alles," originally a creation of the German democratic poet of the 1848 era, Heinrich Hoffmann von Fallersleben, was no longer acceptable after World War II because of its expansionist connotations. President Theodor Heuss then commissioned the poet Rudolf Alexander Schröder to write a new text and the composer Hermann Reuter to create a new melody. However, the resultant "Hymne an Deutschland" did not find acceptance, and in the end the Federal Republic settled on the third verse of the old anthem, "Einigkeit und Recht und Freiheit für das deutsche Vaterland," sung to the original melody, Haydn's Kaiserquartett.

3. 'Ah! que la victoire demeure avec ceux qui auront fait la guerre sans l'aimer!' André Malraux, *Les Noyers de l'Altenburg* (Paris, 1948), 271.

4. Joseph Wechsberg, "Somnambulistic Certainty," *New Yorker*, 16 September 1961, 51–84.

5. The O5 movement—so named because "Oe" stood for "Oesterreich" (Austria), and the "e" is the fifth letter in the alphabet—at first comprised a number of individual resistance groups. In the fall of 1944, the movement was consolidated under the common leadership of a Committee of Seven led by Dr. Hans Becker. On the side of the main portals of St. Stephan's Cathedral, the letters "Oe," deeply carved into the stone, are visible today to all who approach them, and they are meant to be preserved in this condition forever.

6. As soon as the Nazis had been chased out of the Tyrol, Otto drove into the Tyrolean mountains. There he discovered a solitary village, Alpbach, which so appealed to him that

he decided then and there to stage annual forums, which would take place every summer, bringing together academics, writers, business leaders, and statesmen to stimulate European fellowship. He collected the initial funding from Dr. Karl Gruber, whom he knew from the resistance days and who by then had become governor of the Tyrol, later was Austria's first foreign minister, and eventually became ambassador to the United Nations. Not many weeks later, the first European Forum was convened in this idyllic mountain village, and to this day forums are held every summer. European unity has become Otto's paramount concern, not to say obsession. Tante Jani, who observed his comings and goings with great sympathy, often referred to him as "the indomitable one."

7. "Molden. Non-Stop," *Der Spiegel*, no. 26 (1967).

8. A well-known café by the Michaelerplatz, Café Griensteidl was the meeting place of the Viennese literati.

9. Written on 7 December 1937 in the Hospiz of St. Christoph on the Arlberg in the Tyrol.

10. Fritz Molden, *Fepolinski und Waschlapski auf dem berstenden Stern* (Vienna, 1976), 157.

11. Letter from Kurt v. B. to K. v. K., 20 December 1962.

12. "You know that I was enthusiastic, and by virtue of my total seclusion in the army, it remained that way. Things took me wherever there was action. After Poland came France, then preparation for [the invasion of] England, East Prussia, on the first day across the frontier to Russia, and then that uncanny impact of dust, stench, and wild fights up to Leningrad. First impression: here blows another wind; marching in formation is out. Then advance towards Moscow despite filth and indescribable cold, first retreat and flight. Then two years in central Finland, a peaceful war in an enchanting landscape—some very nice comrades in an advanced post, only thirteen men and every fortnight mail and rations ..., battery-operated radio with good programs, good books, many letters. What one wrote during the war one can no longer read today—too kitschy. And then, imagine, I felt embarrassed about sitting up there in relative peace while the Reich was more and more endangered and my friends, many of whom were in disagreement with me, were fighting and dying in droves. Then I had myself transferred to a panzer division of the Waffen-SS and was among the first deployment in Normandy. It was simply horrible. Shortly before that I had met Sonja, whom I married just before my transfer to the Western front. She comes from Silesia.... After the attempt against Hitler [of 20 July 1944], her relatives were one by one jailed, killed, and persecuted.... Feelings of doom accompanied by the bloody deployments by day and by night.... One was not so stupid as not to recognize that the end was in sight and that it would be a terrible end. But somehow one steels oneself with contempt—I certainly never was a hero—and somehow one casts off all fear and imagines oneself in the hall of the Nibelungs. Then flight even there, soon followed by the English being parachuted into Arnhem ... then the Ardennes offensive ... nothing was spared the SS divisions, they were always in the forefront—once defeated there, on to Hungary ..., then the collapse of the Hungarians, again encirclement, flight, fighting.... One thing I must record: there really was something of old Prussia in this outfit. In short ..., I would not for anything have missed this horrifying but truly soldierly experience. We certainly hope that this spelled the end of a historical era and not the start of a new one."

13. Letter from K. v. K. to Kurt, 26 February 1998.
14. Letter from Thomas Mann to Hermann Hesse, Küsnacht, 3 January 1934. Anni Carlsson, ed., *Hermann Hesse–Thomas Mann Briefwechsel* (Frankfurt am Main, 1968), 42.
15. The "little castle" got its name from its owner, Countess Fuchs. She had been a tutor of Empress Maria Theresa, who gave the house to her as a present.
16. Of distinctly more help, I am sure, was another visitor to Rodaun, a young impecunious Germanist, who with his family arrived in Vienna as the first stop during their flight from Nazi Germany. His name was Richard Alewyn, and he turned out to be one of the most distinguished scholars of modern German literature and especially of Hofmannsthal. During the war years, he taught in the United States; after the war, he returned to Germany, where he last occupied a chair at Bonn University.
17. K. v. K., notebook, August 1938.
18. Letter from K. v. K. to C. T., spring 1938.
19. Letter from K. v. K. to Otto Molden, 4 October 1938.

Chapter 4: America—Coming Down to Earth

1. From August 1939 until October 1941, I kept a journal from which in subsequent pages I shall quote selectively. These selections begin with "(J.)."
2. At the initiative of Harvard undergraduates, the Harvard Corporation awarded a number of scholarships to refugee students from Germany, Austria, and Czechoslovakia. The students, faculty, staff, and alumni from Harvard collected the necessary funds, with President Roosevelt, himself an illustrious alumnus of the college and now "deeply interested" in the plan, giving his endorsement. An intercollegiate conference on the refugee problem, which was subsequently convened in New York, was attended by delegates from 100 colleges and universities. Early in June 1990, at a reunion of the recipients of the scholarships, a tree was planted and a brass plaque installed in front of Boylston Hall in Harvard Yard to commemorate the act. The university had originally offered to provide an oak tree for the occasion. For many of the one-time refugees, however, an oak tree had too strong a military connotation, including its use in German war insignia. A linden tree was planted instead. The preference for the linden tree was dictated by memories of the cherished Schubert lied, "Am Brunnen vor dem Tore, da steht ein Lindenbaum, ich träumt' in seinem Schatten so manchen süßen Traum" (At the fountain in front of the door there stands a linden tree, I dreamt in its shade so many a sweet dream). No echo, then, of German militarism; but an echo nevertheless of the German romantic tradition. In a way, this meant a return for the exiles to the better tradition of their homeland. The text of the plaque reads as follows: "To Harvard University Students Faculty Staff Alumni/Whose Generosity Fifty Years Ago Opened Doors to Student Refugees from Nazi Persecution/May This Tree Express in Grace and Beauty/The Abiding and Heartfelt Gratitude of the Recipients/June 1990."
3. The six-year-old daughter of my host family.
4. The German invasion of Poland of 1 September 1939 and the subsequent declaration of war on Germany by Great Britain and France of 3 September.

5. Charles William Eliot (1834–1926) was President of Harvard University from 1869 to 1909.

6. Inaugural address of Charles William Eliot as President of Harvard College, 19 October 1869.

7. Charles Bulfinch (1763–1844) was a major Bostonian architect who designed the state houses in Boston and Hartford, Connecticut, and a number of Harvard buildings.

8. Jakob Rosenberg (1893–1980), a German refugee scholar, who was formerly the keeper of Berlin's Kupferstichkabinett, a museum of prints and drawings, became a professor in the Department of Fine Arts at Harvard. At the Fogg Art Museum he came to be known as "der heilige Jakob," due to his gentle nature. His wife Ellie was the daughter of the German philosopher Edmund Husserl. Since our families had been friends, the Rosenbergs were extremely hospitable to me during my student days in Cambridge, and I experienced much kindness from them. But quite apart from family friendship, as a historian I was especially intrigued by one story Jakob related to me. During World War I, as a wounded German prisoner of war in France, he was sent in an exchange of prisoners to Switzerland, where he was free to study art history. In Zurich he rented a room, bare as a monk's cell, whose former occupant had left without leaving a trace. Later Jakob was told that this former occupant was none other than Vladimir Ilyich Lenin, who in April 1917 had, by arrangement with the German army general staff, boarded the famous sealed train for the Finland station in Petrograd, where he launched his revolution.

9. Novalis was the pseudonym for Friedrich von Hardenberg (1772–1801), one of the outstanding poets of German Romanticism.

10. I am grateful to my friend Justina Gregory for the identification of the passage and the translation from the Greek.

11. Hans Rothfels, a German refugee historian, temporarily interned together with my father on the Isle of Man. He later became a professor at Brown University and the University of Chicago. After the war he returned to Germany, where he taught at Tübingen University.

12. Meanwhile, I have come into possession of the original document. It reads as follows: "Academia Manxiana/Doctorem Herbert de Klemperer a Klemenau/Qui Ipse Fabri Arte Imbutus Permultas/Variasque Machinas Vapore Vel Aere/Motas Construxit Homines et Res Ex-/Imia Mentis Acumine Moderans et Semper/Publicae Saluti Inserviens/In Numerum Sociorum Honoris Causa Recepit/Die Ii Mensis Septembris MCMXL/In Campo Hutchinson" (The Academy of the Isle of Man Is Pleased to Accept as a Member, *Honoris Causa*, Dr. Herbert von Klemperer von Klemenau/Who with Profound Technical Expertise Manufactured Many Different Engines by Steam or by Air; a Moderating Force on Men and Their Affairs Due to the Extraordinary Incisiveness of His Intellect, and a Devoted Servant of the Common Welfare/Camp Hutchinson, 2 September 1940).

13. The Bartols were a Bostonian family that, upon my arrival in Cambridge, opened their house to me. Their hospitality and friendship have meant much to me.

14. Alexander Böker, a Rhodes Scholar from Germany (1934–1937), later studied at Harvard (1939–1943), where he functioned as assistant to the exiled German ex-Chancellor Heinrich Brüning.

15. Jani and her sister Hedwig had been taken away by the Vichy police, leaving their mother alone in Beaulieu sur Mer in southern France. My aunts were turned over to the Nazis, never to return. Granny took her plight stoically. In earlier letters she had written: "All of us had to learn to accept our fate" (Easter Monday, 1939); "I accept my fate because it cannot be changed. Above all, I thank God that I have the strength for it and that I am healthy" (6 January 1940).

Chapter 5: Going To and Fro upon the Earth

1. In the same letter, however, in answer to one written by Franz in which he lamented that his physical strength was not up to army life, Fred wrote that, indeed, the Klemperers, unlike the American pioneers, had "tired blood" in their veins.

2. I have always understood that Fred had at one point distinguished himself and that his unit staged a parade in his honor. But as they failed to call him out, he marched with the rest in formation. Fred later on would not confirm this story.

3. Hans J. Epstein was a fellow student at Harvard and a friend of mine. When I returned from army service, his mother welcomed me into her house in Providence, Rhode Island.

4. Hans W. Gatzke was a former German exchange student and a friend of mine at Harvard. He later became Professor of History at Yale University.

5. Lothar Bossle, ed., *Pforten der Freiheit: Festschrift für Alexander Böker zum 85. Geburtstag* (Paderborn, 1997).

6. In February and March 1943, I kept a journal. Quotations from it will be marked with a "(J.)."

7. "Fas est ab hoste doceri" (It is allowed to learn from the enemy).

8. Victory Mail. In wartime the messages going overseas to the troops were photocopied and sent out in miniature format to save weight and space.

9. Dr. Jeidels, originally managing director of the Berliner Handelsgesellschaft, emigrated to America in 1938, first becoming a partner of Lazard Frères and then vice president of the Bank of America. Back in Germany, he had been a close business associate of Father, and once my brothers and I arrived in America, he took a fatherly interest in us.

10. The "V" in V-1 stood for *Vergeltung*, meaning retribution.

11. Haras-de-Bel-Ebat means in Arabic "May God preserve this beautiful outpost."

12. Previously, on 12 September 1943, Skorzeny had freed the deposed Mussolini from captivity in the Central Italian Apennines and had brought him to Salò by Lake Garda, where Il Duce established the short-lived Republic of Salò.

13. The Molden parents were not spared the worst indignities of Nazi rule. Towards the end of the war, both were imprisoned and indeed tortured by the authorities, who wanted to know their sons' whereabouts. But neither of them told. For the story of the part played by the Moldens in the Austrian Resistance, see Radomir V. Luza, *The Resistance in Austria, 1938–1945* (Minneapolis, MN, 1984); Fritz Molden, *Fires in the Night: The Sacrifices and Significance of the Austrian Resistance* (Boulder, CO, 1989), esp. 93–100; F. Molden, *Fepolinski und Waschlapski auf dem berstenden Stern*, esp. 311f.;

Otto Molden, *Der Ruf des Gewissens: Der österreichische Freiheitskampf, 1938–1945* (Vienna, 1958).

14. In this connection, see Nicholas (William Baron) Bethell, *The Last Secret: The Delivery to Stalin of Over Two Million Russians by Britain and the United States* (New York, 1974).

15. In August 1941, that is, before the United States entered the war, President Roosevelt and Prime Minister Churchill issued a joint declaration of peace aims, the so-called Atlantic Charter, in which they made known "certain common principles." In their eight-point message, they announced that they were seeking "no aggrandizement, territorial or other," and that they respected "the right of all peoples to choose their form of government." After the "final destruction of Nazi tyranny," they pledged to establish a peace that would "afford all nations the means of dwelling in safety within their own boundaries" and all men in all lands "freedom from fear and want."

16. For details, see Robert Wolfe, ed., *Captured German and Related Records: A National Archives Conference* (Athens, OH, 1974), and US Department of State, *Foreign Relations of the United States: Diplomatic Papers 1945*, vol. 3 (Washington, DC, 1945).

17. But when Berlin, besieged by the Russians, turned out to be too risky, the archives were transported to Whaddon Hall in Buckinghamshire, England, where they were microfilmed before eventually being returned to the Federal Republic in Bonn.

18. Women's Auxiliary Army Corps.

Chapter 6: "Du bist ein Wanderer …"

1. Letter from Otto Molden to K. v. K., Innsbruck, 23 May 1946.
2. Letter from Victoria von Schweinitz to K. v. K., Crottorf, 4 January 1947.
3. Letter from Dr. Otto Jeidels to K. v. K., San Francisco, 26 September 1946.
4. Friedrich Meinecke, *Weltbürgertum und Nationalstaat: Studien zur Genesis des deutschen Nationalstaates*, 7th ed. (Munich, 1928).
5. In this connection Meinecke actually mentioned Felix Gilbert, Hajo Holborn, and Hans Rosenberg, but he could as well have mentioned Fritz Epstein, Dietrich Gerhard, Gerhard Masur, Hans Rothfels—all students of his. Letter from Friedrich Meinecke to Ludwig Dehio, Berlin, 21 July 1947; Friedrich Meinecke, *Ausgewählter Briefwechsel*, ed. Ludwig Dehio and Peter Classen (Stuttgart, 1962), 281.
6. Karl Marx, *Economic and Philosophic Manuscripts of 1844*, in Karl Marx and Frederick Engels, *Collected Works*, vol. 3 (New York, 1975).
7. See Sigmund Freud, *Civilization and its Discontents* (New York, 1961), 22, 92.
8. Ibid., 23.
9. H. Stuart Hughes, *Consciousness and Society: The Reorientation of European Social Thought 1890–1930* (New York, 1958).
10. Charles M. Gray, *Hugh Latimer and the Sixteenth Century* (Cambridge, MA, 1950).
11. Sidney Bradshaw Fay, *The Origins of the World War* (New York, 1928). At the time that the book was published, there had been only one world war.

12. The thesis was to be my first book, *Germany's New Conservatism: Its History and Dilemma in the Twentieth Century* (Princeton, NJ, 1957). The volume reflected and tried to translate into scholarly language the concerns that have always been with me: What is the place of conservatism in the modern mass age? Can conservatism—that is, a position of acceptance of the created order of living, as Edmund Burke put it, "in a just correspondence and symmetry with the order of the world"—be reinvented in our age without succumbing to the lure of new allegiances that are essentially intoxicating and manipulative? Germany has not had the benefit of a healthy conservative tradition. Thus, I felt that it was all the more important to identify Germany's proliferating neo-conservative movement in the 1920s and 1930s and its potential for a sound definition of the conservative position, as well as its yielding to the lure of National Socialism.

13. Letter from Heinrich Brüning to Mona Anderson, Lowell House, 24 November 1938, in Heinrich Brüning, *Briefe und Gespräche 1934–1945*, ed. Claire Nix, with Reginald Phelps and George Pettee (Stuttgart, 1974), 220.

14. See Klemens von Klemperer, *Ignaz Seipel: Christian Statesman in a Time of Crisis* (Princeton, 1972). This was my second book, once again about a chapter of German conservatism. Ignaz Seipel (1876–1932), an Austrian statesman—priest and chancellor—was the dominating conservative figure in the First Austrian Republic. He died in August 1932 and was succeeded in the chancellorship by Engelbert Dollfuss. After the latter's assassination by the Nazis in July 1934, Schuschnigg took the helm, to be finally swept from office in March 1938 by Hitler's annexation of Austria.

15. See Klemens von Klemperer, "Kurt von Schuschnigg," *Neue Österreichische Biographie*, vol. 22 (Vienna, 1987), 44–57.

16. For the discussion of Werner Jaeger's advocacy of a "third humanism," I am indebted to Donald O. White, "Werner Jaeger's 'Third Humanism' and the Crisis of Cultural Politics in Weimar Germany," in *Werner Jaeger Reconsidered*, ed. William M. Calder III (Atlanta, GA, 1992), 267–288. See also Reinhard Mehring, "Humanismus als 'Politicum': Werner Jaegers Problemgeschichte der griechischen 'Paideia,'" *Antike und Abendland* 45 (1999): 111–128.

17. On 23 November 1934, however, when Jaeger was a guest professor at the University of California, Berkeley, and evidently still undecided about his future, he went to the German Consulate General in San Francisco to swear the oath of loyalty to Hitler, obligatory for all civil servants; Mehring, "Humanismus als 'Politicum,'" 119.

18. Fritz Stern, "National Socialism as Temptation," in *Dreams and Delusions* (New York, 1987), 147–191.

19. Bonhoeffer wrote a piece for his friends on New Year's Day in 1943. Dietrich Bonhoeffer, "After Ten Years," in *Letters and Papers from Prison*, ed. Eberhard Bethge, trans. Reginald Fuller and Frank Clark, enlarged edition (New York, 1971), 4.

20. I should mention here that there was an angel at work in this institute, Miss Ruth Hubbard. When I arrived in New York, trying to orient myself in the American academic landscape, she was ever so kind and helpful in paving the way for me. She had done the same for my friends, Alex Böker and Hans Gatzke, who had found themselves in a similar situation.

21. Letter from John H. Finley to K. v. K., 21 September 1949.

22. William Allan Neilson addressing a public meeting in Northampton on 1 December 1938.

23. In German, the word *Sie* is used for more formal relationships, while *Du* is reserved for family members and close friends.

24. The highly acclaimed British film *The Third Man* (1949) portrays Vienna of the immediate post-war period from the perspective of the bombed-out city's sewers.

25. Robert Musil, *Der Mann ohne Eigenschaften* (Hamburg, 1952), 12f.

26. Letter from Friedl Lehne to K. v. K., Gösing (Styria), 29 March 1962.

27. Letter from K. v. K. to J. Jean Hecht, 26 January 1963.

28. Letter from K. v. K. to Charles and Isabel McClumpha, Bad Godesberg, 29 November 1963.

29. See Alexander and Margarete Mitscherlich, *Die Unfähigkeit zu trauern: Grundlagen kollektiven Verhaltens* (Munich, 1967).

30. Once, while still a newcomer to this rocky, wooded countryside, I detected smoke coming out of what seemed to be a little barn. I stopped my car instantly and ran up to an obviously insouciant farmer, shouting, "Your barn is on fire!" Laughing, he pointed to his sugarhouse: "I'm sugaring."

Chapter 7: "Mit dem Gesicht nach Deutschland"

1. Joseph Brodsky, "The Condition We Call Exile," in *Altogether Elsewhere: Writers on Exile*, ed. Marc Robinson (San Diego, 1996), 4.

2. Quoted in Peter Steinbach, ed., *Widerstand im Widerstreit: Der Widerstand gegen den Nationalsozialismus in der Erinnerung der Deutschen* (Paderborn, 2001), 155.

3. Wels died in Paris soon after the outbreak of World War II. In exile since July 1933, the Social Democratic Party called itself Sopade. After the Nazi occupation of Paris, it moved on to London.

4. Erich Matthias, ed., *Mit dem Gesicht nach Deutschland: Eine Dokumentation über die sozialdemokratische Emigration* (Düsseldorf, 1968), 7.

5. The vowels in question have been interpreted to stand for the Latin "Austriae Est Imperare Orbi Universo" or "Austria Erit in Orbe Ultima" and the German "Alles Erdreich Ist Österreich Untertan," meaning roughly "Austria is supreme" or "Austria will stand forever."

6. See in particular John Charmley, *Churchill, the End of Glory: A Political Biography* (London, 1993); Clive Ponting, *Churchill* (London, 1994).

7. Letter from Karola von Kempis to K. v. K., 17 February 1965.

8. "Troubled Resistance," *The Times Literary Supplement*, 27 March 1969, 322.

9. As late as 1993, I got involved in an argument with the celebrated American journalist William L. Shirer, who insisted on minimizing "the so-called German *Widerstand*," which "scarcely constituted a genuine Resistance," and maintained that "only the certainty of defeat" had aroused them into action. I in turn chided him for his "patronizing dismissal of the German resisters" who "under the most adverse circumstances stood up for their convictions." I urged him to face up to the complexities of the problem "with the appropriate sense of professional responsibility and humility."

William L. Shirer, "Resistance Scarcely Existed," *Smith Alumnae Quarterly* (Spring 1993): 3; Klemens von Klemperer, "More on the German Resistance," *Smith Alumnae Quarterly* (Summer 1993): 5. In the 1990s, there also appeared Daniel J. Goldhagen's *Hitler's Willing Executioners: Ordinary Germans and the Holocaust* (New York, 1990) and Theodore S. Hamerow's *On the Road to Wolf's Lair: German Resistance to Hitler* (Cambridge, MA, 1997). The first author, referring to the "fabled German Resistance" (page 114), stirred up much argument on both shores of the Atlantic. The latter emphasized the predominantly anti-democratic, nationalistic, and anti-Semitic bias of the German *Widerstand*, which acted largely in the face of defeat. As Shirer's version of German history and his negative assessment of the German Resistance became, if anything, the dominant voice in America, I felt more and more the need to shout against the wind. What actually fired me up was an article, based on a PhD dissertation written under the direction of Hannah Arendt at the University of Chicago, by a colleague of mine on the German Resistance against Hitler; George K. Romoser, "The Politics of Uncertainty: The German Resistance Movement," *Social Research* 31 (Spring 1964): 73–93. With the supreme benefit of hindsight, Romoser came to judge the German resisters for their "political romanticism" devoid of political direction (page 84). This kind of Monday morning quarterbacking I found offensive, and it prompted me to tell the story of those who, under the most adverse conditions, stood up to devilishly organized evil.

10. As it turned out, Clarita was the guardian of the extensive Trott archive, now in the Federal Archive in Koblenz, which was one of the chief repositories for my work and occupied me for many weeks.

11. One factor that fanned Shiela's suspicions was Adam's friendship with David Astor, the second son of Lord and Lady (Nancy Langhorne) Astor. The Astors welcomed Adam to their London house in St. James's Square and their country estate Cliveden whenever he was in England. Lord and Lady Astor were the hosts of the "Cliveden Set," which included the architects of the British appeasement policy of the latter half of the 1930s. Adam's relation to the Astors, however, was defined by his friendship with David. David by no means followed in the footsteps of his parents. A thoroughly independent person, he harbored no illusions about appeasing Hitler. He never wavered in his loyalty to Adam and his faith in Adam's cause—the overthrow of the tyrant. But Shiela did not understand.

12. See Klemens von Klemperer, ed., *A Noble Combat: The Letters of Shiela Grant Duff and Adam von Trott zu Solz, 1932–1938* (Oxford, 1988).

13. Shiela Grant Duff, *The Parting of Ways: A Personal Account of the Thirties* (London, 1982), 61. See the excellent review of the book by Karl Heinz Bohrer, "Schwierige Freundschaft," *Frankfurter Allgemeine Zeitung*, 26 May 1982.

14. Letter from Adam to Shiela, Bellers, Hessen, 7 September 1936.

15. Letter from Adam to Shiela, Peking, 8 September 1938.

16. Letter from Shiela to K. v. K., Castlehaven, 25 January 1979.

17. Letter from Shiela to K. v. K., Castlehaven, 6 October 1978.

18. Letter from K. v. K. to Shiela, Thanksgiving 1978.

19. Letter from Adam to Shiela, 30 December 1938. The passage in question referred to the "Generals' Plot" under General Franz Halder, the objective being to

arrest or to shoot Hitler and to take over the government in Berlin. The venture was foiled largely by British Prime Minister Neville Chamberlain's last-minute decision to visit Berchtesgaden (15 September) and Bad Godesberg (22–24 September), and by the subsequent conclusion of the Munich Agreement between the Western powers, Germany, and Italy, which maintained the peace at the expense of the truncation of Czechoslovakia.

20. Christabel Bielenberg was a distinguished English author who, with her German husband, survived the war in Germany. They were close friends of Adam and Clarita. See Christabel Bielenberg, *When I Was a German, 1934–1945: An Englishwoman in Nazi Germany* (Lincoln, NE, 1998).

21. A pre-Socratic philosopher (ca. 490–421 BC), Protagoras asserted that "man is the measure of all things"—a statement that was intended to express the relativity of all human perceptions.

22. Letter from Shiela to K. v. K, 29 January 1979.

23. Letter Michael Sokolov Grant to K. v. K., 24 April 1982.

24. Grant Duff, *The Parting of Ways*, 141f.

25. Letter from Shiela to K. v. K., 13 July 1985.

26. Letter from Shiela to Ivon Asquith, 19 October 1985.

27. Compared with Churchill College in Cambridge, Trinity was an old institution and a much smaller one, and therefore all the more intimate. John Henry Newman, who had entered the college in 1817, had commented rather wryly that, if asked what qualifications were necessary for it, he had this answer ready: "Drink, drink, drink." I hasten to add that the climate in the college had changed by the time we arrived. Conversation in the common room was, even if at times frivolous, explorative and inspiring.

28. Letter from Ivon Asquith to K. v. K., 14 January 1986.

29. Letter from K. v. K. to Tim Mason, 24 November 1986.

30. Letter from Tim Mason to K. v. K., Rome, 29 December 1984.

31. Otto John had been best man at the wedding between Adam von Trott and Clarita Tiefenbacher in June 1940.

32. See Giorgio Colli and Mazzino Montinari, eds., *Friedrich Wilhelm Nietzsche: Kritische Studienausgabe*, 15 vols. (Munich, 1988).

33. In this connection I particularly treasure a small volume that Montinari gave me: Mazzino Montinari, ed., *Nietzsche lesen* (Berlin, 1982).

34. One of the few statesmen I know of who seems to have been aware all along of the shaky situation of the German Democratic Republic was General Vernon A. Walters, American ambassador to the Federal Republic of Germany from 1989 to 1991, who at the beginning of his tenure in Bonn is quoted as having said that before leaving his post, the GDR would have collapsed.

35. Charles S. Maier, *The Unmasterable Past: History, Holocaust and German National Identity* (Cambridge, MA, 1988).

36. See Heinrich Heine, "Denk' ich an Deutschland in der Nacht/Dann bin ich um den Schlaf gebracht" (When I think of Germany in the night/I sense that something is not right); Heinrich Heine, "Nachtgedanken," in *Gedichte*, ed. Bernd Kortländer (Stuttgart, 1995), 127.

Chapter 8: Living in a "World Come of Age"

1. Robert Musil was influenced by Nietzsche's diagnosis of the unease within European civilization. In Musil's great work *Der Mann ohne Eigenschaften* (Hamburg, 1952), published as *The Man without Qualities*, 3 vols. (London, 1953–1960), which Jamie had read, he exposed this condition with unsparing irony.
2. Letter from J. v. K. to K. v. K., Cambridge, MA, 4 February 1978.
3. These passages stem from notes that I made in the course of a similar, earlier exchange between us in the same vein; letter from K. v. K. to J. v. K., 15 November 1976.
4. Karl R. Popper, *The Open Society and Its Enemies*, vol. 1: *The Spell of Plato* (Princeton, NJ, 1962; 5th rev. ed., 1966).
5. Ibid., 57.
6. George Orwell, "Reflections on Gandhi" (1949), in George Orwell, *The Orwell Reader: Fiction, Essays and Reportage* (New York, 1956), 332.
7. Aristotle, *Poetics* (Harmondsworth, 1962), 38.
8. Karl W. Deutsch, "Introduction," in Karl Jaspers, *Tragedy Is Not Enough*, translated by Harald. A. Reiche, Harry T. Moore, and Karl W. Deutsch (London, 1953), 17.
9. Draft of letter from K. v. K. to Tim Mason, 26 November 1986.
10. Søren Kierkegaard, "Concluding Unscientific Postscript to the 'Philosophical Fragments,'" in *A Kierkegaard Anthology*, ed. Robert Bretall (Princeton, NJ, 1947), 220.
11. Letter from Carl Schorske to K. v. K., 23 May 1998.
12. Lord Hugh Cecil, *Conservatism* (London, 1912), 9f.
13. Edmund Burke in the House of Commons, 19 April 1774, in *Burke's Politics*, ed. Ross J. S. Hoffman and Paul Levack (New York, 1949), 58.
14. Edmund Burke, "Reflections on the Revolution in France" (November 1970), in Hoffman and Levack, *Burke's Politics*, 290.
15. Peter Viereck, *Conservatism from John Adams to Churchill* (Princeton, NJ), 101. Since the 1950s, a brand of conservatism, the New Right, has surfaced in the United States and become dominant on the American political scene, giving a new direction to the conservative agenda. It may not want to acknowledge the parentage of Senator Joseph McCarthy, but its chief advocate came to be the publisher William F. Buckley, Jr., who made the *National Review* the mouthpiece of all self-avowed "radical conservatives" (W. F. Buckley, Jr., "Publisher's Statement," *National Review*, 19 November 1955). During the Bush presidencies, father George H. W. and son George W. legitimized the new version of American conservatism. Must I therefore face up to the paradox that America, once the land of faith in progress and one of the mainstays of the "age of democratic revolution," as R. R. Palmer called it (*The Age of Democratic Revolution: A Political History of Europe and America, 1760–1800* [Princeton, NJ, 1959–1964]), has become a pillar of counter-revolution? What, I keep asking myself, has happened to "my America," in which the "vital center," as Arthur M. Schlesinger, Jr., put it, could celebrate discourse between the right and the left to the benefit of the commonweal and in which I myself so much benefited from the debates with my leftist friends at Harvard? Besides, the one-sided business orientation of this brand of conservatism evokes for me Theodore Roosevelt's characterization of American big business as "glorified pawnbrokers," whose materialism has betrayed America's nobler older traditions (Viereck, *Conservatism*, 101).

16. Letter from Metternich to Guizot, Vienna, 15 June 1847; Klemens Wenzel von Metternich, *Mémoires*, vol. 7 (Paris, 1883), 402.

17. Hugo von Hofmannsthal, *Das Schrifttum als geistiger Raum der Nation* (Munich, 1927).

18. Referring to the speech, Thomas Mann wrote in a letter dated 4 December 1946 to Professor Karl Viëtor: "I remember well that when Hofmannsthal's speech appeared, I warned him in a conversation of the impending threat, to which to some extent he had thus given support. With some uneasiness he passed over the subject." Later, however, Hofmannsthal confided to his friend Leopold von Andrian that he had been "careless" to take on the Munich address, which "after all" had brought him "no satisfaction"; letter from Hugo von Hofmannsthal to Leopold von Andrian, in *Briefwechsel* (Frankfurt am Main, 1968), 392.

19. In this connection, let me mention a book by a cousin of mine from Vienna, Hermann Dorowin, a scholar of Austrian literature teaching in Perugia, Italy. Published in 1991, it deals with a number of European Catholic thinkers, including Leopold von Andrian, a close friend of Hugo von Hofmannsthal, whose conservatism became reality in Austria between 1933 and 1938 under the chancellors Engelbert Dollfuss and Kurt von Schuschnigg. They constituted, Dorowin argues, the "breeding ground" (*Vorfeld*) of European fascism. See Hermann Dorowin, *Retter des Abendlandes: Kulturkritik im Vorfeld des europäischen Faschismus* (Stuttgart, 1991). I reviewed this book in *German Studies Review* 16, no. 1 (1993): 146–148.

20. Friedrich Nietzsche, *Also sprach Zarathustra: Ein Buch für Alle und Keinen. Kritische Gesamtausgabe, Werke*, section VI, vol. 1 (Berlin, 1968), 97.

21. The word *eigentlich* has been translated here as "word for word"; Thomas Mann, *Nietzsches Philosophie im Licht unserer Erfahrung*, in *Gesammelte Werke*, vol. 10 (Berlin, 1956), 669.

22. Hamburger, "A Craving for Hell," 32.

23. These are the words of Mazzino Montinari, the co-editor of the definitive Nietzsche edition; Montinari, *Nietzsche lesen*, 2.

24. Friedrich Nietzsche, *The Use and Abuse of History*, trans. Adrian Collins (New York, 1957), 70f.

25. Ibid., 48, 51f.

26. Ibid., 69.

27. Friedrich Nietzsche, *Die fröhliche Wissenschaft, Kritische Gesamtausgabe, Werke*, section V, vol. 2, ed. Giorgio Colli and Mazzino Montinari (Berlin, 1973), 158–160.

28. William Butler Yeats said of poets that they write out of a quarrel with themselves, a turn of phrase that Michael Hamburger, himself a poet and translator, applied to Nietzsche; Michael Hamburger, "What to Do about Him?" *New York Times*, 2 December 1979, Sunday Book Review Section.

29. Letter from Friedrich Nietzsche to Heinrich Köselitz in Venedig, Sils-Maria, late August 1881; Friedrich Nietzsche, *Briefwechsel, Kritische Gesamtausgabe*, in *Briefe Januar 1880–Dezember 1884*, section III, vol. 1, ed. Giorgio Colli and Mazzino Montinari (Berlin, 1981), 122.

30. Friedrich Nietzsche, *Jenseits von Gut und Böse, Werke*, section VI, vol. 2 (Berlin, 1968), 188.

31. Friedrich Nietzsche, "Vorwort," *Der Fall Wagner, Werke*, section VI, vol. 3 (Berlin, 1969), 413.

32. Letters from Friedrich Nietzsche to Franz Overbeck, Nice, 25 January and 7 April 1884, in Nietzsche, *Briefwechsel*, section III, vol. 1, 467, 494.

33. Friedrich Nietzsche, *Menschliches, Allzumenschliches II, Werke*, section IV, vol. 3 (Berlin, 1967), 84.

34. Friedrich Nietzsche, *Götzen-Dämmerung, Werke*, section VI, vol. 3 (Berlin, 1969), 98.

35. Letter from Friedrich Nietzsche to Franz Overbeck, Sils-Maria, 14 July 1886, in Nietzsche, *Briefwechsel*, section III, vol. 3, 206.

36. Letter from Friedrich Nietzsche to Carl von Gersdorff, Basel, 21 June 1871, in Nietzsche, *Briefwechsel*, section III, vol. 1, 203.

37. Nietzsche, *Menschliches, Allzumenschliches*, 138.

38. Walter Kaufmann, *Nietzsche: Philosopher, Psychologist, Antichrist* (New York, 1956), 26.

39. Peter Meier-Bergfeld, "Im 'nächsten Leben' am liebsten Theologe," *Rheinischer Merkur*, 3 November 2002, 7.

40. Steven Aschheim, *The Nietzsche Legacy in Germany 1890–1990* (Berkeley, 1992), 2. The book is a comprehensive survey of the many readings of Nietzsche in Germany.

41. Crane Brinton, *Nietzsche* (Cambridge, MA, 1941).

42. Hamburger, "A Craving for Hell," 32ff.

43. Crane Brinton, *Ideas and Men: The Story of Western Thought* (New York, 1950), 473.

44. This passage by Nietzsche in fact is quoted by Brinton; ibid.

45. For this reading of Nietzsche, see in particular Kaufmann, *Nietzsche*, 26, 268. Also I owe thanks for the elaboration of these thoughts to a student of mine, Renate Weber, who wrote a paper, "Comparison of Hegel's 'Great Man' and Nietzsche's '*Übermensch*,'" in a course on intellectual history.

46. See Kaufmann, *Nietzsche*, chap. 11.

47. See Brinton, *Nietzsche*, 184f.

48. I have known Ernst Nolte since the winter of 1963–1964, when I taught in Bonn and we lived in Bracher's house next door to the Nolte family. At that time, Nolte, then still a *Gymnasium* teacher, was about to complete his magisterial work, a comparative treatment of fascism in France, Italy, and Germany. The book's main thesis characterizes fascism as "anti-Marxism which tries to destroy the enemy by evolving a radically opposed yet related ideology." Ernst Nolte, *Der Faschismus in seiner Epoche: Die Action Française, der italienische Faschismus, der Nationalsozialismus* (Munich, 1963), translated by Leila Vennewitz as *Three Faces of Fascism: Action Française, Italian Fascism, National Socialism* (New York, 1966). The comparative approach to the various manifestations of fascism, which also connects by contrast fascism and Marxism, foreshadows all of Nolte's subsequent writings. (I had a marginal part in the production of the work inasmuch as Nolte's rather difficult, heavily philosophical style called for special scrutiny in the course of translation.) The book has been attacked by fellow historians and in the media for demonizing Marxism and at the same time trivializing National Socialism and fascism as merely derivatives of and reactions to Marxism. Later, in 1986, Nolte triggered the "German

historians' dispute," which centered on the comparability of Hitler's *Rassenmord* (genocide) and the Stalinist era's *Klassenmord* (class murder), a position that ran into fierce opposition from a large sector of German academia. Led by the philosopher Jürgen Habermas, scholars accused Nolte of relativizing and indeed trivializing the Holocaust, which must be regarded as unique in the annals of horror. Nolte then became identified—all too readily—as an apologist for Hitler's Third Reich.

49. Ernst Nolte, *Nietzsche und der Nietzscheanismus* (Frankfurt am Main, 1990).

50. In 1900, Freud bought Nietzsche's collected works, although, according to historian Peter Gay, he viewed them more as texts to be resisted than to be studied. Still, Freud conceded in 1931 that it had become plain to him that he "would find insights in him [Nietzsche] very similar to psychoanalytic ones." See Peter Gay, *Freud: A Life for Our Time* (New York, 1988), 45, 46n.

51. On this topic, see Nolte, *Nietzsche und der Nietzscheanismus*, 153–167.

52. Karl Marx, *Economic and Philosophic Manuscripts*, in Karl Marx and Frederick Engels, *Collected Works*, vol. 3 (New York, 1975), 341.

53. Friedrich Nietzsche, *The Birth of Tragedy from the Spirit of Music*, trans. Clifton P. Fadiman, in *The Philosophy of Nietzsche*, ed. Willard H. Wright (New York, 1954), 955f.

54. The colloquium, "Art, Politics, Technology—Martin Heidegger 1889-1989," took place on 13–15 October 1989 and was organized by Professors Karsten Harries of Yale University and Otto Pöggeler of the Ruhr University Bochum. See Karsten Harries and Christoph Jamme, eds., *Martin Heidegger: Politics, Art, and Technology* (New York, 1994).

55. Martin Heidegger, *Nietzsche*, vol. 4 (San Francisco, 1982), 393, quoted in Aschheim, *The Nietzsche Legacy*, 262f.

56. Martin Heidegger, *Nietzsche*, vol. 1, *The Will to Power as Art* (New York, 1979), 5.

57. Friedrich Nietzsche, *Werke in drei Bänden*, vol. 3, ed. Karl Schlechta (Munich, 1956), 846.

58. *Ge-stell*=the essence of technology; *Geworfenheit*=thrownness or our being in the world; *das Man*=the average, anonymous person.

59. The term was coined by Julius Seelye Bixler, who was president of Colby College in Waterville, Maine (1942–1960). A philosopher, he studied in the late 1920s in Freiburg under Heidegger; Julius Seelye Bixler, *German Recollections* (Waterville, ME, 1985), 16.

60. Martin Heidegger, *Being and Time*, trans. John Macquarrie and Edward Robinson (New York, 1962), 83.

61. Friedrich Nietzsche, *Thus Spoke Zarathustra: A Book for All and None*, reprinted in *The Portable Nietzsche*, trans. and ed. Walter Kaufmann (New York, 1954), 129ff.

62. Max Weber, *The Protestant Ethic and the Spirit of Capitalism*, trans. Talcott Parsons (New York, 1958), 183. See in this respect Detlev J. K. Peukert's perceptive study *Max Webers Diagnose der Moderne* (Göttingen, 1989), in which (on pages 28f.) he called attention to the previously neglected connection between Nietzsche's and Weber's critiques of the "last" ("modern") man.

63. Marianne Weber, *Max Weber: A Biography* (New York, 1975), 597.

64. This was reported in Theodor Heuss, *Erinnerungen* (Tübingen, 1963), 214.

65. Max Weber, *Wissenschaft als Beruf 1917/1919, Politik als Beruf 1919*, ed. Wolfgang J. Mommsen and Wolfgang Schluchter, in *Max Weber Gesamtausgabe*, section I, vol. 17 (Tübingen, 1992).

66. Weber, *Politik als Beruf*, 249.
67. Weber, *Wissenschaft als Beruf*, 93.
68. Weber, *Politik als Beruf*, 251.
69. Weber, *Wissenschaft als Beruf*, 109.
70. Weber, *Politik als Beruf*, 237.
71. Ibid., 251
72. Martin Broszat, "Widerstand: Der Bedeutungswandel eines Begriffs der Zeitgeschichte," *Süddeutsche Zeitung*, 22–23 November 1986.
73. Kierkegaard, "Concluding Unscientific Postscript," 220.
74. Albert Camus, "The Flesh," in *Resistance, Rebellion, and Death*, trans. Justin O'Brien (New York, 1961), 44; originally published in *Combat*, 27 October 1944.
75. Letter from Dietrich Bonhoeffer to Eberhard Bethge, 30 April 1944, in Bonhoeffer, *Letters and Papers*, 279.
76. Dietrich Bonhoeffer, *Die Nachfolge*, ed. Martin Kuske and Ilse Tödt, in *Werke*, vol. 4 (Munich, 1989), 21.
77. Letter from Dietrich Bonhoeffer to Eberhard Bethge, 9 June 1944, in Bonhoeffer, *Letters and Papers*, 326f.
78. Letter from Dietrich Bonhoeffer to Eberhard Bethge, 16 July 1944, in Bonhoeffer, *Letters and Papers*, 360.
79. Letter from Dietrich Bonhoeffer to Eberhard Bethge, 21 February 1944, in Bonhoeffer, *Letters and Papers*, 217.
80. Ibid.
81. The original text reads "an den Rand der Häresie"; in Eberhard Bethge, *Dietrich Bonhoeffer in Selbstzeugnissen und Bilddokumenten* (Hamburg, 1976), 109.
82. Dietrich Bonhoeffer, "Vorlesung 'Die Geschichte der systematischen Theologie des 20. Jahrhunderts,'" Winter Semester 1931–1932; in Eberhard Bethge, *Dietrich Bonhoeffer: Theologe, Christ, Zeitgenosse* (Munich, 1967), 1053.
83. Albert Camus, "Letters to a German Friend" (fourth letter, July 1944), in *Resistance, Rebellion and Death*, 28.
84. I am referring here to the conservative resistance. The Communists, who initially played a very active part in the German Resistance, had an ideology of their own. Shifting under the impact of the Nazi-Soviet Pact of August 1939, it took a torturous course, left the resisters in confusion, and abandoned them to ineffectualness.
85. In my thinking about the problems of the relationship between totalitarianism and religion, I have much benefited from the work of Karl Dietrich Bracher and in particular from his volume *Zeit der Ideologien: Eine Geschichte politischen Denkens im 20. Jahrhundert* (Stuttgart, 1982).
86. Bonhoeffer, *Ethik*, 268.
87. Nietzsche, *Die fröhliche Wissenschaft*, 264.
88. Ibid., 313.
89. Nietzsche, *Also sprach Zarathustra*, 45.
90. Nietzsche, *Die fröhliche Wissenschaft*, 265.
91. Letter from Dietrich Bonhoeffer to Eberhard Bethge, [Tegel] 8 June 1944, in Bonhoeffer, *Letters and Papers*, 326.

92. Friedrich Nietzsche, *Der Antichrist, Kritische Gesamtausgabe, Werke*, section VI, vol. 3 (Berlin, 1969), 234.
93. Dietrich Bonhoeffer, "What Is a Christian Ethic?" in *No Rusty Swords: Letters, Lectures and Notes 1928–1936*, ed. Edwin H. Robertson, trans. John Bowden (London, 1965), 40.
94. Bonhoeffer, *Ethik*, 301.
95. Bonhoeffer, "What Is a Christian Ethic?" 36.
96. Ibid., 37.
97. Ibid.
98. Ibid., 41.
99. "Dass ich erkenne, was die Welt im Innersten zusammenhält."
100. Marianne Weber, *Max Weber: Ein Lebensbild* (Tübingen, 1926), 339 (italics in the original); quoted in Gerhard Masur, *Prophets of Yesterday: Studies in European Culture 1910–1914* (New York, 1961), 191.
101. Letter from Dietrich Bonhoeffer to Eberhard Bethge, [Tegel] 16 July 1944, in Bonhoeffer, *Letters and Papers*, 359.

Afterthoughts

1. "Denke mit Ehrfurcht stets an Gott, an die Menschen mit Liebe! Und mit Ernst an die Pflicht!" (Think of God with awe, of human beings with love, and of your duties responsibly!)
2. Bonhoeffer, *Letters and Papers from Prison*, 282.
3. Jürgen Habermas, "Vom öffentlichen Gebrauch der Historie," *Die Zeit*, 7 November 1986. See also Maier, *The Unmasterable Past*, 55–57.
4. Yehuda Elkana, "The Need to Forget," *Ha'aretz*, 2 March 1988.

Selected Bibliography

The following listing of references includes titles that evoke the spirit of the various stations of my life and that have accompanied me throughout, helping to shape my ideas and ideals.

Adorno, Theodor W. "Cultural Criticism and Society." In *Prisms*, translated by Samuel Weber and Shierry Weber, 19–34. Cambridge, MA, 1994.
Aschheim, Steven. *The Nietzsche Legacy in Germany 1890–1990*. Berkeley, CA, 1992.
Barea, Ilse. *Vienna*. New York, 1966.
Bethell, Nicholas (William Baron). *The Last Secret: The Delivery to Stalin of Over Two Million Russians by Britain and the United States*. New York, 1974.
Bethge, Eberhard. *Dietrich Bonhoeffer: Theologe, Christ, Zeitgenosse*. Munich, 1967.
_____. *Dietrich Bonhoeffer: Man of Vision, Man of Courage*. Translated by E. Mosbacher et al. New York, 1970.
_____. *Dietrich Bonhoeffer in Selbstzeugnissen und Bilddokumenten*. Hamburg, 1976.
Bielenberg, Christabel. *When I Was a German, 1934–1945: An Englishwoman in Nazi Germany*. Lincoln, NE, 1998.
Bixler, Julius Seelye. *German Recollections*. Waterville, ME, 1985.
Bohrer, Karl Heinz. "Schwierige Freundschaft." *Frankfurter Allgemeine Zeitung*, 26 May 1982.
Bonhoeffer, Dietrich. *No Rusty Swords: Letters, Lectures and Notes 1928–1936*. Edited by Edwin H. Robertson, translated by John Bowden. London, 1965.
_____. *Letters and Papers from Prison*. Edited by Eberhard Bethge, translated by Reginald Fuller and Frank Clarke, enlarged edition. New York, 1971.
_____. *Die Nachfolge*. In *Werke*, vol. 4, edited by Martin Kuske and Ilse Tödt. Munich, 1989.
_____. *Ethik*. In *Werke*, vol. 6. Munich, 1992.

Bossle, Lothar, ed. *Pforten der Freiheit: Festschrift für Alexander Böker zum 85. Geburtstag.* Paderborn, 1997.
Bracher, Karl Dietrich. *Zeit der Ideologien: Eine Geschichte politischen Denkens im 20. Jahrhundert.* Stuttgart, 1982.
Brinton, Crane. *Nietzsche.* Cambridge, MA, 1941.
———. *Ideas and Men: The Story of Western Thought.* New York, 1950.
Brodsky, Joseph. "The Condition We Call Exile." In *Altogether Elsewhere: Writers on Exile,* edited by Marc Robinson, 3–11. San Diego, 1996.
Broszat, Martin. "Widerstand: Der Bedeutungswandel eines Begriffs der Zeitgeschichte." *Süddeutsche Zeitung,* 22–23 November 1986.
Brüning, Heinrich. *Briefe und Gespräche 1934–1945.* Edited by Claire Nix, in collaboration with Reginald Phelps and George Pettee. Stuttgart, 1974.
Camus, Albert. *The Plague.* New York, 1948.
———. "The Flesh." In *Resistance, Rebellion, and Death,* translated by Justin O'Brien, 44. New York, 1961. Originally published in *Combat,* 27 October 1944.
———. "Letters to a German Friend." In *Resistance, Rebellion, and Death,* translated by Justin O'Brien, 28. New York, 1961.
Carlsson, Anni, ed. *Hermann Hesse–Thomas Mann Briefwechsel.* Frankfurt am Main, 1968.
Charmley, John. *Churchill, the End of Glory: A Political Biography.* London, 1993.
Colli Giorgio, and Mazzino Montinari, eds. *Friedrich Wilhelm Nietzsche: Kritische Studienausgabe.* 15 vols. Munich, 1988.
Cordes, Anton. *Löse und Binde: Auf der Fährte der verborgenen Qualität.* Zurich, 1971.
Craig, Gordon A. *The Germans.* New York, 1982.
Des Pres, Terrence. *The Survivor: Anatomy of Life in the Death Camps.* New York, 1976.
Deutsch, Karl W. "Introduction." In Karl Jaspers, *Tragedy Is Not Enough,* translated by Harald. A. Reiche, Harry T. Moore, and Karl W. Deutsch. London, 1953.
Dorowin, Hermann. *Retter des Abendlandes: Kulturkritik im Vorfeld des europäischen Faschismus.* Stuttgart, 1991.
Fay, Sidney Bradshaw. *The Origins of the World War.* New York, 1928.
Freud, Sigmund. *Civilization and Its Discontents.* Translated and edited by James Stranchey. New York, 1961.
Gay, Peter. *Weimar Culture: The Outsider as Insider.* New York, 1968.
———. *Freud: A Life for Our Time.* New York, 1988.
Gerth, H. H., and C. Wright Mills, eds. *From Max Weber: Essays in Sociology.* New York, 1946.
Gilbert, Martin. *Kristallnacht: Prelude to Destruction.* New York, 2006.
Goldhagen, Daniel J. *Hitler's Willing Executioners: Ordinary Germans and the Holocaust.* New York, 1990.
Grant Duff, Shiela. *The Parting of Ways: A Personal Account of the Thirties.* London, 1982.
Grass, Günter. *Im Krebsgang: Eine Novelle.* Göttingen, 2002.
Gray, Charles M. *Hugh Latimer and the Sixteenth Century.* Cambridge, MA, 1950.
Habermas, Jürgen. "Vom öffentlichen Gebrauch der Historie," *Die Zeit,* 7 November 1986.

Hamburger, Michael. "A Craving for Hell: Nietzsche and the Nietzscheans." *Encounter* 19 (1962): 34–40.
Hamerow, Theodore S. *On the Road to Wolf's Lair: German Resistance to Hitler.* Cambridge, MA, 1997.
Handakten des Oberreichsanwalts b. Volksgerichtshof in der Strafsache gegen Georg Hans Hermann von Schweinitz aus Berlin wegen Vorbereitung zum Hochverrat. Berlin Document Center, 1940.
Harries, Karsten, and Christoph Jamme, eds. *Martin Heidegger: Politics, Art, and Technology.* New York, 1994.
Heidegger, Martin. *Being and Time.* Translated by John Macquarrie and Edward Robinson. New York, 1962.
———. *Nietzsche.* Vol. 1: *The Will to Power as Art.* New York, 1979.
Heine, Heinrich. "Nachtgedanken." In *Gedichte*, edited by Bernd Kortländer, 127. Stuttgart, 1995.
Heuss, Theodor. *Erinnerungen.* Tübingen, 1963.
Hofmannsthal, Hugo von. *Das Schrifttum als geistiger Raum der Nation.* Munich, 1927.
———. "Preusse und Österreicher: Ein Schema." *Gesammelte Werke*, vol. 3, 407–409. Frankfurt am Main, 1952.
———. *Briefwechsel.* Frankfurt am Main, 1968.
Hughes, H. Stuart. *Consciousness and Society: The Reorientation of European Social Thought 1890–1930.* New York, 1958.
Johnston, William M. *The Austrian Mind: An Intellectual and Social History 1848–1938.* Berkeley, CA, 1972.
Kardorff, Ursula von. *Berliner Aufzeichnungen aus den Jahren 1942 bis 1945.* Munich, 1962.
Kaufmann, Walter. *Nietzsche: Philosopher, Psychologist, Antichrist.* New York, 1956.
Kierkegaard, Søren. "Concluding Unscientific Postscript to the 'Philosophical Fragments.'" In *A Kierkegaard Anthology*, edited by Robert Bretall, 190–258. Princeton, NJ, 1947.
Klemperer, Klemens von. *Germany's New Conservatism: Its History and Dilemma in the Twentieth Century.* Princeton, NJ, 1957.
———. *Ignaz Seipel: Christian Statesman in a Time of Crisis.* Princeton, NJ, 1972.
———. "Kurt von Schuschnigg." *Neue Österreichische Biographie.* Vol. 22. Vienna, 1987.
———, ed. *A Noble Combat: The Letters of Shiela Grant Duff and Adam von Trott zu Solz, 1932–1938.* Oxford, 1988.
———. *German Resistance against Hitler: The Search for Allies Abroad 1938–1945.* Oxford, 1992.
———. "More on the German Resistance." *Smith Alumnae Quarterly* (Summer 1993): 5.
———. Book review. *German Studies Review* 16, no. 1 (1993): 146–148.
Kohn, Hans. *The Mind of Germany: The Education of a Nation.* New York, 1960.
Kuffner, Hermann Edler von. *Geschichtliche Daten über die Familie Kuffner vom Beginn des XVIII. Jahrhunderts bis zur Gegenwart.* Brünn, 1902.
Laqueur, Walter. *Young Germany: A History of the German Youth Movement.* London, 1962.
Large, David Clay. *Berlin.* New York, 2000.
Lord Hugh Cecil. *Conservatism.* London, 1912.

Luza, Radomir V. *The Resistance in Austria, 1938–1945*. Minneapolis, MN, 1984.
Maier, Charles S. *The Unmasterable Past: History, Holocaust and German National Identity*. Cambridge, MA, 1988.
Malraux, André. *Les Noyers de l'Altenburg*. Paris, 1948.
Mann, Thomas. *Nietzsches Philosophie im Licht unserer Erfahrung. Gesammelte Werke*, vol. 10. Berlin, 1956.
Mannheim, Karl. *Essays on the Sociology of Knowledge*. Edited and translated by Paul Kecskemeti. London, 1952.
Marx, Karl. *Economic and Philosophic Manuscripts of 1844*, in Karl Marx and Frederick Engels, *Collected Works*, vol. 3, editorial commissions. New York, 1975.
Masur, Gerhard. *Prophets of Yesterday: Studies in European Culture 1910–1914*. New York, 1961.
Matthias, Erich, ed. *Mit dem Gesicht nach Deutschland: Eine Dokumentation über die sozialdemokratische Emigration*. Düsseldorf, 1968.
Mehring, Reinhard. "Humanismus als 'Politicum': Werner Jaegers Problemgeschichte der griechischen 'Paideia.'" *Antike und Abendland* 45 (1999): 111–128.
Meinecke, Friedrich. *Weltbürgertum und Nationalstaat: Studien zur Genesis des deutschen Nationalstaates*. 7th ed. Munich, 1928.
_____. *Ausgewählter Briefwechsel*. Edited by Ludwig Dehio and Peter Classen. Stuttgart, 1962.
Metternich, Klemens Wenzel von. *Mémoires*. Vol. 7. Paris, 1883.
Mitscherlich, Alexander, and Margarete Mitscherlich. *Die Unfähigkeit zu trauern: Grundlagen kollektiven Verhaltens*. Munich, 1967. Published in English as *The Inability to Mourn: Principles of Collective Behavior*. Translated by Beverley R. Placzek. New York, 1975.
Molden, Fritz. *Fepolinski und Waschlapski auf dem berstenden Stern*. Vienna, 1976.
_____. *Fires in the Night: The Sacrifices and Significance of the Austrian Resistance*. Boulder, CO, 1989.
Molden, Otto. *Der Ruf des Gewissens: Der österreichische Freiheitskampf, 1938–1945*. Vienna, 1958.
Montinari, Mazzino, ed. *Nietzsche lesen*. Berlin, 1982.
Morison, Samuel Eliot. *Three Centuries of Harvard, 1636–1936*. Cambridge, MA, 1936.
Musil, Robert. *Der Mann ohne Eigenschaften*. Hamburg, 1952. Published in English as *The Man without Qualities*. 3 vols. London, 1953–1960.
Nietzsche, Friedrich. *Der Fall Wagner, Werke*, section VI, vol. 3. Turin, 1888.
_____. *The Birth of Tragedy from the Spirit of Music*. In *The Philosophy of Nietzsche*, edited by Willard H. Wright, translated by Clifton P. Fadiman, 949–1088. New York, 1954.
_____. *Thus Spoke Zarathustra: A Book for All and None*. Reprinted in *The Portable Nietzsche*, translated and edited by Walter Kaufmann. New York, 1954.
_____. *Werke in drei Bänden*. Edited by Karl Schlechta. Munich, 1956.
_____. *The Use and Abuse of History*. Translated by Adrian Collins. New York, 1957.
_____. *Also sprach Zarathustra: Ein Buch für Alle und Keinen. Kritische Gesamtausgabe, Werke*, section VI, vol. 1. Berlin, 1968.
_____. *Jenseits von Gut und Böse, Werke*, section VI, vol. 2. Berlin, 1968.

———. *Der Antichrist, Kritische Gesamtausgabe, Werke*, section VI, vol. 3. Edited by Giorgio Colli and Mazzino Montinari. Berlin, 1969.

———. *Die fröhliche Wissenschaft, Kritische Gesamtausgabe, Werke*, vol. 2. Edited by Giorgio Colli and Mazzino Montinari. Berlin, 1973.

———. *Briefwechsel. Kritische Gesamtausgabe.* In *Briefe Januar 1880–Dezember 1884*, edited by Giorgio Colli and Mazzino Montinari. Berlin, 1981.

Nolte, Ernst. *Der Faschismus in seiner Epoche: Die Action Française, der italienische Faschismus, der Nationalsozialismus.* Munich, 1963. Translated by Leila Vennewitz as *Three Faces of Fascism: Action Française, Italian Fascism, National Socialism*. New York, 1966.

———. *Nietzsche und der Nietzscheanismus.* Frankfurt am Main, 1990.

Orwell, George. *The Orwell Reader: Fiction, Essays and Reportage.* New York, 1956.

Palmer, R. R. *The Age of Democratic Revolution: A Political History of Europe and America, 1760–1800.* Princeton, NJ, 1959–1964.

Peukert, Detlev J. K. *Max Webers Diagnose der Moderne.* Göttingen, 1989.

Ponting, Clive. *Churchill.* London, 1994.

Popper, Karl R. *The Open Society and Its Enemies.* Vol. 1: *The Spell of Plato.* 5th revised edition. Princeton, NJ, 1966.

Romoser, George K. "The Politics of Uncertainty: The German Resistance Movement." *Social Research* 31 (Spring 1964): 73–93.

Rothfels, Hans. *The German Opposition to Hitler: An Assessment.* London, 1970.

Scholl, Inge. *The White Rose: Munich 1942–1943.* Middletown, CT, 1983.

Schonauer, Franz. *Stefan George in Selbstzeugnissen und Bilddokumenten.* Reinbek bei Hamburg, 1960.

Schorske, Carl E. *Fin-de-Siècle Vienna: Politics and Culture.* New York, 1980.

Schuschnigg, Kurt von. *Austrian Requiem.* London, 1947.

Shirer, William L. "Resistance Scarcely Existed." *Smith Alumnae Quarterly* (Spring 1993): 3.

Staël, Madame de. *De l'Allemagne.* Paris, 1813.

Steinbach, Peter, ed. *Widerstand im Widerstreit: Der Widerstand gegen den Nationalsozialismus in der Erinnerung der Deutschen.* Paderborn, 2001.

Stern, Fritz, "National Socialism as Temptation." In *Dreams and Delusions*, 147–191. New York, 1987.

Stern, J. P. *Friedrich Nietzsche.* New York, 1979.

Sykes, Christopher. *Troubled Loyalty: A Biography of Adam von Trott zu Solz.* London, 1968.

US Department of State. *Foreign Relations of the United States: Diplomatic Papers 1945.* Vol. 3. Washington, DC, 1945.

Velder, Christian. *300 Jahre Französisches Gymnasium.* Berlin, 1989.

Viereck, Peter. *Conservatism from John Adams to Churchill.* Princeton, NJ, 1956.

Volke, Werner. *Hugo von Hofmannsthal mit Selbstzeugnissen und Bilddokumenten.* Reinbek bei Hamburg, 1967.

Wagner, Dieter, and Gerhard Tomkowitz. *Anschluss: The Week Hitler Seized Vienna.* New York, 1971.

Weber, Marianne. *Max Weber: Ein Lebensbild.* Tübingen, 1926. Published in English as *Max Weber: A Biography*. Translated by Harry Zorn. New York, 1975.

Weber, Max. *The Protestant Ethic and the Spirit of Capitalism*. Translated by Talcott Parsons. New York, 1958.
Weber, Max. *Wissenschaft als Beruf 1917/1919. Politik als Beruf 1919, Max Weber Gesamtausgabe* XVII. Tübingen, 1992.
Wechsberg, Joseph. "Somnambulistic Certainty." *New Yorker*, 16 September 1961, 51–84.
Weiss, Werner W. *Die Kuffner-Sternwarte*. Vienna, 1984.
White, Donald O. "Werner Jaeger's 'Third Humanism' and the Crisis of Cultural Politics in Weimar Germany." In *Werner Jaeger Reconsidered*, edited by William M. Calder III, 267–288. Atlanta, GA, 1992.
Wolfe, Robert, ed. *Captured German and Related Records: A National Archives Conference*. Athens, OH, 1974.

Index

Some persons are cited by initials only for the purpose of safeguarding their privacy.

absurdity, 123, 125, 128–129
Achenbach, Maimy von, 35, 43, 61, 66
activism, 26, 112
Adenauer, Konrad, 96, 105
Adorno, Theodor, 138
Alewyn, Richard, 144n16
All Quiet on the Western Front (Remarque), 49
Anschluss, 2, 25, 32
Arendt, Hannah, 124, 150
"aristocratic radicalism," 123
Aristotle, 114–115
Armstrong, Sinclair W., 59, 62
Asquith, Ivon, 102–103
Astor, David, 101, 150n11
Atlantic Charter, 58, 147
Austria
    First Austrian Republic, 29, 74, 85
    Second Austrian Republic, 25
Austrian resistance. *See* resistance, Austrian
Austro-Hungarian Monarchy (Habsburg Monarchy), 3, 10, 25

B., Kurt v., 30–32, 64, 118
B., v., family, 38, 43

Balliol College, Oxford, 20, 138
Bartol family, 43, 145n13
Bate, Walter Jackson, 78
Battle of the Bulge, 55
Beaulieu sur Mer, 63, 146, *photo section*
Belvedere Circle, 25
Berlin Wall, 107
Bethge, Eberhard, 130, 133
Bevan, Dr. Edward, 94
Bielenberg, Christabel, 151n20
Birley, Eric Joseph, 51
Bloomsbury Group, 95
Böker, Alexander, 44, 47, 145n14, 148n20
Bolshevism/Bolshevist Revolution, 70–71
Bonhoeffer, Dietrich, 32, 76, 128–133, 137, 139, 148n19
bourgeois, 7, 10, 13, 24, 58, 122–123
Bracher, Karl Dietrich, 87–88, 154–155n48, 156n85
Brandes, Georg, 123
Brecht, Bertolt, 136
Brinton, Crane, 42, 122–123, 126, 154n44
Brodsky, Joseph, 92, 111
Brüning, Heinrich, 42, 44, 47, 72–74, 145n14

Bullock, Alan, 103
Bundy, McGeorge, 70, 78
Bürckel, Josef, 7
Burckhardt, Jacob, 80
Burke, Edmund, 93, 97, 117, 148n12
Byrnes, James, 65

Camp Ritchie (MD), 47–48, 50, 55
Camus, Albert, 69, 116, 128–130
capitalism, 70
Cecil, Lord Hugh, 117
Checkpoint Charlie (Berlin), 107, 109
Churchill, Winston, 51, 93–94, 97–100, 147n15
Churchill College (Cambridge University), 93–94, 98, 151n27
Civilization and its Discontents (Freud), 68
classicism/classicists, 70, 75
Clay, Gen. Lucius D., 59–60
Clemenceau, Georges, 27
Cohen, I. Bernard, 52
Cold War, 70, 106
Columbia University, 36
communism, 1, 68, 108, 123–124
Communist Manifesto (Marx and Engels), 68
Conrad, Joseph, 3, 65
conservative, 30, 41, 50, 64, 66, 73, 76, 87, 93, 97, 104, 106, 116–118, 148n12, 148n14, 152n15, 153n19, 156n84
  "conservative imagination," 97, 118
  "conservative revolution," 118
Conway, John, 71, 78
Cornides, Otto, 35

Dachau concentration camp, 2, 30, 141n3
Der Spiegel, 27
Deutsch, Karl W., 115
Dickinson, Emily, 108–109
displacement and misplacement (Brodsky), 92, 111
Disraeli, Benjamin, 117
Döbling, 5–6, 9, 21, 24, 30, 33, 63–64, 82
Don Quixote (Cervantes), 129

Donne, John, 135
Dorowin, Hermann, 153n19
Dulles, Allen Welsh, 26, 55
Dutschke, Rudi, 89

E., Corporal, 54–55
E., Mrs., and Franzi, 36, 62
Eisenhower, Dwight D., 50, 55, 61
Eliot, Charles William, 38, 145nn5–6
Eliot, T. S., 78, 97
Elkana, Yehuda, 138–139
Emerson, Ralph Waldo, 3, 39
emigration, 3, 19, 32, 39, 64–65, 77
  inner emigration, 19, 64, 110, 136
Enabling Act, 92
Epstein, Fritz T., 58, 77, 147n5
Epstein, Hans J., 47, 53, 78, 146n3
Epstein, Klaus, 77–78
exile, 10, 14, 32–33, 51, 63, 71–72, 75, 83, 92–93, 105, 109, 144n2, 145n14, 149n3, *photo section*

fascism, 1, 71, 73, 116, 118, 124, 153n19, 154n48
fatherland, 15, 30, 38, 64, 97, 110, 142n9. See also *Heimat*
Fay, Sidney Bradshaw, 43, 70, 79
Finley, John H., Jr., 13, 40–41, 50–52, 70, 80, 115
Fischer, Fritz, 70
Förster-Nietzsche, Elisabeth, 122
Fort Devens (MA), 46, 48
Francis, Joseph I, Emperor of Austria, 9, 84
Francis Ferdinand, Archduke of Austria, 9, 25
Französisches Gymnasium, 12, 17, 135
Frederick III, Elector of Brandenburg (King Frederick I), 12
Frederick III, King of Habsburg, 93
French resistance. *See* resistance, French
Freud, Sigmund, 68, 123, 133, 155n50
Friedrich August III, King of Saxony, 9

Gatzke, Hans W., 47, 51–52, 78, 146n4, 148n20
Gaulle, Gen. Charles de, 59

Geest, Pastor, 8
George, Stefan, 15–17
German Resistance (*Widerstand*). See resistance, German
German Youth Movement, 13, 24, 26
Germany
　Federal Republic of Germany, 47, 97, 106–107, 110, 142n2, 147n17, 151n34
　German Democratic Republic (GDR), 107–108, 110, 151n34
Gerschenkron, Alexander, 75
Gersdorff, Carl von, 121
Gestapo, 2, 14, 30, 35, 138
Geyl, Pieter, 70
Gilbert, Felix, 147n5
Goebbels, Josef, 34
Goethe, Johann Wolfgang von, 14, 58–59, 87, 121, 127
Göring, Hermann, 29
Grant Duff, Shiela, 99–104, 150n11
Grass, Günter, 138
Guizot, Guiillaune, 117
Gustav, Crown Prince of Sweden, 6

Habermas, Jürgen, 138, 155n48
Habsburg, Archduke Otto von, 33, 43
Habsburg, Felix von, 43
Hamburger, Michael, 17, 119, 153n28
Hardenberg, Friedrich von (Novalis), 130, 145n9
Harvard, 2, 13, 16, 37–41, 43, 47, 51, 67, 69, 71–72, 75, 77, 79–81, 87, 112, 116, 144n2, 145nn5–8, 145n14, 146nn3–4, 152n15, *photo section*
Hausmann, J. von, 81
Hegel, Georg Wilhelm, 119, 123
Heidegger, Martin, 124–126, 155n54, 155n59
Heimat, 4, 8, 36–37, 42, 63, 64, 66, 121
Heine, Heinrich, 7, 110
Hermlin, Stephan, 109–110
Hesse, Hermann, 32
High Table (Churchill College, Cambridge), 94
Hindenburg, Paul von, 8, 14, 73, 141n9

Hitler, Adolf, 4, 12, 14, 17, 18, 24, 27, 31, 34, 39, 47, 53, 73, 76, 84, 92, 98–103, 105–106, 118, 122, 128, 141nn8–9, 143n12, 148n14, 148n17, 150n9, 150n11, 151n19, 155n48
Hofmannsthal, Hugo von, 8, 12, 32–33, 97, 118, 136, 144n16, 153nn18–19
Hofmannsthal, Tante Gerty, 32, 56
Hogg, Quinton, 97
Hohenberg, Duchess of, 9
Hohenberg, Prince Ernst, 9
Hohenberg, Prince Max, 9
Holborn, Hajo, 39, 77, 147n5
Holyoke Community College, 130
Hughes, H. Stuart, 69
Hugo, Howard E., 78
Hugo, Victor, 92
humanism/humanist, 68, 76–77, 93, 123
　Third Humanism, 75–76, 148n16
Husserl, Edmund, 21, 86, 125, 145n8

idealism/idealist, 27, 39, 86–87, 112–113, 125–128, 133
Iron Curtain, 107

Jaeger, Werner, 52, 75–76, 148nn16–17
Jandorf, Ernest, 2
Jeidels, Otto, 52, 56–57, 65–66, 146n9
John, Hans, 105, 108, 110
John, Otto, 105–106, 151n31
John Paul II, Pope, 141n3 (chap. 1), *photo section*
Jordan, Herr von, 18–19
Jörg, Helmut, 2, 30, 64, 118
Josten, Kurt, 18, 64
Jung, Carl Gustav, 133
Jünger, Ernst, 124

Kardorff, Jürgen von, 18, 65
Kardorff, Klaus von, 18, 65
Kardorff, Ursula von, 18
Karpovich, Michael, 52, 71
Kaufmann, Walter, 121, 123, 154n45
Kempis, Carola von, 27
Kennedy, John F., 25, 88–89
Kerensky, Alexander, 71–72, 74

Khrushchev, Nikita F., 25
Kierkegaard, Søren, 116, 128–129, 135
Kitzburg, the, 27, 96
Klausa, Ekkehard, viii, 141n8
Klausa, Georg Michael, viii, 141n8
Klemperer, von, family, 15, 146n1
Kohl, Helmut, 138
Kuffner family, 5, 7, 21, 33, 82, 140nn1–2

Langer, William L., 70–71
Lehne, Friedl, 24, 87
Leynaud, René, 129
liberalism/liberal, 30–31, 122
Lichtenberg, Provost Bernhard, 8, 141n3 (chap. 1)
Lindsay, A. D., 20
Loewenstein, Dyno, 55
Lowell, A. Lawrence, 81
Löwenstein, Prince Hubertus zu, 14

Maier, Charles S., 110
Malraux, André, 26
Mann, Thomas, 32, 58, 69, 119, 153n18
Marcel, Gabriel, 15
Marx, Karl, 68, 123–124, 126
Marxism/Marxist, 68, 108, 154n48
Mason, Tim, 103, 116
Matthiessen, F. O., 52, 69
Mautner-Markhof, Charlotte, 35
Meinecke, Friedrich, 63, 67, 147n5
Mendelssohn-Bartholdy, Felix, 17
Merriman, Roger B., 40, 52, 71
Merritt, A. Tillman, 58
Metternich, Prince Klemens von, 117
Mitteis, Heinrich, 24–26, 83
Mitteleuropa, 8, 42
Molden, Ernst, 25, 82, 146n13
Molden, Fritz, 26–27, 55–56, 64, 118, 136, 146n13
Molden, Otto, 2, 28, 30, 33, 36, 55, 82, 84, 136, 146n13
Mommsen, Theodor, 73
Montinari, Mazzino, 107, 151n33, 153n23
Morgenthau, Henry, 65
Munich Agreement (September 1938), 122, 151n19

Musil, Robert, 86, 112, 149n25, 152n1
Musset, Alfred de, 101

Napoleon I, 9, 24
Napoleon III, 92
National Socialism, 1, 3, 19, 67, 76, 118, 148n12, 154n48
nationalism, 57–58, 118, 121
Nazi Girls' League (BDM), 59
Nazi-Soviet Pact (August 1939), 109, 156n84
Needham, Joseph, 95
Neilson, William Allan, 80, 149n22
Neue Freie Presse, 21, 25
New Yorker, The, 26
Nietzsche, Friedrich, 7, 15–17, 20, 68–69, 83, 107, 119–126, 131–133, 135, 153n28, 154n40, 154nn44–45, 155n50, 155n62
Nock, Arthur D., 52
Nolte, Ernst, 123, 126, 154n48
November Revolution (1918), 6

O5 movement, 26, 142n5
Office of Strategic Services (OSS), 55, 71
Orwell, George, 114
Ozawa, Seiji, 90

Parker, Hosea, 79
Pascal, Blaise, 114
patriotism, 47, 57, 99, 101, 118, 121
Patton, George S., 58
philosopher-king (Plato), 113–114
Pius XII, Pope, 13
Plague, The (Camus), 116
Plato, 53, 113–114, 126
Plessen, Thilo von, 13, 65
Popper, Karl, 113–114
Potter, John Milton, 40
pragmatism/pragmatic, 3, 39, 65, 85, 117
Preradović, Paula von, 25
Preradović, Petar, 25

radicalism, 74, 118, 123
Ranke, Leopold von, 31

Rathenau, Walther, 106
rationalism/rational, 19, 66–68, 74, 104, 113, 125, 127–129
re-education, 66, 88, 95
refugee, 55–56, 75, 92–93
    refugee scholar/scholarship, 37–38, 67, 77, 80–81, 144n2, 145n8, 145n11
Remak, Heinrich H. H., 17, 142n1
Remarque, Erich Maria, 49
Republic, The (Plato), 113–114
resistance, 97, 128–129
    Austrian, 3, 26, 31, 55, 146n13
    French, 128–129
    German, 3, 20, 47, 97, 100, 106, 118, 128–129, 131–132, 139, 149–150n9
"responsible action" (Bonhoeffer), 128, 131
Richards, I. A., 52
romanticism/romantic, 3, 8, 13, 26, 28–30, 42, 65, 82–83, 116–117, 126, 130, 144n2, 145n9
Roosevelt, Franklin Delano, 65, 75, 97, 144n2, 147n15
Roosevelt, Theodore, 152n15
Rosenberg, Jakob, 41, 145n8
Roskill, Stephen, 94–95
Rothfels, Hans, 43, 145n11, 147n5
Rudolf, Karl, 25–26
Rundstedt, Field Marshal Gerd von, 55

Salvemini, Gaetano, 71
Sand, George, 101
Sch., Rolf, 64
Sch. family, 107–108, 110
Schinkel, Karl Friedrich, 108
Schleiermacher, Friedrich, 7
Schnabel, Franz, 83
Scholl, Hans, 2
Scholl, Sophie, 2
Schorske, Carl E., 116, 152n11
Schuschnigg, Kurt von, 29, 72–74, 119, 148n14, 153n19
Schweinitz, Christoph von, 65
Schweinitz, Friedrich von, 2, 13, 65
Schweinitz, Georg von, 2, 15, 65, 98, 118
Seipel, Ignaz, 74, 85–86
Seznec, Jean, 52
Shakespeare, William, 53, 100
Shirer, William L., 149n9
Siemens, Frau von, 35
skepticism/skeptic, 15, 30, 89, 112–114, 127–128, 131–133, 137
Skorzeny, Otto, 55, 146n12
Smith College, 70, 79–81
Social Democratic Party, 92, 149n3
Socrates, 1, 32, 82, 113
Sokolov Grant, Michael, 102
Sophocles, 124
Soviet occupation zone, 59, 82, 107
Spencer, Theodore, 52
Spengler, Oswald, 95
Spranger, Eduard, 76
Staël, Germaine de, 12
Steiner, George, 95
Steiner, Zara, 95
Stendhal (Henri Beyle), 69
Stern, Fritz, 76
Summersby, Kay, 61
Sumner, B. H., 20
Supreme Headquarters Allied Expeditionary Force (SHAEF), 50, 56, 59
Sz., Bobby, 43

T., Francis von, 49
Tertullian, 128
Teuber, Hans-Lukas, 15, 65
Thiess, Frank, 19
Third Man, The, 85, 149n24
Third Reich, 17, 24, 27, 31, 53, 76, 88, 99, 106, 109, 130, 155n48
Tiefenbacher, Clarita. *See* Trott zu Solz, Clarita von
Tolstoy, Leo, 69
totalitarianism, 114, 123, 156n85
traditionalism, 33, 76, 117
treason, 14, 97–98
Treaty of Versailles, 3
Trott zu Solz, Adam von, 20, 47, 98–104, 150n11, 151n20, 151n31

Trott zu Solz, Clarita von, 27, 98, 101–102, 105, 107, 130, 133, 150n10, 151n20, 151n31
Trott zu Solz, Heinrich von, 99
Trott zu Solz, Vera von, 99

U. family, 61–62
Ulich, Robert, 38–39
University of Bonn, 87
University of Munich, 2, 83, 118
University of Vienna, 3, 25, 30, 67, 80, 83
Ussner, Wilfried, 30

V-E Day, 59
Viereck, Peter, 80, 117
Viëtor, Karl, 75, 153n18

"Waste Land, The" (Eliot), 78
Weber, Max, 126–132, 135, 155n62
Wehrmacht, 2, 7, 17, 26, 65, 96, 141

Weimar Republic, 72, 74, 106
Wels, Otto, 92, 93, 97, 111, 149n3
Weyl, Heinz, 17, 65
White Rose Group, 2
Wilhelm II, Kaiser, 5, 14, 141n4
Wilmowsky, Thilo von, 34
Wilson, Woodrow, 58

Yale, 39, 124
Yalta Conference, 56

Zarathustra (Nietzsche), 15, 69, 119, 131, 132
Zeissl, Hermann, 6, 63

Also by Klemens von Klemperer

Germany's New Conservatism, Princeton, 1957

Mandate for Resistance: The Case of the German Resistance to Hitler,
Northampton, MA, 1968

Ignaz Seipel: Christian Statesman in a Time of Crisis,
Princeton, NJ, 1972

Der einsame Zeuge: Einzelkämpfer im Widerstand,
Passau, 1990

*German Resistance against Hitler: The Search for Allies
Abroad, 1938–1945*, Oxford, 1992

German Incertitudes: The Stones and the Cathedral,
Westport, CT, and London, 2001

Editions

*A Noble Combat: The Letters of Shiela Grant Duff and
Adam von Trott zu Solz, 1932–1938*, Oxford, 1988

"*Für Deutschland*": *Die Männer des 20. July*,
Frankfurt am Main and Berlin, 1994,
reprinted as *Das Attentat*, Vienna, 2006,
with Enrico Syring and Rainer Zitelmann

www.ingramcontent.com/pod-product-compliance
Lightning Source LLC
Chambersburg PA
CBHW072155100526
44589CB00015B/2243